John Dewey's

Liberalism

John Dewey's Liberalism

Individual, Community, and Self-Development

Daniel M. Savage

Southern Illinois University Press
Carbondale and Edwardsville

Library of Congress Cataloging-in-Publication Data

Savage, Daniel M., 1956–
    John Dewey's liberalism : individual, community, and self-development /
    Daniel M. Savage.
        p. cm.
    Includes bibliographical references and index.
        1. Dewey, John, 1859–1952—Contributions in political
    science. 2. Dewey, John, 1859–1952—Contributions in
    liberalism. 3. Individualism. 4. Communitarianism. I. Title.
    JC251.D48 S18 2002
    320.51'092—dc21   2001018402
    ISBN 0-8093-2410-5 (alk. paper)

The paper used in this publication meets the minimum requirements of American National Standard for Information Sciences—Permanence of Paper for
Printed Library Materials, ANSI Z39.48-1992. ∞

For Joyce and Hannah

Contents

Acknowledgments

I owe a lot to Peter Digeser for his numerous rereadings, criticisms, and suggestions, not to mention the insights I picked up from his seminars in contemporary political thought. Tom Schrock, because he doesn't share my admiration for Dewey, acted as the perfect foil when my arguments became too utopian or superficial. He is responsible, I believe, for my emphasis on the concept of virtue. I owe a lot to both Peter and Tom for the encouragement they gave me. Those were good days.

I am grateful for my wife, Joyce, for her patience and support during our moves around the country for university positions and throughout the numerous late nights and weekends I spent revising the manuscript. Thanks also to Hannah, for being patient with Dad despite all the times he was too busy at the computer to play with her. I'm happy that she seems to love books as much as I do.

John Dewey's

Liberalism

Introduction

Pragmatic Instrumentalism

This study is not entitled "The Political Thought of John Dewey" for good reason. Although I will try to flush out his political thought as much as possible, my project is not to offer yet another interpretation and critique of Dewey's political theory. Rather, my goal is to use Dewey's philosophy as a whole to justify a conception of liberalism based on self-development that, although it remains true to both the letter and spirit of Dewey's writings, applies his thought to problems that he did not explicitly address.

My interest in this project began when I noticed that Dewey treated many of the dualisms that are central to the current liberal/communitarian debates in political theory as if they did not exist. The "many" dualisms can, I believe, be reduced to one main distinction—the supposed dichotomy between a community that is constructed around a particular conception of the "good life," on the one hand, and a society that is concerned solely with the protection of individual rights and freedoms, on the other. Dewey's philosophy treated many of the problems that contemporary political theorists derive from this dichotomy as pseudoproblems. My immediate concern was to determine whether Dewey's perspective had been considered and, with good reason, rejected by contemporary political theorists, or whether Dewey offered a neglected but genuine third perspective that helped to remove the problematic aspects of the current impasse.

There are a number of contemporary theorists, of course, both liberal and communitarian, who are working toward, or have developed, perspectives intended to dissolve the supposed dichotomy between individual freedom and the good life. It is only natural that this kind of development will occur. Some of these theorists, whether they acknowledge it or not, depend on Deweyan arguments.[1] In this book I offer a purely Deweyan perspective on the relationship between liberal freedoms and the traditional concept of the good life. It is a perspective that is derived directly from Dewey's writings. My hope is that when I am through, readers will understand that Dewey was not trying to reconcile two opposing goods; rather, he saw freedom and community as necessarily contiguous, that is, freedom is a universal and immutable principle because it is the means to a good that is bounded by time and space.

The key to my particular interpretation and use of Dewey's thought is my explication of a Deweyan conception of autonomy. Although my conclusions are all backed up textually by Dewey's writings, nowhere does Dewey himself say: "this is my conception of autonomy." This explication is important because the rest of my argument (and the rest of my interpretation of Dewey's political philosophy) is based on it.

Although I believe that the central dualism of the liberal-communitarian debate can be summed up by the supposed dichotomy between freedom and the good, my analysis of the supposed distinction breaks down the debate into several component parts. Thus, the first four of my six chapters are concerned with the relationship between freedom, on the one hand, and virtue, context, objectivity, and authority, respectively, on the other. These four analytical chapters allow me to discuss the relationship between freedom and the good (as a synthesis of its component parts) in the fifth chapter, which explicates a justification of liberalism. In the final chapter, I discuss the importance of a Deweyan conception of liberalism for the notion of cultural evolution or development.

The absolutization of method. Dewey offered a justification of liberalism based on self-development as opposed to the dominant rights-based (or contractual) justifications. Dewey's conception of liberalism may also be said to be an ideal-based model in that it justifies liberalism as central to a particular theory of the good life. Rights-based theories, by contrast, typically attempt to put forth a neutrality-based conception of justice that is neutral between competing conceptions of the good. John Rawls's *A Theory of Justice* is an example of a neutrality-based justification of liberalism. Stephen Macedo refers to Rawls's theory as a "minimalist" justification because, when searching for liberal principles, Rawls asks, "what is the least that must be asserted; and if it must be asserted, what is its least controversial form?"[2] Neutrality-based justifications do not interpret liberal values as representing a particular conception of the good. Instead, they promote liberalism as a neutral framework within which a plurality of conceptions of the good can coexist peacefully.

By contrast, Dewey's ideal-based model of liberalism, like those put forth by contemporary theorists such as Joseph Raz and Will Kymlicka, is partisan in its contention that liberal principles are superior to those offered by alternative cultures. Dewey's conception of culture is "functional" in the sense that cultures have functions to perform and can be judged by their capacity to perform them better or worse than other cultures. Dewey believed that social, political, and economic institutions and norms could be evaluated on the basis of their ability to adapt individual quests for the good life, that is, self-development, to the objective environmental conditions in which the individual exists. Cultural institutions and norms should evolve over time because they are contingent on the changing context provided by objectively real natural, social, and technological environments. A culture should provide the social environment in which a continual cooperative inquiry into the most beneficial institutions and norms can be conducted. Liberalism, as Dewey conceives of it, provides the best social environment for this type of cultural inquiry or dialogue. Liberal principles such as free expression, reflective criticism, individuality, and impartiality are valuable, as J. S. Mill would say, precisely because they enable us to choose intelligently between competing goods. These liberal principles enable institutions, rules, and norms to evolve over time to meet the changing needs of a society's members—change brought on by technological and economic innovations. Thus, liberal principles offer a superior mode of inquiry to those prevalent in cultures characterized by dogmatism, conformity, or blind faith in authority.

Implied in my exposition is a somewhat radical departure from existing scholarship concerning Dewey's philosophy. I argue that Dewey's conception of individual autonomy and his defense of liberalism contain the basis for general moral and political principles. Although Dewey went to great lengths to repudiate the "quest for certainty," it is precisely the absence of absolute goods that makes necessary a general method of inquiry, and a general process of growth.

Dewey based his argument for the tentative and hypothetical nature of knowledge on certain generic traits of nature—in particular, the traits of contingency, change, continuity, and qualitative individuality that characterize the phenomenal world. That these generic traits are accepted by most philosophers as characteristic of the phenomenal world is evident from the fact that so many philosophers have found it necessary to transcend the phenomenal realm in their search for absolutes. The phenomenal world has been viewed as less noble by these thinkers precisely because it *is* distinguished by change, contingency, and a narrative continuity. Unlike the fixed and universal realm that supposedly transcends it, the historical world changes technologically and environmentally, is subject to contingencies that produce qualitatively unique situations, and is continuous in the sense that the present is a product of the past and, in turn, helps to produce the future. Because these traits are themselves generic—or, in other words, universal and unchanging—certain processes and methods must also be generic. For example, the generic traits of nature provide a "groundmap"[3] for inquiry. The very flux and change that make the value of goods tentative is the foundation for fixed principles of inquiry. Only if the generic traits were also subject to change, meaning that the ubiquitous nature of change itself could someday be replaced by fixity, would the groundmap of inquiry not be absolute. But this is clearly not the case in Dewey's description of nature.

Although Dewey repudiates the quest for certainty when the focus of inquiry is the essence of a particular thing or good, there can be no doubt that he thought that there is a single general method of inquiry. He wrote, for example: "The necessary . . . is conditioned by the contingent." And: "Timeless laws, *taken by themselves,* like all universals, express dialectic intent, not any matter of fact existence. But their ultimate implication is application; they are methods, and when applied as methods they regulate the precarious flow of unique situations."[4]

Consider also the following: "In doing their specific jobs scientific men worked out a method of inquiry so inclusive in range and so penetrating, so pervasive and so universal, as to provide the pattern and model which permits, invites and even demands the kind of formulation that falls within the function of philosophy. It is a method of knowing that is self-corrective in operation; that learns from failures as from successes." And: "Natural science is forced by its own development to abandon the assumption of fixity and to recognize that what for it is actually 'universal' is *process;* but this fact of recent science still remains in philosophy, as in popular opinion up to the present time, a technical matter rather than what it is: namely, the most revolutionary discovery yet made."[5] Dewey believed he could deny that his philosophy contained absolutes because he distinguished general functions from universal existences. "In one case we are dealing with something constant in *existence,* physical or metaphysical; in the other case, with something constant in *function* and operation. One is a form of independent being; the other is a formula of description and calculation of interdependent changes."[6] I maintain that Dewey must and does carry this general method over into his theory of the self and his political philosophy. As such, general method tells us something about the good life and provides us with a standard of right that is independent of positive law.

Before I start my argument in favor of a Deweyan conception of liberalism, I will sketch the background of Dewey's pragmatic instrumentalism.

The origin and obfuscation of the instrumental nature of knowledge. We have seen that Dewey grounds his justification of liberalism on what he calls the generic traits of nature. By "nature," Dewey refers to the phenomenal realm of objects. Knowledge about the world of phenomenal objects is derived from the natural sciences. One of the functions of philosophy is to interpret what implications this knowledge has for human beings. Dewey believed that the idea from natural science that had the most important implications for humanity was Darwin's theory of the origin and development of species through natural selection; from this, Dewey derived the basis for his defense of liberalism. Three key components deserve particular attention: the refutation of all divine/nature dualisms; the generic inclination of all life toward development or adaptation; and a groundmap for the correct method of practical inquiry.

No *divine/nature dualisms*. First, the Darwinian explanation for the origin of species makes all religiously inspired nonphenomenal explanations of nature superfluous. Dewey pointed out that there is no reason to believe that any part of nature exists outside of space and time. All of the philosophical dualisms that had their origin in religious-based cosmologies and that located the source of value in a transcendental realm are exposed as artificial constructs.[7] Platonic and Kantian dualisms that posit the mind or soul, and hence ethics, in a higher nonphenomenal realm are merely remnants of a religious dualism that separates thought from experience. Darwin's theory of evolution and the histories of anthropology, biology,and social psychology should relieve us of this false dualism and the pseudoproblems (epistemological and political, for example) to which it leads. More recently, Daniel Dennett expresses the implications of Darwin's theory on philosophy when he says that "the idea of evolution by natural selection unifies the realm of life, meaning and purpose with the realm of space and time, cause and effect, mechanism and physical law."[8]

The will to harmony. The second principle that Dewey derived from the evolutionary nature of life is the principle of growth itself, that is, the generic inclination of all life toward development or adaptation. The natural history of adaptation through natural selection shows that the law of all life is not bare survival but the optimization of each species' capacities as these capacities are called out by their environment. Dewey interpreted this natural inclination as a quest for perfection.[9] Perfectionist theories claim that the objective needs of organisms dictate their "good." The needs of humans are partly constituted by their natural organism and partly by the environment in which they live. Thus, human needs are a result of the interaction between the necessary (the needs of our physical and psychical selves) and the contingent (our natural, social, and technological environment) and are subject to change. This quest for harmony with the environment is generic to all living organisms.[10] In humans, this quest for harmony is identical with a quest for the good, or self-development. "That which was unconscious adaptation and survival in the animal, taking place by the 'cut and dry' method until it worked itself out, is with man conscious deliberation and experimentation."[11]

Bacteria, vegetation, and all species of animals constantly strive to achieve a healthy and productive harmony with their environment, whatever it may be. This striving is reflected in a cycle of rest, tension, and movement that characterizes the growth of all living things. Even the simplest of life forms experience need, such as hunger, as a kind of tension that causes movement toward the satisfaction of the need. When the movement is successful, the organism experiences rest. This cycle is important for all those who take Darwin's theory of evolution seriously. First, because progress, development, and growth will be seen as cyclical and continual rather than as a linear progression toward a fixed end. Second, because the ability to reason, if humans evolved from lower life forms, must have developed from a preconscious origin, and thus the generic cycle of rest, tension, and movement would necessarily have been implicated in that development. Reason, in this case, is naturally practical problem solving in situational contexts as opposed to transcendental contemplation of final ends.

Using the cycle to explain human behavior, we can say that people are at rest when they are in a state of harmony with their natural and social environment. When their harmony is disturbed by a problematic situation, a tension is experienced that leads to impulsive (possibly prerationally instinctive) action. In the absence of a problematic, they are complacent—satisfied. Problems are thus the necessary condition for growth. After the development of the ability to reason, human activity becomes potentially thoughtful, or intelligent, rather than merely habitual or impulsive. If reason originates as a tool for problem solving in a given environmental context, then its operations are essentially practical, and knowledge is essentially experiential.[12] Before the development of intelligence, growth is accidental and is the result of cause and effect; after, it is purposeful and is the result of means and ends. Preintelligent development was maintained by the preconscious desire in all living organisms to satisfy their needs. If the good for humans is determined by distinguishing needs from wants or, in other words, by determining what is *really* good for us, then for intelligent beings inquiry into the good becomes a matter of giving direction to unintelligent impulse.

Dewey interpreted this intelligent satisfaction of needs as a kind of growth: not growth toward a fixed essence as in Aristotle,[13] but growth that is characterized by a continuous cycle of dissatisfactions, quests, and consummations. Goods are thus instrumental because they are determined by their ability to meet our needs. No goods are fixed but those that are part of the general process or procedure for realizing future consummations. The contingent and evolutionary nature of existence forced Dewey to rely on a universal method rather than on the fixed and substantive ends called for by other teleological theories. This appears to be the main difference between Dewey's conception of "growth" and that held by most teleological theorists. While others tend to see growth as merely the process of reaching the end, or telos, Dewey understood the process, or growth itself, to be the final end. But because Dewey's method of growth requires certain general principles, it can simultaneously be said to have a substantively defined telos—that is, realization of the general principles necessary for growth.[14]

Dewey's philosophy, therefore, contains two senses of the concept of growth. The first is a continuous cycle of readapting to a contingent and changing environmental context in which the telos is growth itself. In this first sense of growth, the specific goods that result in harmony are contingent on the needs of the current problematic. The second sense of growth is that of realizing the general method (or principles) of growth—that is, the method that results in the kind of growth required in the first sense. I will argue that for individuals, this second sense of growth has for its telos the Deweyan conception of autonomy I will explicate in part one (chapters 1–3). For the community, the second sense of growth has for its telos the Deweyan conception of liberal democracy I will explicate in part two (chapters 4–6). The continual adjustments of institutions, laws, and norms that liberal principles make possible are an example of adaptive growth. The ideal realization of liberal principles would in itself provide the telos for growth in the second sense—toward a general method of adaptive growth.

The groundmap of inquiry. The third principle that Dewey derived from Darwin's idea is the correct method of rational inquiry. After the development of the human mind, growth (or development) became intelligent. Selection is no longer an unconscious reaction to tension but rather the result of purposive inquiry. This is why reason should not be conceived of as dealing with abstractions, because reason is not disinterested. In contrast to Kant's categorical imperative, which stresses an impartiality that is blind to context, Dewey's practical reasoning is selective. It has a purpose, which is adaptation to the environment, and an interest, which is finding the best means of reestablishing harmony in a particular context. Through trial and error, or experience, humans learn which behavior is most conducive to harmony with their environment.

Primitive humans learn, as a group, through a form of intersubjective verification, the best ways to hunt and gather food in their particular environment. They live in the types of dwellings that prove, through experience, to be the most useful. Some of the tools that they use to habituate themselves to their environment are material (technological artifacts) and some are modes of behavior (normative artifacts). These inventions, both material and conceptual, originate either accidentally or through imaginative innovation.

The tools humans invent to help them live harmoniously with their environment become part of the environment to which they must adjust. Technological innovations generally precede and make necessary subsequent innovations in cultural institutions, laws, and norms. As technology advances, the conceptual tools a society depends on may no longer be useful for adapting its members. Growth becomes necessary. The invention of agriculture, for example, required the replacement of a nomadic existence with a more stable village life. The norms and values that enable an agricultural society to harmonize with its environment are different from those that work for a nomadic tribe of hunters and gatherers. Different character types become useful.

The main obstacles, Dewey explained, to the smooth transition from old to new norms are the divinization and habituation of the old. Divinization is related to the interests of those who see their position in society threatened by change. The result is what Dewey called cultural lag. A culture holds on to the norms and institutions of a bygone era, resulting in social dissonance in the current era. Revolution, or violence in some other form, may be the consequence. The attempt of the *ancien régime* to retain an aristocratic feudal social structure after the development of capitalism is an example.

Why do cultures tend to absolutize their beliefs despite its adverse effects? One reason is that some members of society are invariably advantaged by the status quo and so do not wish to see change. These members are usually those who possess the most power under the existing social and political arrangements and are thus able to block normative and institutional change. Another reason is the divine/natural dualism discussed above. Philosophy and politics inherited the habit of seeking divine truth from religion. In other words, thinking of reality in dualistic terms has become a habit that is difficult to break. Whatever has become habitual seems normal and natural despite its contingent origin. Religion cultivates the belief that whatever is fixed and universal is of superior value to that which is changing and contingent. The effect on philosophy has been a dualistic conception of reality. There is a phenomenal realm that is characterized by contingency and change and an ideal realm of immutable and universal "Truths." Although modern science, including Darwinism, has given us every reason to believe that all of nature exists within space and time, philosophy continues to operate on the religious assumption of an ideal realm. Once the existence of a nonphenomenal realm is rejected, we are left with the realization that theory is not separate from (or more noble than) practice but is itself derived from practice, and all practical knowledge is hypothetical, tentative, and experiential.

Historically, those societies that did not absolutize their beliefs were also those that experienced the fullest development or growth. The practical arts do not look to some higher realm of knowledge for the best way to perform their craft—they rely on the intersubjective experience of trial and error. Individual innovations eventually become a part of common knowledge if they work in practice. An example is the practice of medicine. As long as methods of healing were tied to religious or supernatural beliefs, progress was nonexistent. The more the practice of healing came to rely on trial and error and on the intersubjective verification of techniques, the more progress it made, until eventually the practice (or art) of medicine came to be called the science of medicine.

Science, in fact, is merely the application of practical reasoning to the inquiry of natural phenomena. As long as the questions dealt with by physics and astronomy were in the domain of an ideal realm (religion), growth or development of knowledge was nil. It was only when men like Galileo applied the method of practical knowledge to these questions that the world realized that theory by itself was insufficient; or rather, that our theories are derived from our experience, or practice.

The religious leaders of the time were threatened by Galileo's methods. Like the powerful of all ages, they feared that their position was threatened if the source of knowledge were seen to be practical. Practical knowledge is, by its very nature, more conducive to democratic methods of inquiry. Religion eventually agreed to give up its claim to absolute knowledge in the realm of the physical sciences as long as it could retain sole authority in the transcendental realm of moral Truth. With the secularization of the West, philosophers such as Kant, while rejecting the church, held fast to the dualistic division of knowledge. Kant's noumenal realm became the source of a moral truth that transcended culture and history. The phenomenal realm remained the source of knowledge about the practical world.

How degrading it is, dualistic philosophers are habituated to think, to lower questions of morality to the *merely* practical realm—to be concerned, when dealing with moral questions, with what is expedient, beneficial, helpful, and useful. To the contrary, moral principles must be absolute, they must be good in themselves. As such, the genuinely moral person must obey them regardless of the consequences in the actual world of experience.

For Dewey, by contrast, moral knowledge, like all other knowledge, was practical. We cannot deal with a moral question without dealing with the context within which the question arises. Rather than do what is "inherently" right regardless of the consequences, Dewey taught that it is only by looking at the consequences of our actions and beliefs that we can tell whether they are moral. The moral and intellectual virtues do not provide us with ready-made answers to specific moral problems. Rather, they provide us with a practical and general method for conducting moral inquiry. We must approach a moral question or problem with self-discipline, courage, and impartiality, and we must subject hypothetical answers to critical reflection, imaginative reconstruction (if necessary), and intersubjective verification.[15] Antecedent principles and generalizations are useful as hypotheses, and we can assume the appropriateness of particular principles that have always worked in the past, but the ultimate test is experience.

Pragmatic instrumentalism. The three principles discussed above have important consequences for moral and political theory. First, the repudiation of divine/natural, theory/practice dualisms leads to the consequence that moral and political inquiry are practical—that they deal with hypotheticals rather than with categoricals. Second, the recognition of growth (interpreted as a continual quest for reharmonization with our natural and social environment) as the purpose of life provides the end, or telos, of moral and political theory.[16] In other words, the good of the individual is both the end of morality and the end of the political regime. Third, the generic traits of nature provide a groundmap for practical inquiry. The cycle of problem, inquiry, and consummation calls for the practical intellectual principles of critical reflection (the end of philosophy), creative imagination (necessary for "reconstruction in philosophy"), and intersubjective verification. Critical reflection helps us to avoid divinizing existing institutions and norms; creative imagination (or individuality) provides a source for potential new institutions and norms; and intersubjective verification is the necessary condition for common institutions and norms.

Reflective criticism, creative imagination, and intersubjective verification can be seen as components in the life histories of both technological and normative concepts. The invention of the heavy plow, for example, in medieval Europe revolutionized agricultural output. Motivation for the invention came from dissatisfaction with, or criticism of, current methods of cultivation. Although the idea for the new design must have originated in a single individual's imagination, this individual did not have to start from scratch. His or her idea contributed to a progressive development of cultivation methods. Nor was the idea a product of private fantasy—its efficacy was determined by the objective conditions of the soil and the laws of nature regarding the growth of plants. On the other hand, I do not believe that we can say that in devising this new plow, the individual had tapped into the essence of "plowness," it was simply the best tool developed up to that point for accomplishing a specific purpose. It was verified as the best existing plow through the intersubjective experience of individual farmers. The spread of its use all across Europe was the result of the communication of its effectiveness.

The concept of individual rights has a similar history. It was motivated by criticism of, and thus dissatisfaction with, existing political institutions. Although particular thinkers— Locke, for example—provided imaginative visions of a future society in which individual rights were recognized and protected, their theories were not devised from scratch. As Burke helpfully reminds us, the notion of rights gradually evolved through the history of a particular culture.[17] So while Locke's particular notion of individual rights was not the product of private fantasy, it is also doubtful that it represents the discovery of a preexisting natural Truth. It was merely the best idea regarding the organization of a political community devoted to the good of its members that had been devised up until that time. This was verified intersubjectively through the experience and communication of the populations of western Europe and North America. Just as the heavy plow remained subject to subsequent criticism and reconstruction, so should the notion of presocial natural rights. We know that the plow will improve rather than deteriorate as long as the end remains improved agricultural productivity. The organization of the political community will grow as long as the end remains the good (moral and intellectual development) of the community's members and the method of growth maintains the components of critical reflection, creativity, and intersubjective verification.

In this book I will argue, in part one, that this groundmap of inquiry provides the basis for the moral and intellectual virtues required of individuals if they are to strive for self-development and, in part two, that it provides the cultural and political principles of a community that has as its end the good of its members.

In explicating a theory of autonomy from Dewey's philosophy, we will see that the good life must be seen as a personal quest. In other words, our moral meanings must be authentically our own, not the product of conformity or blind obedience. Autonomy thus requires the capacity for reflective criticism and imaginative reconstruction of inherited meanings. But, because idiosyncratic moral meanings lack significance, this criticism and reconstruction must take place within a cultural context of meanings—they must receive some form of intersubjective verification. Meanings are thus, ultimately, products of a communal dialogue—of interaction between our communities and our selves. The capacities that are needed for autonomy are properly called virtues, and they are the product of a certain kind of socialization. The first chapter, therefore,

argues that there exists a natural unity between virtue and a conception
of autonomy that is based on liberal notions of voluntarism and individuality. Freedom and virtue will thus be shown to be harmonious.

The second chapter develops Dewey's conception of the construction
of the self. It argues that identity, and thus a quest for the good life, requires both the liberal notion of autonomy and the communitarian
notion of a cultural context. Cultural context furnishes the starting point
for a quest for the good life by providing individuals with moral orientation. Self-development thus requires the virtue of sociableness, which
can be understood as the antithesis of an atomized individualism that
conceives of the individual as being only artificially related to the community. Culture cannot, however, provide an antecedently fixed end for
the quest, lest a notion of the good life devolve into mere blind conformity. The chooser is thus not only a free chooser (autonomous) but an
intelligent and moral chooser (contextual). Dewey's conception of the
self, when coupled with his notion of autonomy, shows the unity of freedom and context.

The gradual transformation of existing institutions and norms requires the innovative quality of creative individuality. It is the only source
of innovation besides accident (Darwinian mutations, for example). The
virtue of creative individuality is important both for individual quests
for the good life and for the evolutionary growth of culture. In Dewey's
theory of art, creativity is shown to be the interaction of subjectivity and
objectivity. While pure objectivity leaves no space for innovation, pure
subjectivity is by definition idiosyncratic and thus incommunicable. The
third chapter accordingly argues that the liberal notion of individuality
(uniqueness, creativity) does not require a subjective notion of the good
but, on the contrary, is compatible with objective facts and intersubjective norms. The objective (or intersubjective) elements of our environment (facts, technology, existing institutions, and the like) constrain our
subjective interpretations of it, while our subjective interpretations, in
turn, transform the way we perceive objective phenomena. Freedom is
thus compatible with objectivity in that our interpretations are not completely determined by the external world—rather, the two have a reciprocal influence on each other.

According to pragmatic instrumentalism, unique ideas or interpretations may or may not eventually receive communal assent (intersubjective verification) based on experience, that is, based on the consequences the new ideas or interpretations have when put into practice.
Communal meanings are thus a product of dialogue. By the same token, the political decisions of the community ought to be the product
of dialogue between autonomous participants. The legitimacy of a political decision hence ought to rest on its ability to withstand a continu-

ing process of critical reflection and public deliberation. Chapter 4 argues that a Deweyan participatory democracy reconciles freedom and authority in two ways: first, by grounding the authority of the community in the freedom of individuals to subject existing political beliefs to criticism and competing imaginative policy alternatives; second, by institutionalizing a decision-making method in which verification is based on the intersubjective experience of the community as a whole. The authority of the community is thus based on a decision-making method that requires the participation of autonomous (critically reflective, imaginative, and communicative) individuals. Decisions made by the community are authoritative because of the self-correcting method it uses to arrive at them.

The first four chapters set up chapter 5, which argues that the virtues inherent in Dewey's notion of autonomy—reflective criticism, creative individuality, and sociability—imply the necessity of liberal cultural and political principles such as toleration, pluralism, and freedom. Dewey's philosophy thus provides a defense of liberalism that is not only compatible with but requires the communitarian concepts of virtue, cultural context, participatory democracy, and political authority.

Finally, chapter 6 maintains that the same critical reflection, creative individuality, and communal dialogue (sociability) that enable the individual to be an autonomous chooser constitute the best means for a culture to gradually evolve and adapt to a changing technological and economic environment. Cultures that discourage criticism, individuality, and dialogue are less likely to be able to adapt smoothly to a changing world. Dewey's justification of liberalism can thus be seen to be generally applicable to a variety of cultures: because his liberalism is based on a fixed method or process rather than on a fixed body of goods, its general acceptance would not lead to cultural homogenization.

Part One

The Individual

1

The Unity of Freedom and Virtue: A Deweyan Conception of Autonomy

John Dewey believed that the purpose of life is self-development and that perfectionism is a characteristic of life per se. All life seeks to preserve itself, but no life is satisfied with mere self-preservation. Such a faith in a higher end is necessary, I think, for a pragmatist—otherwise pragmatism risks degenerating into a mere theory of means. The term self-development, like self-realization, has accumulated many negative associations in the late twentieth century. What Dewey means by the term is the development of capacities (in humans, the cognitive, creative, moral, and the like) to an ever higher degree. He also means the realization of a human life that is meaningful and satisfying, and this is achieved only by developing the intellectual and moral capacities or virtues.[1]

For Dewey, self-development is a continual process; there is no point at which the optimal development of one's capacities has been achieved. Satisfaction is not something that we rest in; it is derived from the process of growth itself and is part of the neverending cycle of problem, inquiry, and solution that characterizes life in general. As Dewey points out, "the process of growth, of improvement and progress, rather than the static outcome and result, becomes the significant thing. . . . The end is no longer a terminus or limit to be reached. It is the active process of transforming the existent situation. Not perfection as a final goal, but the ever-enduring process of perfecting, maturing, refining is the aim of living."[2]

There are two senses in which growth is continual. In the first sense, growth is adaptation to change, and change is a generic trait of nature. Harmony with one's present environment is always temporary. Life is a continual cycle of rest, tension, and growth. One might also say that dissatisfaction is a good because it leads to growth. Dissatisfaction is accounted for in Dewey's theory by reflective criticism. In the second sense, growth is toward a perfecting of the general method of adapting to change contained in the Deweyan conception of autonomy. Because in their ideal sense the intellectual and moral virtues that together make up Dewey's notion of autonomy can never be perfectly attained, we are always in the process of attainment. Thus, in both senses of growth, the process is continual.

Self-development is not something that other people can undertake for us. It is a quest, and quests, by their very nature, are not passive enterprises. Self-development is thus a personal achievement. Dewey's notion of self-development is therefore similar to what is usually referred to in moral philosophy as the "good life." For many classical and communitarian thinkers, the ends or goals that we must achieve in order to live the good life are defined for us by nature, God, or culture. The part played by the individual is the attainment of this inherited goal. The individual quest is thus concerned with means, not ends. A particular way of life has been determined for us in advance by tradition or religion, usually a mixture of both, and individuals are deprived of the element of choice.

Dewey argues that when our definition of the good life is inherited—when a particular conception of the best way of life, or self-development, is decided for us antecedent to our experiencing the consequences of this particular way of life—it is likely to prove inadequate to the full cultivation of our capacities. One reason for this is that our cognitive, creative, and moral capacities are most fully developed by the process of discovering our own ends. Another reason is that in a world that is characterized by change and flux, no single, unchanging conception of the good life can continue to provide meaning or satisfaction unless it takes the form of a general process or method that can allow us to adapt to changes in the world.

Fixed forms and ends, let us recall, mark fixed limits to change. Hence, "they make futile all human efforts to produce and regulate change except within narrow and unimportant limits. They paralyze constructive human inventions by a theory which condemns them in advance to failure."[3] Dewey's conception of self-development depends on a method of adaptation. The method justifies a body of fixed intellectual and moral virtues that makes up what I will call Dewey's conception of autonomy. As I pointed out in the introduction, nowhere does Dewey argue that there are no fixed principles per se, only that there are no fixed principles that are not part of a method or process. I will take the liberty of referring to the fixed principles in Dewey's philosophy as *virtues* to distinguish them from the more transient and contextual goods, which I will refer to as *values*.

Autonomy is the means of striving for one's personal good, which, Dewey was convinced, is the only good each of us has. If autonomous persons are "those whose ends and purposes are authentically chosen,"[4] then individuals who do not have the intellectual capacity to determine better from worse ends or the free will to choose their own ends do not have the capacity for self-development. Autonomy is thus a necessary prerequisite for living the good life. There should be nothing particularly controversial about this. To unreflectively do what others have determined that we ought to do can hardly be conceived of as being the means to a satisfying or meaningful way of life. To act reflectively we must, first, know what we are doing and, second, choose to act.[5]

For Dewey, self-development is the end of life and autonomy is the means. The question remains, however, what precisely is meant by the term *autonomy*. The conception of individual autonomy that can be explicated from Dewey's philosophy satisfies the criterion for a reflective, and thus knowledgeable and free, chooser of the good. In this chapter, we begin with a critique of Immanuel Kant's conception of autonomy, which is abstracted from any particular cultural context of meaning and value. Next, Alasdair MacIntyre's communitarian theory is used to demonstrate the necessity of the virtues of critical reflection, individuality, and sociability within a cultural moral context that has become, as MacIntyre terms it, a tradition of rational moral inquiry. Finally, the discussions of Kant and MacIntyre are used to explain specifically how the elements of Dewey's conception of autonomy meet the criteria of knowledge and free choice.

Kantian autonomy. Kantian autonomy is important in an analysis of Dewey because rights-based theories of liberalism (from Robert Nozick's to John Rawls's) depend on it. Since Dewey's conception of autonomy differs significantly from Kant's and provides the justification for his theory of liberalism based on self-development, it is important to differentiate the theories and the practical consequences they have for individuals and society.

For Kant, autonomy means free will, but a will is only free if it is good and only good if it is rational. Autonomous persons freely and rationally adopt their own moral principles, while heteronomous persons either accept the moral principles of others (the state, society, or God), or they act according to "contingent drives or sentiments."[6] Autonomous moral principles will have an internal and rational source; heteronomous moral principles will have either an external or an irrational source, or both.

Because Kant believes that a free will is a rational will and that there is a common method of reasoning, he concludes that objective and universal moral principles are compatible with autonomy. The common method of reasoning is summarized by Kant's notion of the categorical imperative, which demands that all potential moral principles be able to pass the test of universalization. Genuine moral principles (those that pass the test) are objective and fixed. In order to be autonomous moral agents, therefore, we must recognize and endorse the validity of these objective moral principles and, in effect, make them our own.[7]

It is important to note that for Kant objective and universal moral principles exist in what he calls the noumenal realm, which is abstracted from the realm of concrete particulars (which he labels the phenomenal realm). The phenomenal realm is the realm of cause and effect—the realm of nature, in which there is "necessity" but "no oughts." The moral realm, being that of "freedom" and of "oughts," must be distinct from the realm of nature. Kant argues that only nonmoral (if/then) principles can be derived from the phenomenal realm of concrete particulars. Moral principles are thus categorical while nonmoral principles are merely hypothetical. For Kant, moral reasoning requires that we transcend the concrete world of change and flux and reflect the noumenal itself. Nonmoral reasoning, on the other hand, is practical reasoning— discovering the right means to specific ends in particular contexts.

There are four specific problems with Kant's notion of autonomy, which I will return to later to argue for the superiority of Dewey's conception. First, Kant's bifurcation of persons into both phenomenal and transcendental creatures does not stand up to analysis. Second, the categorical/hypothetical dualism created by Kant's division of moral and practical realms renders his moral principles of little practical use. Third, morality, seen as obedience to categorical imperatives, becomes wholly a matter of rules and duty rather than of virtue. Morality thus becomes unnecessarily formalized. And finally, the absolute nature of the categorical imperative has unfortunate (mainly antidemocratic) political consequences. Political rights and rules become absolutes based on abstract reasoning rather than on the practical results of trial and error experimentation and democratic deliberation. Rights become ends in themselves rather than what they are to Dewey: means to the equal liberation of individuals to pursue self-development.

First, Kant's notion of autonomy requires a dualistic conception of the self. One aspect of the self exists in the moral realm of freedom and reason, the other in the phenomenal realm of sense and experience. Kant makes this dualism clear in his "Metaphysical Foundations of Morals": "[R]eason . . . transcends anything that the senses can offer it and so proves its most important function in distinguishing the world of sense from that of the intellect. . . . A rational being must regard himself *as an intelligence* belonging, not to the world of sense, but to that of the intellect. Hence man can regard himself from two points of view . . . so far as he belongs to the intelligible world, [man is] under laws independent of nature which are founded not on experience but on reason alone."[8] We thus have the disembedded and disembodied self of Kantian liberalism; the free will is a will that is free from sensual desire and cultural inclination. Yet, when I make moral choices, I am conscious of myself as a creature within the phenomenal realm of sensual desire and social habits. Plus, if my moral choice is to have any practical use, if it is to have any effect on my desires and habits, it must operate within the realm of cause and effect. In fact, I cannot imagine myself as the particular self that I am without my particular combination of desires and habits; otherwise I fade into the universal and unconscious self that is the source of nirvana in the Buddhist religion—wholly transcendent.

Second, because Kant's imperative is abstracted from experience, it provides little practical guidance, only general rules for all rational creatures at all times and places without regard for the circumstances of a particular context. "Unless we deny that the notion of morality has any truth or reference to any possible object, we must admit that its law must be valid not only for men, but for all *rational creatures generally,* not only under certain contingent conditions or with exceptions, but with absolute necessity." And: "Just as pure mathematics is differentiated from applied and pure logic from applied, so, if we choose, we may also differentiate pure philosophy of morals (metaphysics) from applied (viz., applied to human nature). Also, by this designation we are at once reminded that moral principles are not based on properties of human nature, but must exist *a priori* of themselves."[9]

The problem is that all of the concrete moral questions that I encounter in real life occur within specific contexts with peculiar, often difficult, circumstances. Thus, Kant's imperative can only say, "thou must not lie," but I must ask if this imperative applies to the situation in which a murderous mob asks me for the whereabouts of its intended victim, who is hiding in my closet. Kant already infringes on the purity of his moral realm by allowing practical consequences to enter into his method of reasoning when he asks what the consequences would be if everyone made lying a principle of behavior. According to Kant's own theory, moral reasoning becomes wholly practical/hypothetical when we have to ask questions that involve the "if/then" of such particular situations as the one mentioned above.

The question may be raised whether a universal is necessary at all, even when asking practical moral questions. The answer is yes, but the universal must supply a *method* of practical moral reasoning rather than an abstract rational *rule.* A general method of moral reasoning requires the concept of virtue. The capacity for practical moral reasoning consists of both moral and intellectual virtues. In Dewey, for example, we can find the virtues of persistence (courage), wholeheartedness (self-discipline), and impartiality (justice), which together make up his conception of moral wisdom. Thus, the third problem with Kant's notion of autonomy is that it is based on a formal duty to obey abstract rules rather than on the type of moral character (attitudes, dispositions, virtues, and the like) that makes courageous and just decisions. Kant's belief in the sufficiency of formal rules derives from his belief that moral reason must be distinguished from the inclinations of desire and experience. A virtue-based morality, on the other hand, is concerned with making one's inclinations (desire and habits) courageous, self-disciplined, and impartial.

The fourth problem with Kant's notion of autonomy is the unfortunate political consequences that follow from adherence to abstract rules. If the right, or justice, is determined by Kant's transcendent moral reasoning, then political rules, laws, and rights will be based on abstract reasoning as opposed to trial-and-error experience. Rights, for example, will be based on truths and reasons determined antecedent to their actual use in concrete experience and thus antecedent to knowledge of their practical consequences. Rights will be prepolitical or, in other words, not subject to democratic deliberation.

Democratic deliberation is desirable for two reasons: because it is necessary for self-rule and because it is the means of generalizing the intersubjective experiences of a people. Under a system of prepolitical rights, persons are treated as incapable of governing themselves and their practical needs are ignored when seeking the good. Kantian liberals fear that individual rights are precarious if based on an "instrumental" foundation. But unless particular individual rights are justified as a means to the equal liberation of all individuals to seek self-development, there can be no assurance that they will not end up hindering, rather than aiding, individuals in their quests for the good life.

The consequence of prioritizing the right can be seen clearly in subsequent theories of liberalism that depend on a Kantian notion of autonomy and moral reasoning. In such theories, the right is necessarily abstracted from any particular quests for self-development and is absolutized. Libertarian liberalism, like Nozick's, absolutizes Locke's individual natural rights, while egalitarian liberalism, like Rawls's, posits fixed "principles of justice." Thus, Locke argued: "The *State of Nature* has a Law of Nature to govern it, which obliges every one: And Reason, which is that Law, teaches all Mankind, who will but consult it, that being all equal and independent, no one ought to harm another in his Life, Health, Liberty, or Possessions."[10] Libertarians then use such antecedent reasoning to sanctify property rights so that an unequal liberation of individuals to seek self-development is protected under the guise of justice.

Egalitarian liberals, on the other hand, use prepolitical rights to justify redistributive principles: "The principles of justice are also categorical imperatives in Kant's sense. For by a categorical imperative Kant understands a principle of conduct that applies to a person in virtue of his nature as a free and equal rational being. The validity of the principle does not presuppose that one has a particular desire or aim. Whereas a hypothetical imperative by contrast does assume this: it directs us to take certain steps as effective means to achieve a specific end. . . . The original position may be viewed, then, as a procedural interpretation of Kant's conception of autonomy and the categorical imperative."[11]

The "reflective equilibrium" that Rawls uses in his theory is not capable of replacing democratic deliberation in the real world. As Jurgen Habermas explains in his comments on Rawls's theoretical method of public discussion: "The theory as a whole must be subjected to criticism by citizens in the forum of public reason. But this now refers not to fictionalized citizens of a just society about whom statements are made within the theory but to real citizens of flesh and blood. The theory, therefore, must leave the outcome of such a test of acceptability undetermined." Otherwise, "all the essential discourses of legitimation have already taken place within the theory . . . [and] the public use of reason does not actually have the significance of a present exercise of political autonomy."[12] Thus, the political consequences of the Kantian notion of autonomy are inherently undemocratic.

Now let's turn from Kantian liberalism to its main contemporary critical opponent—communitarianism—to see if we can find the basis for an alternative theory of individual autonomy there.

MacIntyre's communitarianism. The preceding critique of Kantian moral theory and autonomy is similar to critiques leveled against Kantian liberalism by "soft" communitarian thinkers such as Michael Sandel, Robert Bellah, and Charles Taylor.[13] Dewey, however, while recognizing the need for community, is firmly within the liberal camp. Dewey's critics question whether he is trying to create an untenable reconciliation between liberal freedoms and communitarian concerns for the good.[14] I will argue that he is not. A false dichotomy between the individual and the community was created by the contract theorists of the seventeenth and eighteenth centuries, who erroneously posited the naturalness of isolated individuals in opposition to the artificial authority of the community. Contemporary communitarians, instead of pointing out the falsity of the dichotomy, have simply decided to argue from the other side of it. Alan Ryan has it right when, speaking of such communitarians as Michael Sandel and Robert Bellah, he claims: "This communitarian strain is often thought to be anti-individualist and antiliberal, even by its own supporters. It is not. It is not a reversion to a nineteenth-century conservative or backward-looking emphasis on *Gemeinschaft;* it is much more nearly a rehearsal of Durkheim and

Dewey. Individuals need communities, and liberal communities consist of associated individuals. Modern individuals need flexible, forward-looking, tolerant communities to live in, and such communities can be sustained only by modern individuals who are looking for a meaning-ful existence in association with similarly autonomous people."[15] Rather than trying to reconcile two incompatible goods, Dewey simply recognized that the supposed incompatibility was itself untenable. This will be clear when we understand that the components of a Deweyan conception of autonomy are implied by a communitarian conception of life as a quest for the good. We will focus on MacIntyre because he is the most virulently antiliberal of the communitarians. He represents "hard" communitarianism. If MacIntyre's theory of community implies a Deweyan notion of autonomy, then it should be easy to apply the argument to less hardline communitarian theories.

The most common liberal criticism of communitarianism is that such theories, if put into practice, will require closed, authoritarian societies that deny, or are at least a threat to, basic liberal freedoms of speech, association, religion, and others. Many liberals also fear that the type of individual required by communitarian theories is one without individuality or the capacity for critical reflection. In short, rights-based liberals fear that communitarianism requires unthinking conformists whose ends are provided for them by others.

Communitarians are quick to defend their theories against such charges. MacIntyre, for instance, claims that the traditional community that he advocates in books such as *After Virtue* and *Whose Justice? Which Rationality?* is dynamic and evolves through a kind of internal dialectic—it is "sustained and advanced by its own internal arguments and conflicts."[16] It is to this internal dialectic that we must now focus our attention.

MacIntyre tells us that individuals' ends (by which we are referring to particular conceptions of the good life) are provided by the traditions of their particular communities. Thus, the good life for individuals will, according to MacIntyre, be contingent on the moral tradition within which they happen to find themselves.[17] Goods evolve contingently within a tradition and are subsequently rationalized by philosophers. MacIntyre gives Aristotle credit, for example, for rationalizing the heroic tradition of ancient Greece.[18] A particular moral tradition provides the context within which moral inquiry is conducted. While goods are contingent, virtues are rational because they are the means to the good. *"A virtue is an acquired human quality the possession and exercise of which tends to enable us to achieve those goods which are internal to practices and the lack of which effectively prevents us from achieving any such goods. "*[19] Without a common conception of the good, according to MacIntyre, it is logically impossible to derive a common conception of virtue. If virtues are the means to the good, then a plurality of goods will require a plurality of means. Liberal society is moral chaos precisely because it is characterized by a plurality of private goods.[20] Virtues, MacIntyre points out, are not merely means, because living the good life is a process, not an end-state.

The virtues, therefore, are to be understood as those dispositions that "will not only sustain practices and enable us to achieve the goods internal to practices, but will also sustain us in the relevant kind of quest for the good, by enabling us to overcome the harms, dangers, temptations and distractions which we encounter, and which will furnish us with increasing self-knowledge and increasing knowledge of the good. . . . The good life for man is the life spent in seeking for the good life for man, and the virtues necessary for the seeking are those which will enable us to understand what more and what else the good life for man is."[21] MacIntyre then claims that the contingently evolving goods of a traditional community can be rationalized by philosophy. By "rationalized," he means that conflicts and inconsistencies between goods are eliminated, resulting in an internally rational hierarchy of goods. This is not a onetime event but a continual process. Ends, while relatively stable, are not fixed; they evolve over time through an internal dialectic. The dialectic is driven by internal inconsistencies between two or more goods, between different interpretations of the same goods, and by the insufficiency of existing goods for solving problems or providing meaning in a changing environment.[22] A consequence of the fact that conflicts, inconsistencies, and insufficiencies internal to a community or practice need to be resolved is that goods and standards are subject to criticism and reconstruction.[23] "Thus the standards are not themselves immune from *criticism,* but nonetheless we cannot be initiated into a practice without accepting the authority of the best standards realized so far. . . . In the realm of practices the authority of both goods and standards operates in such a way as to rule out all subjectivist and emotivist analysis of judgment."[24] He goes on: "For all reasoning takes place within the context of some traditional mode of thought, transcending through *criticism and invention* the limitations of what had hitherto been reasoned in that tradition: this is as true of modern physics as of medieval logic" (my emphasis).[25] MacIntyre seems to be arguing that in a community of shared goods and virtues, "criticism" and "invention" are necessary ingredients if the tradition is to remain both internally rational and externally efficacious. If existing goods are subject to criticism, then it is implied that they are subject to alteration or outright replacement. The source of new or evolving goods, according to MacIntyre, is "the invention or discovery of new concepts. . . . Imaginative conceptual innovation will have . . . to occur."[26] MacIntyre is therefore arguing that if a community wants to avoid holding as dead dogma its existing (and possibly inconsistent and inadequate) body of goods, it must practice reflective criticism and imaginative innovation.

It is not clear who does the criticizing and imagining in MacIntyre's traditional community. He may wish to limit critical reflection and imaginative innovation to a small group of philosophers. After all, philosophers are responsible for rationalizing the tradition in the first place. But how realistic would this be? Reflective criticism is concerned with internal conceptual inconsistencies and practical external inadequacies of traditional norms and beliefs. Who is in the best position to detect these inconsistencies and inadequacies: ivory tower philosophers or the population that actually experiences the consequences of the inconsistent and inadequate concepts? It is simply another way of asking who is best able to determine where the shoe pinches. Even if criticisms need to be articulated by philosophers and artists, if they are to be concrete rather than abstract, they must originate within the community. Some institutional means of communication and intersubjective verification are thus necessary.

Imaginative innovation, likewise, requires an open and participatory society. A state may encourage individuality or it may discourage it, but it cannot limit it to a particular class. It cannot predict where valuable ideas will come from. This is one of the lessons we can learn from the former Soviet Union's failed experiment with totalitarianism. It wanted to discourage individuality in its people while simultaneously competing with the West in technological innovation. But no centralized authority can cultivate and control an elite class of innovators while discouraging originality in the mass of its citizens.

If MacIntyre wants reflective criticism and creative individuality in his traditional community, he will need to have the types of citizens for whom reflective criticism and creative individuality are character traits. Like all character traits, or virtues, they cannot be turned on and off like an electric lamp for the convenience of the state. As MacIntyre himself points out, "although the virtues are just those qualities which tend to lead to the achievement of a certain class of goods, nonetheless unless we practice them irrespective of whether in any particular set of contingent circumstances they will produce those goods or not, we cannot possess them at all. We cannot be genuinely courageous or truthful and be so only on occasion."[27] Neither, I submit, can we be genuinely reflective and creative only on occasion.

Reflective criticism and creative individuality imply another aspect of society that would help MacIntyre to refute liberal charges that he favors a closed and authoritarian society—open communication. It is conceivable that an authoritarian state may instruct its members that they may reflect critically on the goods of the community and even imagine innovative alternatives to them, as long as they keep such musings to themselves. This hypothetical state may threaten to imprison anyone who attempts to publicize or otherwise communicate their critiques and ideas to others by way of pamphlet, book, public address, or even personal conversation. But critical reflection and creative individuality would have absolutely no practical benefits for such a state. For a community such as that envisioned by MacIntyre, that is, one that is evolving to meet the needs of its members, communication of these critiques and innovative ideas is essential.

The internal dialectic that results in the evolving standards within one of MacIntyre's traditional communities must be the product of an inclusive communal dialogue that encourages reflective criticism and creative individuality. Therefore, the members of MacIntyre's traditional communities will have to possess the internal capacities that enable them to reflect critically on the beliefs they have been habitualized to accept as valid, to imagine alternative possibilities to those current in existing society, and to actively contribute to a communal dialogue the criticisms and ideas they have developed internally. A cultural tradition whose citizens do not possess these virtues and freedoms will not be able to adapt smoothly to change.

I suggest that a Deweyan comprehensive liberalism based on self-development, as opposed to a rights-based political liberalism or a "traditional" community, is the type of political culture that best exemplifies the reflective criticism, imaginative innovation, and communal dialogue that would be necessary for the kind of dynamic cultural tradition of which MacIntyre speaks. While MacIntyre is critical of liberalism, his argument focuses mainly on Kantian rights-based models. He identifies the good of a liberal tradition, for example, with the market, while a liberalism of self-development has the good life for individuals as its final end. MacIntyre rejects the Kantian disembedded and disembodied self, but the Deweyan conception of autonomy provides for reflective choice within a cultural context. MacIntyre criticizes the notion of the priority of the right with its abstract rules, but Deweyan liberalism provides an instrumental justification of rights and focuses on development of the moral and intellectual virtues. In short, Deweyan autonomy is able to provide the freedom and practical rationality of a genuine conception of autonomy within a cultural framework of meanings and virtues.

A Deweyan conception of autonomy. To avoid the flaws of the Kantian notion of autonomy, it is necessary to show how the individual elements contained within a Deweyan concept of personal autonomy can be conceived of as dispositions or virtues. This can be done by using Aristotle's notion of virtue as a just proportion between two extremes.[28] Thus, for example, as Aristotle situates courage as the just proportion between the extremes of cowardice and foolhardiness critical reflection—a Deweyan virtue—can be conceived of as the just proportion between the extremes of dogmatism and moral skepticism.

By setting up the intellectual virtues of autonomy in this way, we can better see how a conception of liberalism based on self-development can achieve a golden mean between a virtue-based communitarianism that shortchanges individual initiative and freedom and a postmodernist glorification of difference that shortchanges objective and/or intersubjective standards of value. Deweyan liberalism achieves a level of complexity that accommodates both the integrative aspects of communitarianism and the differentiating aspects of postmodernism. Differentiation, conceived as individuality, is necessary for a community that wants to adapt to change, but by itself it threatens disintegration. Integration, conceived as shared ends, is necessary for meaning and significance, but by itself it threatens stagnation. If a culture wishes to be dynamic and evolving and yet provide a stable context of shared ends, it must contain the conceptual tools to accommodate both differentiation and integration.

Critical reflection. A dogmatic disposition tends toward integration in that it treats existing beliefs as absolute truths that are above criticism and the test of experience. Moral skepticism tends toward differentiation in that it treats all moral beliefs as subjective. The moral skeptic accords all beliefs equal value because they are all explained by personal preference or particular interest. Occupying the middle ground between these two dispositions is critical reflection, which holds that no belief is above criticism or the test of experience precisely because some beliefs are superior to others, and that criticism and experience are the best means for distinguishing the better from the worse. Dewey spoke of criticism as an intrinsic good in *Experience and Nature:*

> Because of . . . [the] uncertainty of what used to be called ends . . . the important consideration and concern is . . . a theory of criticism; a *method* of discriminating among goods on the basis of the conditions of their appearance, and of their consequences. . . . [my emphasis]

> [A] brief course in experience enforces reflection; it requires but brief time to teach that some things sweet in having are bitter in after-taste and in what they lead to. Primitive innocence does not last. Enjoyment ceases to be a datum and becomes a problem. As a problem, it implies intelligent inquiry into the conditions and consequences of the value-object; that is, criticism.

Criticism . . . occurs whenever a moment is devoted to looking to see what sort of value is present; whenever instead of accepting a value-object wholeheartedly, being rapt by it, we raise even a shadow of a question about its worth, or modify our sense of it. . . .

Conscience in morals, taste in fine arts, and convictions in beliefs pass insensibly into critical judgments; the latter pass into a more and more generalized form of criticism called philosophy. . . .

[S]ince reflection is the instrumentality of securing freer and more enduring goods, *reflection is a unique intrinsic good.* Its instrumental efficacy determines it to be a candidate for a distinctive position as *an immediate good,* since beyond other goods it has the power of replenishment and fructification. In it, apparent good and real good enormously coincide. [my emphasis]

[P]hilosophy is inherently criticism, having its distinctive position among various modes of criticism in its generality; a criticism of criticisms, as it were . . .

Philosophic discourse partakes both of scientific and literary discourse. . . . Its business is to accept and to utilize for a purpose the best available knowledge of its own time and place. And this purpose is criticism of beliefs, institutions, customs, policies with respect to their bearing on the good. . . .

Thus philosophy as a critical organ becomes in effect a messenger, a liaison officer, linking reciprocally intelligible voices speaking provincial tongues . . . [for example, anthropology, biology, social psychology, and others].[29]

Because critical reflection focuses on existing beliefs, it assumes a preexisting body of goods. It does not subject the entire body of goods to criticism all at once, or all of the time, but it does subject a particular good or belief to criticism if it becomes problematic. When Dewey speaks of a good or belief being "problematic," he is referring to the same kind of conceptual inconsistencies and concrete inadequacies that were discussed by MacIntyre. Critical reflection focuses on the conditions (or causes) of an existing problematic belief and its practical consequences in the believer's life. It also reflects on the conditions and consequences of hypothetical alternative beliefs. Although the consequences of alternative hypothetical goods must be rehearsed imaginatively, the final test is always actual experience. Kantians may object that goods that are verified by their efficacy at obtaining particular consequences are merely hypothetical because they are merely means to an end. The final ends that provide these means with a goal must, therefore, be determined by some other method, or they must simply be inherited. But when we understand, as Dewey does, the purpose of the political community as liberating all members equally for self-development, we see that pragmatism rests on the same kind of initial assumption as Kant's elevation of each individual to an end in him or herself. With the exception of this ultimate goal, all ends are tentative because all ends are themselves means to the final good of growth. Pragmatic consequentialism is thus based not on mere expedience but rather on the need to make rules and duties relevant to a practical or concrete quest for the good life. Thus, for Dewey, the value of goods and beliefs is determined by their consequences. In other words, we must ask which ends, or which dispositions, have as their consequence the final good that we are seeking?

The autonomous person applies critical reflection not only to habits and beliefs but to desires and impulses as well. "We estimate the import or significance of any present desire or impulse," Dewey explains, "by forecasting what it will come or amount to if carried out; literally its consequences define its *consequence,* its meaning or import."[30] Immediate, unreflective desires must be subjected to the test of conditions and consequences because moral agents are responsible for the consequences of their actions. Those whose actions are determined by unreflective desires are by definition irresponsible and nonautonomous.[31] They are nonautonomous because they cannot meet the criterion for reflective action that calls for agents to *know* what they are doing. To know what you are doing means that you have reflected on the causes and consequences of your behavior. Dewey's focus on consequences is common to most contemporary theories of autonomy and responsibility. "The root idea of autonomy," says Richard Arneson, "is that in making a voluntary choice a person takes on responsibility for all the foreseeable consequences to himself that flow from this voluntary choice."[32]

Although Dewey offered a practical method of moral reasoning that transcends any particular cultural context, he understood that the material his autonomous chooser must work with differs from one cultural context to the next. Thus, critical reflection must begin with the institutions, rules, and norms of the culture in which we find ourselves. No rational inquiry can begin from scratch—all ultimately depend on a background of unquestioned assumptions. Kant's categorical imperatives are no exception. Nietzsche recognized this when he referred to Kantian liberalism as secularized Christianity.[33] "Right, law, duty," Dewey reminds us, are not the products of a moral reasoning that abstracts from experience; they "arise from the relation which human beings intimately sustain to one another, and. . . their authoritative force springs from the very nature of the relation that binds people together."[34]

Postmodern "pragmatists" such as Richard Rorty share the Kantian noncontextual conception of the self when they speak of a "thus I willed it" self-creation that abhors social influences. A classical pragmatist such as Dewey, while he insisted that existing institutions, rules, and norms be subjected to reflective criticism, realized that this was an exercise that could only be performed within a particular framework of meanings. The necessity of a cultural context is taken into account in most contemporary theories of autonomy. Joel Feinberg, for instance, asserts: "To reflect rationally, in the manner of the autonomous-authentic person, is to apply some already accepted principles, in accordance with the rules of rational procedure, to test the more tentative principles or candidates for principles, judgments, or decisions. Rational reflection thus presupposes some relatively settled convictions to reason from and with. If we take authenticity to require that all principles (beliefs, preferences, etc.) are together to be examined afresh in the light of reason on each occasion for decision, then nothing resembling rational reflection can ever get started." Therefore, "[s]elf-creation in the authentic person must be a process of self-*recreation*, rationally accommodating new experiences and old policies to make greater coherence and flexibility. Self-creation is possible but not *ex nihilo*."[35] Gerald Dworkin seconds Feinberg's analysis: "We simply find ourselves motivated in certain ways, and the notion of choosing, from ground zero, makes no sense. Sooner or later, we find ourselves, as in Neurath's metaphor of the ship in mid-ocean, being reconstructed while sailing, in mid-history. But [insofar as we are autonomous] we always retain the possibility of stepping back and judging where we are and where we want to be."[36] Thus, the Deweyan notion of reflective criticism within a cultural context accords well with recent conceptions of autonomy that have acquired a relatively wide acceptance. It also fits into the communitarian conception of the individual's relationship with the community, while the Kantian conception of autonomy does not.

Now let us turn to the second intellectual virtue contained within a Deweyan conception of autonomy: creative individuality.

Creative individuality. The virtue of individuality can be conceived of as the just proportion between the extremes of conformity and eccentricity. A conformist disposition lacks what Emerson called self-reliance. It looks to others, the group or an authority figure, for confirmation of its beliefs. Dworkin uses a quote from Tolstoy's *Anna Karenina* to exemplify the conformist, or nonauthentic, disposition: "Stepan Arkadyevitch took in and read a liberal paper, not an extreme one, but one advocating the views held by the majority. And in spite of the fact that science, art, and politics had no special interest for him, he firmly held to those views on all these subjects which were held by the majority and by his paper, and he only changed them when the majority changed them—or more strictly speaking, he did not change them but they imperceptibly changed of themselves within him."[37] Arkadyevitch lacked the confident self-reliance to establish his own views on important moral and political questions. Dewey taught that confidence in one's own thought is a social product: "[T]here are variations of point of view . . . from person to person. When these variations are suppressed in the alleged interests of uniformity . . . [o]riginality is gradually destroyed, confidence in one's own quality of mental operation is undermined, and a docile subjection to the opinion of others is inculcated."[38]

Self-reliance is essential to the notion of autonomy. David Riesman explained that "the idea that men are created free and equal is both true and misleading: men are created different; they lose their social freedom and their individual autonomy in seeking to become like each other."[39] In the pecuniary society in which he lived, Dewey saw that the consequence of conformity was individualism in business and the suppression of individuality in thought and speech.[40] Without self-reliant individuality, the quest for the good life becomes impossible. Contemporary theorists of autonomy seem to have gravitated to the point of view of non-Kantian liberal theorists such as Dewey, T. H. Green, and Riesman; the following statement from Feinberg could have been made by any of them: "A person's highest good in life is self-fulfillment, and by its very nature, fulfillment is not something that can be achieved for the self by someone else."[41]

The opposite extreme is the eccentric disposition. It tends to understand *all* socially influenced behavior as inauthentic. To be one's self means to be different, idiosyncratic. Richard Rorty expresses a postmodern conception of authenticity when he claims that "[t]he vocabulary of self-creation is necessarily private, unshared, unsuited to argument."[42] When carried to its logical conclusion, it leads to a desire for difference for difference's sake. Nonconformity for the eccentric disposition means much more than merely following your conscience rather than the crowd; it means taking positive action to differentiate yourself from the crowd whenever possible.

The virtue of individuality, while it seeks authenticity and self-reliance in the formation of character, recognizes the necessity for a context of meaning within which character building is accomplished. Creative innovation in the realm of moral concepts does not require romanticist escape from the community any more that it requires Kantian abstraction from it. Dewey assures us that "originality and uniqueness are not opposed to social nurture; they are saved by it from eccentricity and escape."[43] He goes on: "Individuality itself is originally a potentiality and is realized only in interaction with surrounding conditions. In this process of intercourse, native capacities, which contain an element of uniqueness, are transformed and become a self. Moreover, through resistances encountered, the nature of the self is discovered. The self is both formed and brought to consciousness through interaction with [the] environment."[44]

Dworkin dismisses postmodernist notions of authenticity when he asserts that "[i]t makes no more sense to suppose we invent the moral law for ourselves than to suppose that we invent the language we speak for ourselves."[45] Creative individuality, rather than being opposed to social context, is the source of imaginative innovation within society. It is "an agency of novel reconstruction of a pre-existing order."[46] It is responsible not only for conceptual innovations but for adapting existing habits to new conditions and for coherently integrating new ideas into an existing body of meanings. "Custom is Nomos, lord and king of all, of emotions, beliefs, opinions, thoughts as well as deeds. Yet mind in an individualized mode has occasionally some constructive operation. Every invention, every improvement in art, technological, military and political, has its genesis in the observation and ingenuity of a particular innovator. All utensils, traps, tools, weapons, stories, prove that someone exercised at sometime initiative in deviating from customary models and standards. Accident played its part; but *some one* had to observe and utilize the accidental change before a new tool and custom emerged."[47] Individuality is thus the subjective operating within an objective context. "Imagination as mere reverie is one thing, a natural and additive event, complete in itself, a terminal object rich and consoling, or trivial and silly, as may be. Imagination which terminates in a modification of the objective order, in the institution of a new object is other than a merely added occurrence. It involves a dissolution of old objects and a forming of new ones in a medium which, since it is beyond the old object and not yet in the new one, can properly be termed subjective." But "[u]nless subjective intents and thoughts are to terminate in picturesque utopias or dogmas irrelevant to constructive action, they are subject to objective requirements and tests."[48]

Charles Taylor, whom Alan Ryan describes as "for the most part a Deweyan without knowing it,"[49] gives what I consider to be the best argument for a Deweyan conception of individuality in his book *The Ethics of Authenticity*. Taylor asserts that our choices are trivial and insignificant if they are made outside of a context by which we may judge some choices as being more worthy than others. If all of our choices are equally worthy by virtue of being freely chosen, he contends, then all difference becomes insignificant.[50] Dewey explains that the self we converse with while introspecting is a dialogical product. "When the intro-spectionist thinks he has withdrawn into a wholly private realm of events disparate in kind from other events, made out of mental stuff, he is only turning his attention to his own soliloquy. And soliloquy is the product and reflex of converse with others; social communication not an effect of soliloquy. If we had not talked with others and they with us, we should never talk to and with ourselves."[51] Thus, in effect, to follow one's con-science rather than the crowd is to rebuke the crowd for deviating from its own standards of worth. The reformer who practices civil disobedi-ence is trying to shame the crowd into acknowledging the attitudes and behavior called for by its own tradition of moral judgment. The true strong poet, revolutionary, reformer, or prophet creates a vision for the crowd that is simultaneously "change" *and* continuous with the crowd's existing body of goods.

Sociability. Dewey makes much of the common etymological roots of the words *community* and *communication*. Community is created by and consists in communication. "Society not only continues to exist *by* transmission, *by* communication, but it may fairly be said to exist *in* transmission, *in* communication. There is more than a verbal tie between the words common, community, and communication. Men live in a community by virtue of the things which they have in common; and communication is the way in which they come to possess things in com-mon. What they must have in common in order to form a community or society are aims, beliefs, aspirations, knowledge—a common under-standing—like-mindedness as the sociologists say."[52] When we speak of the scientific community, we do not refer to a specific city or region pop-ulated by scientists, we refer to the fact that scientists, from the farthest corners of the earth, communicate their ideas, criticisms, and experiences to each other. It is proper, therefore, to speak of the scientific commu-nity as a cooperative endeavor. No single member has the breadth of experience or the imaginative capacity of the community as a whole. The same applies to moral communities in which meanings are dialogical.

If we want our moral choices to be intelligent (as opposed to impul-sive or habitual) and meaningful (as opposed to trivial and insignificant), then we must be part of a communal or cultural dialogue. I will call the virtue that provides for this need "sociability." By sociability I mean the disposition of being sociable; and by sociable I mean the tendency to identify our own good and well-being with the good and well-being of the community of which we are a part. This identification is necessary for three reasons: first, because our understanding of the good is neces-sarily dialogical, or social; second, because the dispositions necessary to live the good life—that is, the dispositions contained within Dewey's conception of autonomy—are social products; and third, because to conduct a quest for our own good and well-being without regard for social demands or commitments is narcissistic and will necessarily lead to us into nihilism.[53] The quest for the good life is thus a social endeavor. Although we are naturally social creatures we must learn to be sociable. Society can just as easily habituate us to be antisocial.

Sociability is the just proportion between the two extremes of docility and rebelliousness. The docile disposition is compliant and submissive, characterized by unquestioning obedience to authority. It is not autonomous because it is the surrender of autonomy to an outside authority. It is sociability without individuality or critical reflection. Thoreau was referring to the docile disposition in his essay "Civil Disobedience," when he discussed the soldiers marching off to the Mexican-American War. The soldiers believed that the moral rightness or wrongness of the war was not their concern—their only concern was to obey orders. Thoreau compares such men to an inanimate object, a stick for example, which, if used by person A to smash person B over the head, is not held responsible because it is not a free moral agent but merely a tool in the hand of a free moral agent (person A). These soldiers, in effect, saw themselves as less than human, as mere objects or tools to be used for some other persons' ends.

Dewey saw the creation of docile individuals through education as intrinsic to the desire by some to use others as means for their ends. "[H]is [the student's] seeming attention, his docility, his memorizings and reproductions, will partake of intellectual servility. Such a condition of intellectual subjection is needed for fitting the masses into a society where the many are not expected to have aims or ideas of their own, but to take orders from the few set in authority. It is not adapted to a society which intends to be democratic."[54] Docile citizens are fit for authoritarian regimes and cultures where individual autonomy is not valued. They are not fit for participatory democracies.

The rebellious disposition, by contrast, is asocial and anarchic. It sees an unjustified intrusion into its personal or private affairs in every attempt to exercise political, communal, or even familial authority. The rebellious disposition interprets freedom as absolute self-will. Its motto is "I am my own." Politically it can be seen in the atomized individualism of the libertarian liberal. This rebellious, or asocial, disposition should not be mistaken for the self-reliance of Emerson who, though he was concerned with self-development through self-reliance, was anything but asocial and was wholly critical of the hedonistic individualism of the libertarians. Dewey complains that the "idea individuals are born separate and isolated and are brought into society only through some artificial device is pure myth."[55] By characterizing freedom as individualism, rights-based liberalism has succeeded in convincing many that there is some kind of natural opposition between the individual and society.[56]

While the docile disposition is agreeable to life in a community that lacks participatory institutions in that it encourages a form of collective activity that requires no communicative input from the participants other than the giving and receiving of instructions, the rebellious disposition is agreeable only to self-directed activity devoid of common direction or purpose. The sociable disposition, being the just proportion between the two extremes, is characteristic of a community of autonomous participants. Activity is cooperative in that individuals contribute their unique perspectives to a common dialogue, while authority is derived from the cooperative process of decision making itself. The sociable disposition is thus neither docile nor rebellious; it is cooperative. It seeks harmonious relations within a pluralist society. It is not equivalent to a disposition that seeks to lose itself in continual involvement in associative activity. The sociable disposition recognizes the importance of private life, of introspection, of quiet—it simply does not regard its own good as in competition with the good of others.[57]

Sociability integrates the virtues of critical reflection and individuality into the community. Although critical reflection represents a just proportion between two extremes, it tends away from dogmatism and toward skepticism—and thus toward differentiation. Individuality, likewise, tends away from conformity and toward the differentiating pole of eccentricity. The virtue of sociability tends in the opposite direction— away from differentiating rebelliousness and toward integrating docility. The three virtues should not, therefore, be conceived of separately. The tension created by the synthesis of the three keeps each from degenerating into the excess toward which it tends. *Together* they constitute the autonomous individual.[58]

There is a natural interaction between the critical self-reflection of the individual and the shared ends of the community in that they are partially dependent on one another. To borrow Taylor's terms, while introspection is performed in an isolated *manner,* the *matter* it deals with refers to something beyond the self.[59] The matter that introspection deals with is the body of goods provided by a moral community. Personal identity is thus as much the product of dialogue as it is of reflection. From the perspective of the community, consciousness of itself (social awareness) requires communication between critically reflective individuals.

The relation between individuality and community is, I hope, already much clearer. From the perspective of the individual, the necessity of communication prevents innovation from becoming eccentric and thus incommunicable. From the perspective of the community, communication of the unique ideas of individuals is the source of innovative progress. An assembly either of conformists or eccentrics would be equally ill-suited for the purpose of inquiry. An assembly of creative individuals would, on the other hand, be very profitable.

The virtue of autonomy. The disposition to reflect critically on existing beliefs and immediate desires is more conducive to well-being than are dogmatic or skeptical dispositions because it provides a better method or process for evaluating goods. The disposition of self-reliant and creative individuality is more conducive to well-being than are conformist and eccentric dispositions because it provides a better source of conceptual innovation. The disposition of sociability is more conducive to well-being than are docility and rebelliousness because it is a better means of communicating our critical and creative thoughts.

The three intellectual dispositions together make up a Deweyan conception of autonomy. They are properly called virtues because, as MacIntyre has already informed us, a virtue is a *"human quality the possession and exercise of which tends to enable us to achieve those goods which are internal to practices and the lack of which effectively prevents us from achieving any such goods."*[60] In this case the good we are seeking to achieve is self-development. The difference between Dewey's conception of virtue and MacIntyre's concerns the distinction between intellectual and moral virtues. MacIntyre, with Aristotle, claims that "intellectual virtues are acquired through teaching; the virtues of character from habitual exercise. We become just or courageous by performing just or courageous acts."[61] Dewey argues that intellectual virtues are as much a product of habituation as are moral virtues. We cultivate all of our capacities by practicing them; we are not taught them prior to practicing them except in the sense of becoming cognitively aware of their value. There is as big a difference between cognitively affirming the value of individuality and practicing it as there is between cognitively affirming the value of courage and practicing it.

Because the components of Deweyan autonomy are virtues that must be cultivated, autonomy becomes an achievement. Moreover, because the virtues are more than merely a means to the good life—because they are part of the good life itself—the greater the autonomy we achieve, the greater the degree to which we will realize the good in our lives. Conceptualized thus, autonomy can be seen as a potentiality that all humans possess, a potentiality that may be realized by degrees. Further, because it is the means to the good, and human society is concerned with the good of its members, it becomes the responsibility of society to cultivate this potentiality in all of its members.

Conclusion. The conception of autonomy that I have explicated from Dewey's writings meets the criterion of the reflective chooser set out in the beginning of this chapter. That criterion required that individuals "know" what they are choosing and that they "choose freely." The three virtues contained within Dewey's conception of autonomy enable individuals to choose freely and intelligently within a cultural context.

My Deweyan conception of autonomy also meets all of the criteria for a conception of autonomy set out by Gerald Dworkin.[62] (1) It is logically consistent in that none of the particular virtues internal to it contradicts one of the others—In fact, they can only be rightly understood as a united whole. (2) It is empirically possible in that meliorative growth in any of the particular virtues contained within the Deweyan conception of autonomy is not only possible per se but is a potentiality of all mentally healthy persons. (3) It has value conditions in that it is explicated in a theory in which it is presented as a good or as desirable. (4) It is ideologically neutral, according to Dworkin's conception of that criterion, in that it can be valued by more than merely individualistic societies. (5) It has normative relevance in that liberal institutions, rules and norms can be grounded on it. (6) It has judgmental relevance in that it provides for conceptual judgments, such as the possession of autonomy is a matter of more or less rather than of all or nothing, and it provides for normative judgments, such as "autonomy is that value against which paternalism offends."

Dworkin also says that the central idea of autonomy is self-determination. A Deweyan conception of autonomy requires self-determination because it requires individuals to reflect critically on inherited norms and institutions as well as immediate desires, and it repudiates conformity in favor of individuality. Unlike the Kantian notion of autonomy, however, it does not require the division of persons into transcendent will, on the one hand, and contextual and sensual inclination, on the other. Rather, critical reflection and imaginative reconstruction are means of controlling and redirecting inclinations. A Deweyan conception of autonomy thus provides a means of practical reasoning within particular contexts by developing within individuals certain moral and intellectual virtues. Kantian autonomy, by contrast, merely provides a set of abstract and formal rules that apply to no situation in particular and require no particular character traits other than obedience to duty. As mentioned above, the difference between the Kantian and Deweyan conceptions of autonomy has important political consequences, particularly in regard to the necessity of deliberative democracy and the relevance of individual rights to individual quests for the good.

We have also seen how the intellectual virtues contained within a Deweyan conception of autonomy are necessary conceptual tools for any theory of traditional community that wants to evolve to meet the needs of a changing technological, economic, and social environment. Even MacIntyre writes of the necessity of critical reflection and imaginative innovation and, as we have seen, critical reflection and imaginative innovation are useless without dialogue. So a dynamic tradition would also seem to require a Deweyan notion of sociability rather than docility.

The Deweyan conception of autonomy is not an individualist concept. This is important because it is my intention to show that liberalism is itself not an individualist concept. To understand Dewey, we have to see beyond the tired division of antiliberal community versus liberal individualism and instead to conceptualize the liberal community of autonomous deliberators. We do not have to choose between the priority of the right or the good but rather begin to see the relationship between the right and the good as reciprocal—and more than in just a political sense. The Deweyan conception of autonomy is concerned with cultivating the intellectual virtues that make the good life possible. Unlike hard communitarianism, it does not require that individuals' choices be made for them in the quest for the good. Unlike liberal individualism, it does not consider negative freedom to be a sufficient condition for a quest for the good. The virtues of autonomy provide the individual with the intellectual means necessary to conduct a quest for the good within the context of a particular cultural community. In the next chapter, on a Deweyan conception of the self, I will explain why the autonomous chooser is not only compatible with the contextual self but is a necessary element in any quest for the good within a cultural context.

2

The Context of Freedom:
A Deweyan Conception of the Self

In the previous chapter, we saw that not all conceptions of autonomy need be individualistic. Communitarian theories imply the need for critical reflection and individuality when they claim, as they all do, that their conceptions of community do not require manipulative control of the populace by those in authority. If the shared norms and beliefs of a traditional community are to transcend superstition, blind obedience, and mindless conformism, its members must to some extent practice autonomy in the way that Dewey conceived of it.

On the other hand, a Deweyan conception of autonomy repudiates the notion that individuals are capable of determining their own moral rules, norms, and institutions outside of the context of a moral community. While critical reflection and individuality are necessary for self-determination, they cannot function in a vacuum. Outside of a context of shared meanings, there are no norms, rules, and institutions to reflect critically on, and there is no historical narrative to be influenced by our imaginative innovations. Dewey was quoted in the previous chapter as saying that community is the result of holding meanings in common which, in turn, is a result of communication. Moral reasoning thus requires social dialogue between critically reflective and imaginative individuals.

The goal of this chapter is to show that Dewey's conceptions of the self and of individual autonomy are able to bridge the gap between the liberal notion of autonomy and communitarian depictions of the socially embedded self, thus eliminating pseudoproblems that have occupied theorists in the liberal/communitarian debate. The tension between autonomous choice and objective moral context disappears when we understand the former as representing the elements of change and innovation and the latter as representing the elements of stability and tradition in a dynamic, interactive, and mutually beneficial relationship.

The argument will be presented in four parts. First, we examine the contextual nature of meaning in Dewey's conception of the self. The relationship between the individual mind and the norms, rules, and institutions of a particular cultural tradition is the same in Dewey's philosophy as it is in the theories of communitarians such as Alasdair MacIntyre and Charles Taylor.[1]

Second, we review Dewey's conception of individual autonomy to demonstrate that it preserves the importance of such liberal values as voluntarism, social criticism, and individuality without having to create an artificial tension between the individual and community. The target of communitarian critiques of autonomy is the Kantian conception, and once we see that the Kantian conception does not reflect actual experience, the autonomous individual need not be understood as being antithetical to community.

Third, we confront an argument that the contextual nature of moral life necessarily implies that life be understood as a narrative quest for the good. It will be suggested that this narrative quest, as portrayed by MacIntyre and Taylor, is not coherent without the element of individual autonomy. While MacIntyre's and Taylor's theories prevent them from accepting the Kantian and postmodern conceptions of autonomy, they are entirely compatible with the conception of autonomy contained in Dewey's interpretation of the self.

Finally, the implications Deweyan conceptions of the self and individual autonomy have for identity theory will be examined. Specifically, Dewey's theory of the formation of personal identity is compared with the theory put forth by Richard Rorty. The argument is that Rorty's neopragmatism, which is a synthesis of two distinct traditions of thought—the classical pragmatist tradition of Pierce, James, and Dewey with the postmodern tradition of Nietzsche, Heidegger, Foucault, and others—is neither a logical continuation of pragmatic theory nor does it adequately meet the individual's natural need for a meaningful existence.

Contextualism. Dewey argued that all meaning is contextual. By "meaning," I am referring to the feelings, thoughts, and behavior that are induced by particular objects and events in our environment. Certain objects, for example, may induce feelings of dread; others will induce feelings of affection. We think of an object that induces a feeling of dread as being dreadful: that is the meaning that particular object has for us.[2] By contextual, I am referring to the belief that all human thoughts and emotions are cultivated within particular frameworks of meanings. A cultural tradition, for example, provides a set of norms, values, and beliefs that, for those who are socialized into that culture, become habitual, unconscious, or what some would refer to as intuitive. These habitual ways of feeling, thinking, and acting provide a background or horizon of meanings within which it becomes possible for individuals to reason.

To reason literally means *to give reasons* for the ways we feel, think, and act. Outside of any particular background or horizon, so contextualists argue, it is impossible to exercise reason. Outside of a particular context of meaning, our feelings, thoughts, and behavior become incoherent, meaningless. Dewey believed that the habitual meanings that we are socialized into within our particular cultural tradition mold or channel the natural instincts and innate needs with which we are born.

In his 1938 essay, "Does Human Nature Change?" Dewey stated that there is no reason to believe that the innate needs or instincts of human beings have ever—or will ever—change. Innate needs (such as food, drink, movement, companionship, cooperation, adapting to the environment, emulation of others, the exhibition of energy, and aesthetic expression and satisfaction) and natural tendencies (such as anger, fear, courage, sympathy, selfishness, and the like) are, in all probability, immutable. But these innate needs and tendencies are channeled in a variety of directions by different cultures. The need for food is universal, but the manner in which the need is satisfied varies from culture to culture. The same can be said for the manner in which the need for companionship, or for aesthetic expression, is satisfied, or in some cases repressed, in one culture as compared to another.[3]

The direction in which culture channels the innate needs and tendencies of members is contingent but not arbitrary. Cultural norms are biases that reflect the innate needs of humans in particular natural and social environments. Nietzsche's Zarathustra recognized that all cultural norms reflect some bias or interest: "Verily, my brother, if thou knewest but a people's need, its land, its sky, and its neighbor, then wouldst thou divine the law of its surmountings, and why it climbeth up that ladder to its hope."[4] But if each culture has its own prejudices, can there be any way of evaluating the biases of a particular culture? Dewey believed that there could. The meanings a culture gives to objects and events can be judged by their effectiveness at meeting its members' innate needs and instincts.

One innate need that we all have is for meaning itself, which is why humans are culture-building animals. But there are two senses in which humans seek meaning. One is the sense in which all of our feelings and actions become unintelligible outside of a context of meaning. This is what Dewey was referring to when he said: "Babies owe to adults the opportunity to express native tendencies in meaningful ways," because "the meaning of native activities is acquired." In this sense, our natural tendencies and instincts obtain meaning when they are channeled in a particular way by a particular culture. Outside of that cultural context, meaning is lost. Dewey was adamant that "it is not an ethical ought that conduct should be social. It is social, whether good or bad." Egoism, selflessness, individuality, and conformity are all equally social products.[5]

The other sense in which meaning is a natural need is the sense in which we all need to feel that our lives are meaningful, purposeful, and significant. This is what Dewey was referring to when he noted that "man is more preoccupied with enhancing life than with bare living."[6] This is why, he explained, the ancients developed the epic drama before they did narrative history, and why the development of religion and ornamental art preceded the development of philosophy and the practical arts.[7] Dewey scholar Thomas Alexander speaks of the "human eros": "a deep-seated drive to exist with a sense of meaning and value" that is sought through "love, friendship, happiness, creative work, curiosity, awareness of mystery and beauty and hope." Meaning, in this sense, is what humans "endure suffering and death for the sake of," and is the primary "subject of literature and religion."[8]

The fact that all living organisms have a natural survival instinct is uncontroversial, but Dewey did not believe it is possible to distinguish the desire to survive from the desire to live the good life. Even animals want more than to just continue their physical existence. All living organisms, according to Dewey, practice "selective bias in interactions with the environment in order to maintain [themselves]. Responses are discriminatory on behalf of some results rather than others."[9] The preferred results are the bias, or interests, of the particular organisms. The desire to live a good life, to enhance the quality of experience, is innate in all humans. Cultural biases, therefore, as discriminations on behalf of preferred results, can be judged both by the results they seek and by their efficacy at achieving them.

Natural and social environments are precarious, ruled to a large extent by fortune and contingency. Humans, unlike the lower animals, are capable of inquiring intelligently into which habits or biases will help them satisfy their natural desires in whatever cultural context they happen to be. Meanings (cultural biases) are thus tools or instruments designed to bring individual members into a more harmonious relationship with their environment. Because our social and technological environments are always changing, this quest for harmony is a continuing process. When the process is working as it should, when our innate physical and psychological needs are being met within a contingent and evolving cultural context, then growth is occurring. In Dewey's philosophy, the process of growth is the final end. Just as eudaimonia is the final end in Aristotle's philosophy and all other ends are efficient, growth is the final end for Dewey, and all other goods are tools, instruments, or methods for its realization.[10] The value of the meanings chosen by any particular culture cannot, therefore, be evaluated according to any "disinterested" or neutral standard, but only by the "interests" (or the good) of the individuals within that culture. An ahistorical and transcultural *method* for determining the most useful meanings within each cultural context is, however, implied.

Dewey's conception of the self is thus based on the contextual nature of all meaning. The meaning that words, objects, and events have for us is always somehow related to a context of cultural habits of thinking, feeling, and acting: "We grasp the meaning of what is said in our own language not because appreciation of context is unnecessary but because context is so unescapably present. It is taken for granted. . . . Habits of speech, including syntax and vocabulary, and modes of interpretation have been formed in the face of inclusive and defining situations of context. . . . We are not explicitly aware of the role of context just because our every utterance is so saturated with it that it forms the significance of what we say and hear."[11]

Dewey assured us that "[w]hat is true of the meaning of words and sentences is true of all meaning." Cultural norms, values, and beliefs provide a field or network of givens, a stable body of assumptions that allows all particular objects and events to become intelligible. "Surrounding, bathing, saturating, the things of which we are explicitly aware is some inclusive situation which does not enter into the direct material of reflection. It does not come into question; it is taken for granted."[12]

"Mind" is the label that Dewey gave to this relatively stable body of habitual meanings that are held by individuals and that are originally transmitted to the young through socialization and education. Meanings, he insisted, are of an aesthetic nature and are arrived at dialogically. Thus, Dewey described mind as "an added property assumed by the feeling creature when it reaches communicative interaction with others."[13] Prior to communication, no meanings are attached to the feelings of living creatures. Mind originates when feelings are intersubjectively verified and habitualized through social interaction. The result is a body of meanings held unconsciously by the member of a particular culture. "The child learns through social intercourse that certain behavior is greedy, rude, anger, and that certain qualities are red, foul odor or musical tone."[14] Mind is thus a function of the physical organ we call the brain, and not a separate thing in itself.

"Consciousness" is also a function—one that constitutes present awareness. It is the individual's focus on immediate experience or, as Dewey explained, "that which is imminent and critical." The objects and events of consciousness receive their meaning from the context provided by mind. Mind allows the individual to fit the objects of immediate experience into a pattern that is organized, ordered, and coherent. Prior to the emergence of mind, the living creature with a brain can act upon impulse or be conditioned by memory (training), but it cannot attach meaning or value to the objects and events of nature. "Objects of knowledge do not come to us pre-defined, classified and labeled." Mind provides the categories, classifications, and values that provide the objects of experience with meaning; it "suffuses, interpenetrates, colors" the objects of consciousness. Meanings provide the "rules for using and interpreting things."[15] In other words, mind provides all of our perceptions with context and makes reasoning possible. Consciousness "denotes the part of the road upon which the spotlight is thrown. The spatial context is the ground through which the road runs and for the sake of which the road exists. It is this setting which gives import to the road."[16]

Dewey's notion of context, I believe, is similar, if not identical, to those of modern communitarian theorists such as MacIntyre and Taylor. Dewey claimed: "There is no thinking which does not present itself on a background of tradition, and tradition has an intellectual quality that differentiates it from blind custom. Traditions are ways of interpretation and of observation, of valuation, of everything explicitly thought of."[17] Speaking of tradition, MacIntyre remarks that "I inherit from the past of my family, my city, my tribe, my nation, a variety of debts, inheritances, rightful expectations and obligations. These constitute the given of my life, my moral starting point." Such traditions, MacIntyre continues, do not represent a fixed body of beliefs but, "when vital, embody continuities of conflict."[18]

The conflict is most significantly over the meanings contained within the cultural context—in particular, those meanings having to do with the tradition's conception of the good life. "A living tradition then is an historically extended, socially embodied argument, and an argument precisely in part about the goods which constitute that tradition."[19]

MacIntyre's notion of tradition is similar to Taylor's idea of horizons of meaning. "My identity is defined by the commitments and identifications which provide the frame or horizon within which I can try to determine from case to case what is good, or valuable, or what ought to be done, or what I endorse or oppose." This frame or horizon is in all cases the product of a language community. "To study persons is to study beings who only exist in, or are partly constituted by, a certain language," and "a language only exists and is maintained within a language community." So therefore, "one is a self only among other selves."[20] Dewey's conception of the contextual self is thus wholly compatible with those offered by communitarians such as MacIntyre and Taylor.

Dewey's autonomy. As we saw in chapter 1, Dewey's conception of autonomy consists of three components, which provide a method of practical rationality: critical reflection, individuality, and sociability. And as we saw above, all moral reasoning takes place within the context provided by a particular cultural tradition. To be autonomous, individuals must reflect critically on the cultural meanings they have inherited. This exercise is necessary not only to make meanings their own but because of the continual need for reconstruction. Dewey tells us that beliefs, ideals, standards, and methods of interpretation are inherited from a previous age and may be at odds with actual conditions.[21] Thus, to accept cultural meanings blindly is to act unintelligently. Reflection, Dewey pointed out, is the "sole alternative to habit, caprice, and random action."[22] The purpose of criticism is not to find correct meanings but to "criticize those already operative" in terms of their conditions and consequences: to determine whether meaning A works better or worse than meaning B, to decide which best harmonizes with the existing body of meanings and which produces the more desirable consequences.[23]

Dewey explained that reflective morals "uses all particular codes as data," including the creative products of our own imagination. The source of creativity in moral inquiry is individuality. Individuality is that aspect of the individual that is genuinely unique, a perspective that only one person can have because it is acquired through a unique personal history. Individuality is "a potentiality and is realized only in interaction with surrounding conditions. . . . Native capacities . . . are transformed and become a self."[24] Dewey defined art as the "authentic expression of any and all individuality."[25] The importance of this creative capacity is not limited to the creation of new meanings but is necessary to adapt alien meanings to one's cultural tradition in a way that is continuous with the preexisting body.

Art, according to Dewey's theory, is the synthesis of subjectivity and objectivity. The subjective component is the imagination of the individual, and the objective component is the preexisting body of cultural meanings. All genuine creativity begins with a unique perspective on an objective (or, more properly, intersubjective) problem or concern. Pure objectivity leaves no room for a contribution from the creativity of the individual. Pure subjectivity, because it is located outside of the context provided by culture, is meaningless.

Dewey's notion of authenticity, therefore, is close to Taylor's.[26] Taylor's argument is that a totally subjective identity, one that rejects all social demands and standards, is ultimately insignificant and trivial. The source of all significance and meaning is a language community. An authentic identity is thus a "non-trivial identity," a product of free choices that are worthy of being chosen according to the standards of a particular language community.[27] Likewise, for Dewey, an individual cannot become authentic without being situated within a context of shared meanings. So, while our choices may be the result of critical reflection and free will, they must take place within a language community for there to be a way of evaluating them.

Choices, as Taylor points out, cannot be valuable simply by virtue of being freely chosen. Even if a particular moral context elevated free choice as the highest value, it could not value the free choice of a lifestyle that rejected the value of free choice. Our cultural tradition provides both the meanings that we subject to critical reflection and the criteria by which they, and any innovations, are judged. Thus, sociabilty, or the disposition to participate cooperatively with others on a common project, is also a necessary virtue for a practical conception of autonomy.

As I pointed out in the previous chapter, the three components—critical reflection, individuality, and sociability—that together comprise Dewey's conception of autonomy cannot be understood in isolation from each other. When we reflect critically, we must reflect on something, and when we criticize, we must do so in terms of a standard. What we are reflecting on is the existing body of cultural meanings. If we reject the notion that we can transcend time and chance and enter into a fixed, universal—and thus neutral—realm of reason, then we must criticize in terms of the standards provided by our own culture. It follows that we can never subject a culture as a whole to reflective criticism without using the standards of an alien culture. Reflective criticism is an exercise that is confined to particular meanings within the culture as a whole. Particular ideals, principles, norms, or beliefs that have become problematic are subjected to critical reflection in terms of the standard provided by the cultural tradition as a whole. Thus, our identity can never be completely the product of subjectivity. Even Heidegger, despite the value he attached to subjectivity, recognized that we can criticize our cultural identity only in terms of the norms and values that we have inherited.[28] The relationship between critical reflection and authenticity is thus reciprocal. To be a reflective individual requires that one also be sociable— that is, that one be securely situated within a horizon of meanings. The reverse is also true. To be a sociable person, one must also be reflective. It is docility and not sociability that requires us to adopt the meanings provided by our culture uncritically.

Individuality is also implicated in the notion of a sociable relationship between the individual and the community. Dewey argued that genuine creativity is purposive—an innovation designed to deal with an objective situation. How well the innovation performs its task can be determined only by experience—and thus a culture's meanings are generalizations of its members' intersubjective experiences. Pure subjectivity is necessarily trivial and eccentric because it is necessarily private and incommunicable. To speak of private meanings is equivalent to speaking of a private language. In Dewey's discussion of art in *Art as Experience,* he explains the synthesis of subjectivity and objectivity in all acts of creativity. "A poem and picture present material passed through the alembic of personal experience. They have no precedence in existence or in universal being. But, nonetheless, their material came from the public world and so has qualities in common with the material of other experiences, while the product awakens in other persons new perceptions of the meanings of the common world. The oppositions of individual and universal, of subjective and objective, of freedom and order, in which philosophers have reveled, have no place in the work of art. Expression as personal act and as objective result are organically connected with each other."[29] One cannot pretend to be sociable and at the same time lack individuality, for conformist sociability is equivalent to docility and, as we have seen, docility is the vice caused by an excess of sociability. On the other hand, it is just as impossible to cultivate one's individuality outside of the context of meaning provided by a cultural tradition. To be an autonomous person is thus, according to Dewey's conception of it, to be an individual who puts into practice his or her capacities for critical reflection and imaginative reconstruction within a body of culturally transmitted norms and beliefs.

The narrative quest for the good. Dewey's conception of the self, like that of most contextualists, is a narrative conception. The context of cultural meanings in which individuals find themselves embedded develops through time. We can fully grasp a meaning's significance only if we know its history. So each cultural tradition can be understood in terms of a narrative. Likewise, the particular lives of individuals can be understood only as narratives within a (cultural) narrative. They have beginnings, middles, and ends, and in the process of moving from beginning to end, development occurs.

MacIntyre helps to clarify the notion of a narrative self when he insists that human behavior must be understood in terms of the intentions, desires, and goals of actors and that these intentions, desires, and goals are only intelligible when understood as episodes in the history of an individual's life.[30] In his essay "Time and Individuality," Dewey asked us to understand that life is characterized by a "temporal seriality":

> Take the account of the life of any person. . . . Everything recorded
> is an historical event . . . or, if you prefer, it is a course of events
> each of which takes up into itself something of what went before
> and leads on to that which comes after. The skill, the art, of the
> biographer is displayed in his ability to discover and portray the
> subtle ways . . . in which one event grows out of those which pre-

ceded and enters into those which follow. . . . That which comes later explains the earlier quite as truly as the earlier explains the later. . . . Individuality is the uniqueness of the history, of the career, not something given once for all at the beginning which proceeds to unroll as a ball of yarn may be unwound.[31]

Each person's biography contains a unique series of interactions with the environment called experiences. These experiences mold each person's mind in a unique way. Because each self is the product of a distinct personal history, mind is individualized.

This is not a deterministic process because, as we have already seen, the autonomous individual has some control over his or her own development. The nonautonomous individual, on the other hand, is the product of external forces. Failure to reconstruct the self leads to the disintegration of individuality.[32] The self is not "something complete, perfect, finished," as it is in a conception of the self that transcends time and chance, it is involved in a continuous process of growth, realizing new imaginative possibilities by the incorporation of new habits. Individuality, Dewey contended, is "something moving, changing, discrete, and above all initiating instead of final."

> Except as the outcome of arrested development, there is no such thing as a fixed, ready-made, finished self. Every living self causes acts and is itself caused in return by what it does. All voluntary action is a remaking of the self, since it creates new desires, instigates new modes of endeavor, brings to light new conditions which institute new ends. Our personal identity is found in the thread of continuous development which binds together these changes. In the strictest sense, it is impossible for the self to stand still; it is becoming, and becoming for the better or the worse. It is in the *quality* of becoming that the virtues reside. We set up this and that end to be reached, but *the* end is growth itself. To make an end a final goal is but to arrest growth.[33]

Thus, for Dewey, narrative provides the "time" dimension of a social context (culture providing the "space" dimension). We can understand ourselves only in terms of where we have been and where we would like to be. The elimination of another philosophical dualism is at work here. The present exists between the past, which can be understood in terms of materialism (mechanistic cause and effect) and the future, which can be understood in terms of idealism (teleological goals). Experience helps us to understand which causes produce the effects, or ends, that we want. For example, in terms of self-development, I might ask which beliefs, if they were to become habits, produce the type of character that I understand as good?

Pragmatism might be understood, then, as the synthesis of material-ism and idealism, and historical narrative as the synthesis of mechanistic and teleological descriptions of the world. In this sense, ideals and teleo-logical ends cannot be preexisting (discoverable truths) *unless they are methods of controlling the process of change.* By control, I do not mean in the sense of overcoming contingency but of dealing with it intelligently and morally rather than impulsively or according to thoughtless habit.

The ultimate end—growth—and the method of attaining it—the moral and intellectual virtues of the autonomous chooser—transcend any particular narrative just as they do any particular culture. Posses-sion of the virtues of autonomy does not tell us, therefore, the specific directions growth will take within a particular context. For example, feminists want to stop the practice of socializing young girls into tradi-tional gender roles, not so they can be socialized into preferable femi-nist roles—this would merely be to replace one preconceived and fixed identity with another—but rather so that they can be socialized to be autonomous choosers, free to develop their own identities. Dewey's conception of autonomy provides the virtues by which an individual can develop a personal identity within a social context. The virtues tell us that the identity will be the product of intelligent and moral choices because of the intellectual and moral virtues, but it does not tell us the specific identity of any particular autonomous chooser.

Dewey does not conceive of a self that *endures* through the changes that take place in this development but rather of a self that is *continu-ally* changing or becoming. Dewey learned from Bergson and James that the distinction between passing from one state into another and con-tinuing in what is called the same state is another false dichotomy. There is no such thing as a desire, feeling, or idea that is not constantly un-dergoing change—even if only the change of becoming one moment older and hence capable of being conveyed from the past into the present by memory. We imagine a difference only when change becomes dras-tic enough for us to notice it. The self, thus, "does not endure through change, but by change."[34] Personal identity is found in the thread of con-tinuous development because we can only understand who we are at age sixty-five in terms of who we were at ages five and twenty-five and so on. Critical reflection requires us to reflect on conditions and conse-quences of, for example, a belief; but this is just another way of saying that we must reflect on the narrative history of the belief—from the conditions of its origin to the future consequences of its continued use.

The contextual and narrative conception of the self necessarily in-vokes the idea of a narrative quest for the good. MacIntyre claims that the "unity of a human life is the unity of a narrative quest."[35] Taylor's spatial analogy provides a good way of explaining the necessity of the quest. The horizon of meanings provided by a cultural tradition situates individuals morally. It enables them to judge the worth of their life choices in terms of a cultural standard. In other words, we can see where we stand in relation to the good when we can locate ourselves within a background of cultural meanings. If the narrative conception of life means that we are developing through time, then the background provided by our cultural tradition tells us in which direction we need to go. "One could put it this way: because we cannot but orient ourselves to the good, and thus determine our place relative to it and hence determine the direction of our lives, we must inescapably understand our lives in narrative form, as a 'quest'. But one could perhaps start from another point: because we have to determine our place in relation to the good, therefore we cannot be without an orientation to it, and hence must see our life in story. From whichever direction, I see these conditions as connected facets of the same reality, inescapable structural requirements of human agency."[36] Compare this with Dewey: "[A]t the time of practical experience man exists from moment to moment, preoccupied with the task of the moment. As he resurveys all the moments in thought, a drama emerges with a beginning, a middle and a movement toward the climax of achievement or defeat."[37] Dewey did not mean by this that we can ever rest from our reconstructive quest for the good life, because "direction of movement, not the plane of attainment and rest, determines moral quality."

Dewey complained: "Practically all moralists have made much of a distinction between a lower and a higher self, speaking of the carnal and spiritual, the animal and the truly human. . . . The only distinction, however, that can be drawn without reducing morals to conventionality, self-righteous complacency, or a hopeless and harsh struggle for the unattainable, is that between the attained static, and the moving dynamic self."[38] Dewey's notion of the autonomous self was necessarily implicated in this narrative quest for the good. The notion of a narrative quest would seem to imply the necessity of certain capacities contained within the Deweyan conception of autonomy: criticism of existing meanings, the application of imaginative alternatives, free will, and the like. As we have seen, even a staunch critic of liberalism such as MacIntyre maintains that reason, operating within the horizon of a particular context, can transcend "through criticism and invention the limitations of what had hitherto been reasoned in that tradition."[39] In the debates between communitarians and liberals, however, the notions of autonomy, individuality, and voluntarism have been linked almost exclusively to the liberal side of the argument. A false dichotomy has developed that asks, "Can individuals decide for themselves what to believe or what not to believe, or are their beliefs determined by their cultural environment?"

Can a critic of liberalism such as MacIntyre equate voluntarism with an arbitrary and noncontextual choice of ends and still speak logically of transcending the limitations of tradition while involved in a narrative quest for the good? Can we transcend the limitations of our existing tradition through "criticism and invention" without being voluntarists?[40] Dewey would agree with MacIntyre that our cultural tradition must provide impersonal criteria in order for genuine moral reasoning to take place, but not that this contextual rationality is incompatible with the autonomous self or with voluntarism. MacIntyre insists that even though "the self has to find its moral identity in and through its membership in communities," this "does not entail that the self has to accept the moral *limitations* of the particularity of those forms of community."[41] But he does not tell us how personal growth or transcendence can take place in a community of shared beliefs where autonomy is not treated as an essential virtue.

MacIntyre's argument can be summarized as the claim that we must choose between living within the rational context of a cultural tradition or adhering to the values of liberal society, in which case all of our moral choices must be noncontextual and thus arbitrary or emotivist. Dewey's conceptions of the self and autonomy show that this choice is unnecessary. There is nothing incompatible between the liberal values of freedom, individuality, autonomy, and voluntarism, on the one hand, and the contextual and narrative conception of the self, on the other. In fact, if, as communitarians such as MacIntyre and Taylor conclude, the contextual and narrative conception of the self necessarily implies the characterization of life as a narrative quest for the good, liberal values are not merely compatible but necessary. Individual growth or perfection within a cultural context necessarily implies the capacities of critical reflection and creative individuality. These two capacities, as well as the third component in Dewey's conception of autonomy—sociability— necessarily imply a society characterized by liberal freedoms, toleration, and democracy.

The reason communitarians tend to think of liberalism as inherently opposed to the notion of contextual rationality can be better understood by confronting an argument put forth by Taylor on the nature of practical rationality. Taylor claims that contextualists depend on a kind of "substantive" rationality that is oriented around "what we think." Liberals, on the other hand, depend on a "procedural" rationality that is concerned with "*how* we think." According to Taylor, procedural rationality necessarily discounts substantive notions of the good because the method of reasoning must be evaluated independently of its conclusions. This involves liberals in a contradiction because they are committed to the substantive goods of liberalism—that is, autonomy, freedom, toleration, and the like. Their procedural method of rationality requires liberals to claim neutrality between alternative goods yet, at the same time, they want to claim the superiority of autonomy, freedom, and toleration.[42]

The incompatibility between procedural rationality and liberal goods can be eliminated by adopting a Deweyan conception of autonomy. As we just saw, the components contained in Dewey's conception of autonomy—critical reflection, individuality, and sociability—are necessary means in the individual's narrative quest for the good within a cultural context. These three components do not merely describe behavior in particular situations, nor are they merely capacities that an individual may possess but not utilize; they are personal attitudes or dispositions and are, thus, elements of character. As such, we must think of them as virtues.

MacIntyre's account of virtue is again helpful to us here. MacIntyre defines a practice as any cooperative activity in which goods are realized. He includes within that definition the "making and sustaining of forms of human community." He then defines virtue as a means to obtain the goods sought by a practice: *"A virtue is an acquired human quality the possession and exercise of which tends to enable us to achieve those goods which are internal to practices and the lack of which effectively prevents us from achieving any such goods."* MacIntyre gives as examples the virtues of honesty, courage, and justice which, he claims, are necessary to all practices regardless of cultural context. Liberalism ultimately fails, he adds, because it promotes external goods (money, material goods, power, and status) at the expense of these internal goods or virtues.[43]

Compare MacIntyre's discussion of virtue to Dewey's: "Accordingly we shall discuss virtue through enumeration of traits which must belong to an attitude if it is to be genuinely an interest, not by enumeration of virtues as if they were separate entities. (1) *an interest must be wholehearted.* Virtue is integrity, vice is duplicity. . . . (2) the interest which constitutes a disposition must be continuous and *persistent.* . . . [And finally,] a complete interest must be (3) *impartial* as well as enduring."[44] A look at the context in which both authors use them shows that the terms *honesty, courage,* and *justice* can be freely interchanged with the terms *wholehearted, persistent,* and *impartial.* As for Dewey's use of the term *interest,* he explained: "Any concrete case of the union of the self in action with an object and end is called an interest. Children form the interest of a parent; painting or music is the interest of an artist. . . . An interest is, in short, the dominant direction of activity."[45] When we compare this to MacIntyre's notion of a practice, we see: "[F]arming is. So are the inquiries of physics . . ., and so are painting and music."[46] Thus the terms *interest* and *practice* are also interchangeable.

Dewey thus argued that certain dispositions or virtues are necessary in the quest for any "object" or "end." If the end in question is the good life—or, in Dewey's terms, "growth"—then the virtues of whole-heartedness, persistence, and impartiality are necessary if the quest is to be successful. Dewey believes that these virtues "interpenetrate one another" and may be called as a whole "moral wisdom."[47] In the same manner, the virtues of reflectiveness, individuality, and sociability are necessary in any quest for the good regardless of the cultural context in which the quest takes place. They also interpenetrate one another and as a whole may be referred to as the intellectual virtues. Together, the virtues constitute a Deweyan conception of autonomy.

When we understand Dewey's conception of autonomy as consisting of virtues internal to a practice, the contradiction between procedural rationality and substantive goods disappears. As MacIntyre points out: "The virtues are of course themselves in turn fostered by certain types of social institution and endangered by others."[48] The virtues of critical reflection, individuality, and sociability and the social institutions that foster them—freedom, toleration, democracy—are not the *products* of procedural rationality, but the *components* of it. Likewise, the virtues are necessary to any particular conception of the good—they in fact place limitations on the desirable conceptions of the good—but they do not prevent the liberal state from being neutral between those conceptions of the good that do not circumvent the virtues of procedural rationality. The plurality of substantive conceptions of the good are thus the product of the liberal method of procedural rationality.

Despite the space provided for a plurality of goods, a Deweyan notion of liberalism is necessarily ideal-based as opposed to neutrality-based because the life of the autonomous chooser, regardless of his or her particular choices, *is itself* the good life. This must not be understood to mean that the worthiness of a choice does not matter as long as it is freely chosen. Rather, it means that the virtues of critical reflection, individuality, and sociability provide individuals with the best method for arriving at the most worthy choices in terms of their particular life histories.[49]

Contrary to Taylor's argument, liberals need not, by emphasizing method or procedural rationality, give primacy to existing desires and will, not when the method is constituted by critical reflection and imaginative reconstruction. Contrary to Taylor's argument, the emphasis on free and autonomous choice does not deny the existence of an objective order—rather, it provides the only rational means of growth within that objective order. Taylor himself reports that within any particular horizon there are a plurality of goods that may conflict, and that any given individual will have to rank them. He also advises that individu-

als are the source of innovations.[50] How can this innovation and rank-
ing proceed in the absence of free and autonomous choice?

Taylor, of course, has in mind the Kantian and postmodernist defi-
nitions of freedom and autonomy when he rejects their compatibility
with an objective horizon of moral meanings. He explains that the rank-
ing and innovation occur in a dialogical context. But as we have seen,
Dewey's conception of autonomy is completely compatible with Taylor's
notion of authenticity and the dialogical nature of moral reasoning. The
key is Dewey's theory of art, in which the opposition between objectivity and subjectivity is seen to be unnecessary. True moral inquiry, and
thus growth, will always involve a dialectical relationship between the
objective context of the community and the subjective imagination of
the individual. Communitarians need to recognize the necessity of autonomous individuality just as much as liberals need to recognize the
necessity of community.

Identity. In the final part of this chapter, we will examine the implications of Dewey's conception of the self for personal identity, specifically by comparing the construction of identity in Dewey's philosophy
with that explicated by neopragmatist Richard Rorty in his book *Contingency, Irony, and Solidarity.* I show that, contrary to Rorty's claim,
Dewey does not stand at the end of the road that postmodernists are
traveling.[51] Dewey, in fact, would have rejected the subjectivity of the
postmoderns as strenuously as he did the objectivity of transcendental
philosophy.

I will begin with the definition of identity offered by Taylor. "My
identity is defined by the commitments and identifications which provide the frame or horizon within which I can try to determine from case
to case what is good, or valuable, or what ought to be done, or what I
endorse or oppose. In other words, it is the horizon within which I am
capable of taking a stand."[52] The questions we will be concerned with
are how individuals come to have the particular set of "commitments
and identifications" (or, in other words, the particular horizons) that
they do, and what part socialization and voluntarism have in the making of personal identity.

Dewey's conception of autonomy suggests the capacity of individuals to mold their own identities but only within the context of a particular framework of meanings. The narrative conception of life implies
that individuals must exercise the virtues of the autonomous chooser
within two contexts. One is the social framework provided by one's
community; the other is the individual's own unique personal history.

Although the mind is saturated with the shared meanings of a cultural tradition, from moment to moment, consciousness is focused on
a continuous series of personal experiences. How individuals respond

to these experiences determines their identity. If a meaning provided by our cultural framework induces feelings and actions that lead to satisfactory consummations in our personal experiences, then this meaning will become habitual, and thus a part of our character or identity. If it leads to unsatisfactory consummations, we have the capacity to reflect critically on the meaning and perhaps imaginatively alter or replace it in a way that is continuous with the remaining body of meanings that constitutes our identity.

Because of the operation of criticism and imagination within a social context, autonomous individuals are able to create a unique and intensely personal perspective. The self is as much a creation of the power of the individual imagination as it is of the community. But individuality can be achieved only within a social context; it is therefore a social product. "The human being is an individual because of and in relation to others. Otherwise he is an individual only as a stick of wood is, namely, as spatially and numerically separate."[53]

Let me turn now to a discussion of the self as explicated by Rorty. Rorty characterizes the conversation between intellectuals over the past couple of centuries on the construction of the self as a battle between philosophy and poetry. Either human nature is fixed by nature and is thus universal, or the identity of each individual is created within a changing and contingent world. Once we recognize that the notion of a fixed and universal human nature is a myth, Rorty explains, we are left with the options of subjectively creating our selves or allowing our selves to be created by others.

Dewey stresses the role cultural meanings play as responses to objective environmental conditions and as constituting in themselves an objective social environment for members. Rorty, on the other hand, stresses the notion that cultural meanings are merely descriptions of the world made by someone else, probably reflecting someone else's interests and needs rather than mine. While this may be partially true, when we understand cultural meanings only in the sense stressed by Rorty, we cannot help but understand freedom—autonomy—as *liberation from* cultural meanings. Thus, reflecting a Nietzschean rather than a Deweyan notion of the relation between the individual and community, Rorty argues that self-perfection is entirely a private affair.[54]

"To create one's own mind is to create one's own language, rather than to let the length of one's mind be set by the language other human beings have left behind." And Rorty is not here referring only to the future direction of one's life, but to a redescription of who and what one is today. "[C]oming to know oneself. . .; tracking one's causes home, is identical with the process of inventing a new language—that is, of thinking up some new metaphors. For any . . . use of an inherited language game for this purpose, will necessarily fail." My individual identity, therefore, must be the product of an "idiosyncratic fantasy."[55] It should be noted, however, that individual identity "must be" the product of idiosyncratic fantasy only if I wish to be autonomous. Otherwise, individual identity is simply a product of someone else's (an inherited) language.

When Dewey spoke of "making oneself," he was speaking of reconstructing meanings, which results in a change in the way we will feel and act in the future from the way we felt and acted in the past. Rorty speaks of redescribing our past feelings and actions so that they now have a different meaning for us. Dewey was concerned with changing character so that it becomes more worthy according to our horizon of meanings. Rorty is concerned with freeing personal identity from any outside evaluation of worth: "The paradigm . . . is the life of the genius who can say of the relevant portion of the past, 'Thus I willed it,' because she has found a way to describe the past which the past never knew, and thereby found a self to be which her precursors never knew was possible."[56]

According to Rorty, Freud democratized this genius by giving everyone a creative unconscious: "By seeing every human being as consciously or unconsciously acting out an idiosyncratic fantasy, we can see the distinctively human, as opposed to animal, portion of each human life as the use for symbolic purposes of every particular person, object, situation, event, and word encountered in later life. This process amounts to redescribing them, thereby saying of them all, 'Thus I willed it.'"[57]

No quest for the good is possible for such persons because they are located in no moral space. Their existing character can simply be redescribed as the good. This is the type of freedom and autonomy that Taylor is referring to when he says that it denies the existence of an objective order and merely gives primacy to existing desires and will. The worth one's identity takes on under a Rortyan conception of the self is the worth of being freely chosen and original. Originality is, for Rorty, a good in itself.[58] For Dewey, originality was *purposeful.* "The artist in realizing his own individuality reveals potentialities hitherto unrealized. This revelation is the inspiration of other individuals to make the potentialities real, for it is not sheer revolt against things as they are which stirs human endeavor to its depths, but a vision of what might be and is not."[59] Dewey, unlike Rorty and postmodernism in general, did not celebrate difference for difference's sake, but rather for the opportunities it lends both individuals and the community as a whole for growth.

Rorty, of course, concludes that "no project of redescribing the world and the past, no project of self-creation through the imposition of one's own idiosyncratic metaphoric can avoid being marginal and parasitic" on existing languages.[60] But Rorty does not see this dependence on a cultural tradition as valuable because it is a source of meaning; rather, he sees it as an unfortunate and inescapable limitation on the project of self-perfection.

The label "authentic" not only implies that something is genuine but that it is worthy of trust. The meanings that make up the identity of a Deweyan self, while they may originally be the product of subjectivity (and hence genuine), are verified through the intersubjective experience of the community as a whole (and thus worthy of trust). They are purposeful tools designed to deal with existential conditions in an objectively real social environment and can therefore be tested. As such, they are more worthy of trust than the untested "idiosyncratic fantasies" of isolated individuals. It follows that Dewey's (and by implication Taylor's) conception of what constitutes an authentic self is superior to the Rortyan conception.

Privatizing self-creation may protect me from the idiosyncratic fantasies of others, but it does not protect me from my own fantasies. "Authenticity," as Heidegger meant it, refers to a personal identity that is worthy of being chosen by virtue of being original as opposed to parasitic. But what standard makes originality more worthy than parasitism? Both Rorty and Heidegger reject the notion of universal standards, so the standard must be cultural. But this means that the standard that judges originality as being more worthy than parasitism is itself parasitic on some cultural context of meanings. Without either a cultural or universal standard of worth, there is no way of positing one way of developing personal identity as more or less worthy than any other way. There is an inescapable theory of self-development in any conception of the self that posits a goal that is worthy of being achieved. If Heideggerian authenticity is seen as an argument for a way of life that is worthy of being chosen, then it is subject to competition from arguments for alternative ways of self-development. Dewey made the argument that while originality is necessary, it is not sufficient for the construction of a worthy identity. Isolated from such goods as critical reflection and intersubjective verification, the originality of my identity may have no connection with the reality of my natural and social environment. Psychologists refer to these kinds of meanings and identities as delusionary.

It does not follow, however, that the identity of a Deweyan self is entirely constituted by the descriptions of others. Dewey's conception of the self is dependent on the notion of a dynamic and interactive relationship between cultural meanings and personal innovations that are the products of unique personal histories. Mind is continually being adapted by small degrees to a changing reality by the experiences of consciousness. Different life histories mean different life experiences, which result in different adaptations of mind. Even infants, Dewey pointed out, because of idiosyncrasies and self-image (based on the way they are treated), have unique personalities although socialized into the same culture.

When individuals in Dewey's theory encounter one another, they do so with unique perspectives. If this were not so, communication would be of no more use in the quest for the good than it is in the idiosyncratic quests of postmodernists. The representative perspective of any particular individual would suffice. Individual creativity would be nonexistent. Intersubjective verification, the criterion of knowledge in Dewey's theory that asks, "Was your personal experience with this particular object or process similar to mine?" would be meaningless. Remove the individualizing effects of personal history, and the self cannot develop and grow. Remove individuality from the community, and culture does not develop and grow. It stagnates. Every time a novel meaning is incorporated into the mind of an individual, the self is changed. Although the greatest part of the self is characterized by stability, the gradual accumulation of numerous small changes in attitude or perspective can, eventually, result in a transformed personality or character. New attitudes and interests are created; old ones are altered. Innovation changes context which, in turn, changes the way we perceive things.

New meanings may originate as impulses or ideas. They may be entirely the product of personal reflection or be adapted from an outside source (a preexisting principle from another culture or from a particular moral philosopher's theory, for example). Regardless of their source, meanings are incorporated into the mind of a reflective individual only when first, the individual is satisfied through experience that the new meaning is valuable, and second, the individual makes a creative effort to incorporate the new value into his or her individualized mind. (The artist can create a new meaning that may be incorporated into the culture at large, but individuals must perform the feat within their own minds.) Thus, by adapting old habits to new circumstances and by intelligently uniting immediate desires into a stable body of meanings, individuals are choosing what kind of a person they want to be. We are making, or remaking, our selves.[61]

Conclusion. Freedom, Dewey maintained, is trivial and meaningless if it simply amounts to the ability to follow the whims of personal preference. We live in an objectively real environment. We can find meaning in our lives, and we can experience fulfillment, only within an objectively real context. It follows that to define freedom as the ability to follow the whims of personal preference is either to ignore this fact or to give up the quest for meaning and fulfillment. Creative individuality is an element of freedom, but it is an element that can be exercised only within a specific context without degenerating into meaningless eccentricity. Freedom is not liberation from objective reality. It is rather a matter of the correct relationship between this objective reality and the functioning of individual imagination. It is the ability to make, and act on, intelligent choices from the base of our own individuality.

Raymond Boisvert compares Dewey's conception of freedom to developing a talent—such as learning to play the piano. "Mere freedom to practice is not enough. For the talent to grow dependencies are necessary."[62] As the talent grows, so does the freedom to play. Dewey's freedom is thus the actual freedom to function meaningfully within an objective context as opposed to the formal freedom we receive from merely being left alone. We will close this chapter with a quote from Dewey's *Theory of the Moral Life:* "The final word about the place of the self in the moral life is, then, that the very problem of morals is to form an original body of impulsive tendencies into a voluntary self in which desires and affections center in the values which are common; in which interest focuses in objects that contribute to the enrichment of the lives of all. If we identify the interests of such a self with the virtues, then we shall say, with Spinoza, that happiness is not the reward of virtue, but is virtue itself."[63]

3

The Freedom of Creativity: A Deweyan Conception of Individuality

In the introduction, I pointed out the importance of complexity for an organism or system that wants to adapt to its environment. "Complexity" was defined as the synthesis of differentiation and integration. The greater the degree of differentiation, the better an organism or system is able to adapt to change because of the larger number of qualities available to meet needs in a new environment. An undifferentiated, or simple, organism or system has fewer qualities with which to respond to the challenge of a changing environment. Environmentalists argue that the ecosystem as a whole, for example, becomes more precarious with each extinction of a plant or animal species. Thus, as differentiation of the ecosystem is minimized, the greater the likelihood that a new, contingent—and possibly catastrophic—problem will occur that humanity is unable to cope with.

Differentiation without integration, however, results in disintegration. All of the differentiating elements must merge harmoniously if there is to be a *system*. It is precisely because humans have not learned to live harmoniously with their environment that differentiation of the ecosystem is being minimized. A complex ecosystem requires both differentiation and integration. The greater the degree of such complexity, the greater the likelihood that it can adapt to contingency. Dewey did not derive his belief in the necessity of the synthesis of integration and differentiation from a study of the ecosystem, however, despite the influence of Darwin on his philosophy. Hegel was a far greater influence in regard to this particular aspect of Dewey's thought. From Hegel, Dewey derived the importance of the simultaneous use of the rational operations of analysis (differentiation) and synthesis (integration) for knowledge of the world.

In the case of the state, this relationship between analysis/differentiation and synthesis/integration takes the form of the interaction between the individual and the community. In regard to the quest for survival, or for knowledge, either of the poles in isolation is insufficient to meet the needs of a state's members. The recognition of both individuals and community requires the type of political system that is characterized by the participation of autonomous individuals in cooperative endeavors to solve problems they hold in common. This type of participatory democracy will be the focus of chapter 4, on social intelligence. Before discussing the ways in which individuals integrate their efforts, however, I must discuss the differentiating element in Dewey's political theory.

Because of the inadequacy of the individual (differentiation) in isolation from the community (integration), the asocial individual*ism* of rights-based liberalism is insufficient to provide this differentiating element. Dewey turns our attention, instead, to the concept of individual-*ity*. Individuality differs from individualism in that it does not require isolation from community but rather emphasizes the unique perspectives and contributions that individual members can make when they are integrated into a community. In this chapter I will discuss, therefore, a Deweyan conception of individuality.

Because individuality refers to the uniqueness of persons, it can be understood as another word for the concept of creativity. To develop one's individuality is to develop one's creative imagination. The concept of individuality is thus intimately related to art or poetry. Dewey draws an analogy between art and the use of imaginative creativity in the process of self and cultural evolution in the same sense that Nietzsche used the analogy between poetry and the creation of personal identity and cultural values. Dewey's theory of art is therefore useful if we would understand exactly what his conception of individuality is.

The debate that Dewey entered when he discussed art and creativity is one that has been in existence, in one form or another, since the classical philosophers. Dewey did not define the terms of the debate but sought to guide it to a successful consummation by helping us to see the futility of the mental tug of war between classicism and romanticism—objectivism and subjectivism. Genuine creativity, Dewey argued, is the interaction of objectivity and subjectivity.

I admit that it is hard for me to understand why Dewey's solution would strike anyone as controversial. Its basic premise seems simple and self-evident: pure objectivity necessarily excludes any creative contribution; pure subjectivity necessarily excludes the possibility of expression. On the one hand, to express one's self artistically requires at least some objective components (material, language, common experiences or values) so that the work is capable of being communicated. On the other hand, for the expression to be creative, as opposed to imitative, some component of the work must be subjective (imagination, innovation, uniqueness, fantasy).

Creativity—individuality—is thus the synthesis of objectivity and subjectivity. This synthesis is expressed in the aforementioned description of individuality as the just proportion between conformity and eccentricity. Emphasis on the use of imitation in the construction of one's identity is commonly referred to as conformity. Emphasis on the use of fantasy in the construction of one's identity is commonly referred to as eccentricity. For an identity that is simultaneously our own, as opposed to an imitation, and meaningful, as opposed to having no significance, we must exercise both imitation and imagination. It is probably true that no one can avoid exercising both, and thus the difference between conformity, individuality, and eccentricity is, in fact, a matter of degree.

The argument in this chapter will be divided into five parts. In the first part, I assert that there is universal agreement among philosophers that the physical/phenomenal world is characterized by change and chance. I contend that because of the ubiquity of change and chance, innovation and creative change are necessary and desirable. The only source of innovation and creativity is the singular individual. In the second part, I argue that Dewey's theories of art and individuality are the same, and that creativity (the common denominator of art and individuality) is the synthesis, or interaction, of subjectivity (the unique perspective of the individual) and objectivity (the existentially real natural and social environment).

In the third part of the argument, I examine alternative theories of art, creativity, aesthetics, and the like to analyze the consequences these theories have for the concept of individuality. This part has five subdivisions. Dualist philosophies are first distinguished from organicist philosophies and, in turn, ancient and modern dualists and organicists are distinguished from each other. Dualist and organicist philosophies are then compared to each other. The argument is that creativity, and thus individuality, is incompatible with theories that divide the world into physical or phenomenal realms, on the one hand, and divine, ideal, or noumenal realms, on the other. Also, the contention is that creativity is limited or curtailed in organic theories of existence to the extent that remnants of the divine, the absolute, or Being are allowed to seep back into them. ·

In the fourth part of the argument, I propose a view of the narrative construction of the self in which the interaction of individuality (subjectivity, difference, creativity) and community (norms, shared goods, common judgments) leads to the elimination of neither. Genuine individuality, like genuine creativity, requires the participation of both the subjectivity of the individual and the objectivity of the community. And finally, in the fifth part of the argument, I clarify the difference between philosophical and asocial individualisms and Dewey's conception of individuality.

The ubiquity of change and chance. Individuality was important for Dewey because of the universality of change and chance. The existence of change and chance within the world of time and space has been recognized historically by most major philosophers. Firm ethical absolutists (from Plato to Kant) posit the existence of a higher realm of fixed universals precisely because they recognize the change and contingency of the phenomenal realm. Other theorists (from Heraclitus to Rorty) limit all existence to the world of time and space and believe that all that exists within time and space is subject to change and chance.

A third alternative (from Aristotle to Dewey) limits all existence to the world of time and space but sees this phenomenal realm as one of continual interaction between the changing and contingent, on the one hand, and the fixed and universal, on the other. Thinkers such as Aristotle and Dewey believed that splitting existence into two realms, a higher and a lower, creates unnecessary philosophical (epistemological) problems. Aristotle avoided transcendence by locating the fixed and universal in the essential nature of things in themselves—change consists of growth toward a thing's essential nature. For Dewey, the fixed and universal consist of methods or processes of change, whether they be accidental—natural evolution—or planned—moral or political reform. Labeling the fixed and universal "reality" and the changing and contingent "appearance" only hinders the process of reconciling the two aspects of existence. Both aspects are just as objectively real.[1]

What, precisely, do we mean when we speak of change and chance? When I speak of chance, I am referring to the unpredictability of the future due to the reality of novelty. Because novelty is a trait of nature, particular situations are qualitatively individualized (or unique). When I speak of change, I am referring primarily to the social alterations that are caused by technological progress, climatic changes, natural catastrophes, wars, and the like. Technological innovations, especially, are the start of an unpredictable chain of reactions in the economic, social, and political spheres. The invention and widespread use of machines, for example, led to a new form of economic organization (mass production, corporations, and bureaucracies) that had a profound impact on the social and political lives of people (altered class relations, decline of extended families and local communities, unequal political relations because of the interrelationship of the economic and political spheres—

what Marx called "relations of production"). Particular economic, social, and political institutions (the contingent and changing) that evolved
in the premachine age may or may not be applicable (for meeting the
fixed and universal needs of humans—that is, what Aristotle called well-
being) in the changed technological environment.[2]

Dewey argued that because of the ubiquity of change and chance,
political, social, and economic norms and institutions must be regarded
as tentative and hypothetical: mere cultural biases as opposed to *methods* of personal and social change, which can be generalized. These
methods consist of virtues (for personal growth) and principles (for
cultural growth).[3] Virtues and principles are absolute if they are processes and methods for controlling and managing change itself.[4] For a
pragmatist such as Dewey, cultural biases are literally generalizations
derived from past experience. The meanings of the past must be adapted
to present experience. Practical rationality for pragmatists is thus the
application to particular individualized situations of generalizations
gleaned from prior experiences.[5] On the other hand, the application to
particular situations of fixed universals that have been abstracted from
practical experience was, to Dewey, the best means of assuring that institutions, rules, and norms will have no relation to concrete conditions
and consequences. The appearance of novel situations implies the likelihood that some of the institutions, rules, and norms of the past may have
to be adapted to the actual conditions of the present. The only source
of innovative norms and ends is the creativity of individuals. "Every
invention, every improvement . . . has its genesis in the observation and
ingenuity of a particular innovator."[6]

The greatest obstacle to the creative innovation of individuality is the
absolutization of existing institutions, rules, and norms. When, in order to escape the uncertainty of change and contingency, metaphysicians
posit the existence of a supranatural realm of fixed universals, they hinder the process of adaptation. Institutions, rules, and norms that are
settled upon because of their appropriateness to a particular social context are made into universal and eternal laws. When change occurs, and
the biases of the past are at cross-purposes with the currents of present
experience, the gap between the beliefs of the people and the existential conditions of the environment widens.[7] "There is always a gap between the here and now of direct interaction and the past interaction
whose funded result constitutes the meanings with which we grasp and
understand what is now occurring."[8] If this gap is maintained and allowed to widen, it can eventually have destructive consequences. Existing norms and ends "lose their immediate certainty and efficiency, and
become subject to all kinds of aberrations. There often occurs systematized withdrawals from intercourse and interaction, from what com-

mon sense calls 'reality': carefully cultivated and artificially protected fantasies of consolation and compensation; rigidly stereotyped beliefs not submitted to objective tests; habits of learned ignorance or systematized ignorings of concrete relationships; organized fanaticisms; dogmatic traditions which socially are harshly intolerant."[9] Consider, for example, the proliferation of right-wing militias and other extremist associations that feed off conspiracy theories and feel threatened by the changes in norms in such areas as gender roles, ownership and usage of firearms, and the teaching of religious values in public schools.

Because contingency and change are universal or, as Dewey called them, generic traits of nature, the only fixed and universal norms and ends are the virtues. They are absolute because they are functional, that is, part of a process or method of adapting to change. Individuality is a virtue because it is the necessary agent of adaptation to change and chance. The social and economic dislocations that sometimes occur when a society is undergoing change (economic change, for example) are not the result of the change per se but rather the insistence by some within the society on retaining the prescriptions of the past and their refusal to adapt to current contingencies. Innovations are appreciated only when the dislocations become so severe that the "demand for initiative, invention and variation exceed[s] that for adherence and conformity."[10] Pragmatism originated as a particularly American phenomenon precisely because of the dislocations connected with establishing a new culture out of the remnants of older European traditions.

Speaking of the application of European traditions of thought in the New World, Horace Kallen has pointed out that because "occasions and difficulties were new, thoughts and actions must be new. Inherited dogma and habit were insufficient. Survival became a consequence of readiness to change." Early Americans did not discard their European traditions, but the settlers were able to survive and thrive because they were progressive, innovative, and creative in their application of those traditions in the New World. Economic, social, and political institutions, although derived from European theories and practices, were also innovative enough to be considered experimental. Kallen argues that Alexis de Tocqueville recognized the pragmatic spirit of Americans when he claimed that whereas the established hierarchy in Europe tended to cultivate "the arrogant and sterile researches of abstract truth," in America "the social conditions and institutions of democracy prepare them to seek immediate and practical results of the sciences." Kallen also recognizes the pragmatic spirit in a speech by Abraham Lincoln after the battle of Fredericksburg: "The dogmas of the quiet past are inadequate to the stormy present. The occasion is piled high with difficulty, and we must rise to the occasion. As our case is new, so must we think anew and act anew. We must disenthrall ourselves, and then we shall save our country."[11]

Dewey's theory of art. Dewey's theory of individuality is inseparable from his theory of art—"a process of doing or making."[12] Genuine art is a creative making, and creativity is always the product of the uniqueness of an individual. The key concept to understanding both art and individuality is, therefore, creativity. Art in the sense used by Dewey is as applicable to science, technology, and ethics as it is to painting and literature. It is the application of imagination to some aspect of objective reality. "Some existent material was perceived in the light of relations and possibilities not hitherto realized when the steam engine was invented."[13] The imaginative perception of possibilities, in the case of the steam engine, were verified by experience. The imaginative possibilities of novel institutions, rules, and norms must also be verified by experience.

Theories of creativity in art are usually distinguished as romanticist (those that see art as the free play of subjectivity) or classicist(those that see art as representing objective reality). Historicists add a third alternative with the claim that art reflects a cultural and hence, an intersubjective perspective. Dewey's theory of art involves the interaction of all three theories. Creativity is the purposeful application of a subjective perspective on an objective problem. The work of art is judged by the intersubjective verification of the community in regard to the creation's concrete or objective consequences.[14] Art, which is the productive aspect of creativity, thus involves the interaction of subjectivity and objectivity, while aesthetics, which is the consumer aspect of creativity (or judgment), involves the interaction of objectivity and intersubjectivity. When I examine alternative theories of creativity below, I will point out how they tend to overemphasize one element of artistic creation and aesthetic appreciation at the expense of the others.

For Dewey, therefore, art is the synthesis of objectivity and subjectivity. "The thoroughgoing integration of what philosophy discriminates as 'subject' and 'object' is the characteristic of every work of art."[15] Art conceived as pure objectivity becomes mere imitation; individuality thus becomes nonexistent.[16] Change, in classical philosophy, can be conceived of only as decay or as discovery of what was preexistent but previously unknown, but it can never be seen as the result of creative imagination. Such a conception of art would necessarily lack the element of creativity, unless creativity is conceived of as private fantasy (in the sense of being meaningless, lacking purpose).

When conceptualized as pure subjectivity, art is indeed reduced to private fantasy. It is idiosyncratic, uncommunicable, and thus insignificant. Its only justification must be, as the subjectivist slogan indicates, "art for art's sake." But, as Dewey pointed out, even fine art is born out of a purpose, to heighten awareness of immediate experience. All art is thus subject to judgment. In one way or another, "all art is a process of making the world a different place in which to live." All art "involves a phase of protest [critique of the existent situation] and of compensatory response [imaginative reconstruction]." Further, "[i]t is [only] owing to frustration in communication of meanings [due to the lack of commonality] that the protest becomes arbitrary and the compensatory response wilfully eccentric." Dewey contends that: "No matter how imaginative the material *for* a work of art, it issues from the state of reverie to become the matter *of* a work of art only when it is ordered and organized, and this effect is produced only when *purpose* controls selection and development of material.[17]

The debate between objectivity and subjectivity in art has been carried on under the headings of classicism and romanticism:

> From the philosophic point of view, I see no way to resolve the continual strife in art theories and in criticism between the classic and the romantic save to see that they represent *tendencies* that mark every authentic work of art. What is called "classic" stands for objective order and relations embodied in a work; what is called "romantic" stands for the freshness and spontaneity that come from individuality. At different periods and by different artists, one or the other tendency is carried to an extreme. If there is a definite overbalance on one side or the other the work fails; the classic becomes dead, monotonous, and artificial; the romantic, fantastic and eccentric. But the genuinely romantic becomes in time established as a recognized constituent in experience, so that there is force in the saying that after all the classic means nothing more than that a work of art has won an established recognition.[18]

Dewey thus exposes another false dualism.

Individuality, as we have already seen, may also be conceived of as the mean between the two opposing extremes of conformity and eccentricity. Conformity refers to unreflective and thus uncritical acceptance of the preexisting norms and ends of the community. Conformity can be justified only by the belief that the norms and ends of the community are derived from a source of fixed and universal truths. Eccentricity refers to acceptance of a wholly imaginative, and thus untested, set of principles and ends that have no objective purpose or relations but are in fact the product of a private fantasy. Eccentricity can be justified only by skepticism that any objective criteria for distinguishing better from worse norms and ends can exist, and thus existing norms and ends are either arbitrary or reflect particularized interests. Thus, to avoid being used or arbitrarily marginalized, such theories encourage people to be eccentric. Like the subjectivist slogan of "art for art's sake," we have the postmodernist call of "difference for difference's sake." Thus, one of the major sources of contention we find between communitarians and liberals—how the individual can maintain autonomy within the language community—is dismissed by Dewey as a pseudoproblem. The individual is simultaneously related to and distinguished from the other members of the community in the same way that a letter is related to and distinguished from the other members of the alphabet. In art, the objective material of a work simultaneously is manipulated by and constrains the possibilities of the subjective imposition of form. This relationship is replicated in the life of individuals by the interaction between the norms and ends of the community and the unique perspective of individual members. The influence the two poles have on each other is reciprocal. Common meanings provide context for individual perspective, while imaginative possibilities produced by individuals gradually adapt common meanings to meet the concrete needs of the community's members.

Dewey explains that "[i]ndividual variations of thought remain private reveries or are soon translated into objective established institutions through gradual accumulation of imperceptible variations."[19] The stable and slowly changing norms and ends of the community are the product of interaction with the imagination and impulse of individuals. This relationship may more properly be referred to as the interaction between intersubjectivity and subjectivity, but objectivity still plays a role, for not only do the community's norms and ends provide an objectively real environment within which the individual must interact but both the community and the individual must work within the constraining limits of objective human needs and impulses.

Thus art, for Dewey, represented interaction between the spontaneous and the habitual, the immediate and the latent, the new and the old, the future and the past. "Imagination . . . is the large and generous blending of interests at the point where the mind [habitual meanings] comes into contact with the world [present experience]. When old and familiar things are made new in experience, there is imagination."[20] Another way of expressing the synthetic nature of art is as the interaction of play and work. Work "is directed by the accomplishment of an objective material result," while play is "an attitude of freedom from subordination to an end imposed by external necessity." Thus, the creative process involves both objectivity and freedom.

> The philosophical implications of the play theory are found in its opposition of freedom and necessity, of spontaneity and order. This opposition goes back to the same dualism between subject and object. . . . There is an assumption that freedom can only be found when personal activity is liberated from control by objective fac-

tors. The very existence of a work of art is evidence that there is no such opposition between the spontaneity of the self and objective order and law. In art the *playful* attitude becomes interest in the transformation of material to serve the purpose of a developing experience. Desire and need can be fulfilled only through objective material, and therefore playfulness is also interest in an object.[21]

Furthermore, "[t]he activity that is free from the standpoint of the self is ordered and disciplined from the side of objective material undergoing transformation."[22] Thus, play represents the freedom of subjectivity (the imaginative source of form), while work represents the objective necessity imposed by the natural and social environment (the preexisting material). In both art and social relations, subjectivity (or form) is constrained by the "objective material undergoing trans*form*ation." In art, the objective material consists of canvas, stone, language; in social relations, it consists of cultural institutions, rules, and norms.

It is easy to see how when we begin speaking of language and cultural norms as the preexisting material on which subjective form is imposed, the distinction between poetry and social reform blurs. In both art and social relations, the objective material constrains and channels subjectivity as much as subjectivity, in turn, transforms the preexisting material.

Alternative interpretations of creativity. We turn now to conceptions of creativity that differ from Dewey's in the way they understand the relationship between objectivity and subjectivity. My hope is that we might be able to understand why Dewey's conception of art and individuality works better (in the pragmatic sense) than the alternatives to explain the way individuals interact with their natural and social environments. The alternative theories that I discuss differ from Dewey's in the following ways: (1) Creativity is divine—thus, humans can approach it only indirectly through divine inspiration. On their own, the most artists can do is imitate nature (Plato). Individuality, as Dewey conceived of it, is not possible. (2) Form is preexisting (natural) rather than imaginative; if human creativity exists at all, it does so in the process of transforming objective material into preexisting objective form (Aristotle). Thus, art is wholly objective. (3) Art exists within a realm of subjectivity, while science and right exist within the realm of objectivity. The two realms never interact. Poetry—individuality—has no role to play in the transformation of cultural institutions, rules, and norms (Kant). (4) Subjectivity is the path to objectivity because objective truth is revealed through the intuition of individuals who open themselves to its influence (Goethe). Individuality is passive in its relation to objectivity rather than actively transforming or reconstructing.

Ancient dualism. The notion of creativity per se is derived from the notion of divine creation; hence, the ancients interpreted creativity as divine inspiration. For Plato, art (or *technē*) is what craftsmen do. In *The Sophist,* Plato defines art not as creative but as imitative.[23] He distinguishes two types of art: one is that of making likenesses and the other the "fantastic art or the art of making appearances." The latter refers to the practice of employing perspective which, according to Plato, is a form of deception.[24] Plato's is thus an objective theory of art. The artist, Plato argued in *The Republic,* produces a copy (the work of art) of a copy (the particular object being imitated, which is an imperfect copy of a universal and perfect form).[25] Thus, art is thoroughly conservative; there is no place for creative individuality.[26]

Beauty, according to Plato, transcends art, which is mere imitation, and finds its source in divine inspiration. Poetry is thus distinguished from, and has a more noble calling than, art. When the poet "sits on the tripod of his muse he is not in his right mind, —like a fountain, he allows to flow out freely whatever comes in. . . . Neither can he tell whether there is more truth in one thing that he has said than in another."[27] Thus, the poet functions as a passive conduit of universal truth. Subjectivity plays no active role. There is the implication of the synthesis of objectivity and subjectivity in this notion of divine inspiration. The subject is temporarily at one with objective reality. The difference between this type of synthesis and the one in Dewey's theory of creativity is that Dewey's subject is an active maker rather than a passive conduit, and the objective reality the subject interacts with is the phenomenal world of time and space rather than a nonphenomenal world of transcendent ideals. Dewey's maker has a hand in altering the objective context in which he or she exists. Creativity thus becomes the basis of a genuine freedom of choice within an objective context. For Plato, on the other hand, the poet achieves freedom only in the sense of a temporary escape from the phenomenal world and subsequent obedience to an objective order that humans have no role in making. The notion of a transcendent realm of objective reality is thus incompatible with the notion of individuality defined as creativity.

Modern dualism. Kant, another philosophical dualist, has an entirely different interpretation of art. In his "Critique of Judgment," Kant claimed that the artist is indeed capable of creativity in the sense of being able to produce the novel and original. But Kant was careful to distinguish a work of art from questions of truth and falsity. Such questions apply to issues of science or right but not to works of art. The latter are products of human creativity, while the former are matters of objective reality. The realms of subjectivity (creative individuality) and objectivity (fixed and universal truths) are subject to their own separate standards of judgment. The standard of judgment for works of art is subjective taste, while the standard of judgment for principles of right or justice is objective universal reason.[28]

Two rather important consequences follow from Kant's distinction between aesthetic and ethical judgment: one philosophical and the other historical. The former refers to the fact that art is located in a realm of subjectivity that has no relation to objective reality (to truth or falsity). Aesthetic judgment is a matter of taste. Freedom, on the other hand, is located in the opposing objective realm: we are free only when we voluntarily choose universal principles determined by reason. Kant thus separates freedom from individuality, perpetuating the Platonic dualism between objectivity (the realm of freedom) and subjectivity (the realm of taste).

The latter, historical, consequence of Kant's distinction between aesthetic and ethical judgments follows indirectly from the philosophical. Kant's distinction was very influential. When, therefore, many thinkers eventually rejected the notion of a universal standard of judgment in morals, they naturally fell back on the only available standard remaining: the standard Kant had reserved for works of art—that is, subjective taste. Richard Bernstein, in his discussion of Hans-George Gadamer's *Truth and Method,* explains how communal taste eventually devolves into personal preference. "Once we begin questioning whether there is a common faculty of taste *(a sensus communis),* we are easily led down the path to relativism. And this is what did happen after Kant—so much so that today it is extraordinarily difficult to retrieve any idea of taste or aesthetic judgment that is more than the expression of personal preferences. Ironically (given Kant's intentions), the same tendency has worked itself out with a vengeance with regard to all judgments of value, including moral judgments."[29] Although, as Bernstein suggests, it is ironic that Kant is given partial credit for the movement toward subjectivism in moral judgments, perhaps it is the inevitable consequence of the dualist mode of thought. The dualist perspective assures that no criteria of objectivity can exist short of eternal, universal truth. Our valuations are either eternal and universal or they are matters of taste. Dewey traces subjectivism in the art world to precisely this cause. "Because the [classicists] set up false notions of objective values and objective standards, it was made easy for the impressionist critic to deny there are objective values at all."[30]

Contemporary subjectivist moral theories, such as Richard Rorty's, imply the same objectivity/subjectivity dualism.[31] Upon examination, Rorty's description of the cultural origin and eventual subjectification of moral judgment is analogous to Kantian aesthetic judgment. Both kinds of judgment are a matter of communal taste with no relation to objective truth or falsity, and because of this, individuality in judgment becomes nonconformity to communal tastes or, in other words, idiosyncratic preference. Both are also concerned primarily with aesthetic judgment because, in Rorty's view, all moral principles are originally the product of the free play of subjectivity, that is, self-creation.

Rorty frames his argument within the same dualistic clash between philosophy and poetry that was used by Plato, with the only apparent difference being that, with Rorty, the poets rather than the philosophers are victorious.[32] We must choose between the poet's "effort to achieve self-creation by the recognition of contingency" and the philosopher's "effort to achieve universality by the transcendence of contingency." Rorty shares a hope that he attributes to Nietzsche "that once we realized that Plato's 'true world' was just a fable, we would seek consolation, at the moment of death, not in having transcended the animal condition but in being that peculiar sort of dying animal who, by describing himself in his own terms, had created himself." The "strong poet," rather than the philosopher, becomes "humanity's hero."[33]

Rorty does not explain why the efforts of thinkers such as Dewey, Heidegger, and Wittgenstein "to exhibit the universality and necessity of the individual and contingent" in the world do not as a consequence lead to universal and necessary functions, processes, or methods of adaptation, nor why individual or specific conditions should be any less objective just because they are the product of contingency. Rorty's analysis antecedently discounts the possibility of any alternative between the absolute/arbitrary dichotomy. Raymond Boisvert puts it well when he argues that Rorty

> is, despite his protestations to the contrary, still drawing upon the capital deposited by modernity: disembodiedness and disembeddedness. The radical redescriptions envisioned and celebrated by Rorty would only work for disembodied intellects envisioning playfully one self-description after another. They do not work so well for concrete human beings who have bodies, are parts of families, make up the fabric of a particular culture, and in general are embedded in a network of caring relations. It is one thing to say as an abstract, general pronouncement that "most of reality is indifferent to our descriptions of it." It is another to be a concrete, embodied individual living in a particular social and natural environment. In the latter case, continuous redescriptions are neither so possible, nor such ideals.[34]

Rorty thinks that the rejection of the notion of a common and fixed human nature frees individuals to create themselves, but while socialization may channel human impulses and needs in a variety of different ways, this does not change the fact that humans do have common natural impulses and needs.[35] It also does not alter the fact that humans live within objectively real social and natural environments and that, within these environments, our descriptions of ourselves and of our world lead to objectively real consequences. Unless, therefore, the "idiosyncratic fantasies" Rorty speaks of are channeled and constrained (in other words, objectified) by objective conditions and consequences, they are meaningless (insignificant and incommunicable).

For example, if the consequence of an equal distribution of freedom is more conducive to the equal opportunity for self-development than is the consequence of a rigid hierarchy in which freedom is unequally distributed, then descriptions of ourselves and of our world that favor one or the other of these options can be judged as better or worse. Our freedom consists precisely in our capacity to reflect critically on existing descriptions, imagine alternative descriptions that might offer more desirable consequences, and test and judge those alternative descriptions experientially.

Ancient organicism. There is another line of thought concerning creativity that aims to recognize within itself both the objective and subjective aspects of art. Aristotle explained the artistic process (literal creation, for Aristotle, equals exnihilation and is thus impossible for humans) as the imposition of form on matter. In sculpture, for example, stone (matter) is the objective aspect of the work of art, and form is the product of subjectivity (of the artist). Matter limits the possible forms that can be imposed on it, containing, as it does, only certain potentialities and not others. The maker is thus free to innovate within the boundaries imposed by objective matter. This formulation seems to imply the interaction of subjectivity and objectivity and can also be applied to Aristotle's distinction between theory and practice. Art can be explained as the application of theory to practice. Practice, like matter, plays the objective limiting role; theory plays the subjective expanding role.[36]

All of this is very similar to Dewey's theory except for Aristotle's essentialism. Aristotle is able to avoid transcendence because he locates the universal in the thing (the material, the practice) itself. But what effect does this have on the role played by art? In his *Poetics,* Aristotle speaks of art as being imitation of the possible, and in *Nicomachean Ethics,* he explains that all art "is concerned with coming to be; and the exercise of the craft is the study of how something that admits of being and not being comes to be, something whose origin is in the producer and not in the product."[37] This sounds very close to the Deweyan notion of creativity. Art is imagination of the possible; it functions in the realm of becoming or process. In fact, the role assigned by Aristotle to art for growth seems entirely compatible with Dewey's until we recall that this development, or growth, is limited to the achievement of a preordained "natural form." Speaking of the development of the Greek concept of tragedy, for example, Aristotle explains: "Tragedy developed little by little as men improved whatever part of it became distinct. Many changes were introduced into tragedy, but these ceased *when it found its true nature*" (my emphasis).[38] Once its natural form has been realized, the object or practice stops growing or developing.[39] Potentiality is determined by the natural essence of the matter or practice. Although the seeds of genuine creativity seem to be in Aristotle's philosophy, we are forced to ask: if art is imitation of the possible, and the possible is predetermined, how much of a role is left for subjectivity?

In Dewey's theory of art, the possible is determined by interaction between the subject and the object. I will quote Dewey at length from his essay "Time and Individuality," in which he discusses potentiality and its genesis in the interaction between subject and object:

> The issue involved is perhaps the most fundamental one in philosophy at the present time. Are the changes which go on in the world simply external redistributions, rearrangements in space of what previously existed, or are they genuinely qualitative changes. . . ? Development and evolution have historically been eulogistically interpreted. They have been thought of as necessarily proceeding from the lower to the higher, from the relatively worse to the relatively better. But . . . [f]rom this point of view cancer is as genuinely a physiological development as is growth in vigor; criminals as well as heroes are a social development.[40]

Thus, development is contingent on conditions. Some physiological conditions have the consequence of producing vigor, others of producing cancer; some social conditions have the consequence of promoting heroism, others of promoting criminal behavior. "If we accept the intrinsic connection of time with individuality, they [developments: physical, social, artistic, and the like] are not mere redistributions of what existed before." Development is contingent because novel conditions are a genuine possibility in the world, and novel conditions produce novel consequences.

> Since it is a *problem* I am presenting, I shall assume that genuine transformations occur, and consider its implications. First, and negatively, the idea is excluded that development is a process of unfolding what was previously implicit or latent. Positively it is implied that potentiality is a category of existence, for development cannot occur unless an individual has powers or capacities that are not actualized at a given time. But it also means that these powers are not unfolded from within, but are called out through interac-

tion with other things. While it is necessary to revive the category of potentiality as a characteristic of individuality, it has to be revived in a different form from that of its classic Aristotelian formulation. According to that view, potentialities are connected with a *fixed* end which an individual endeavors by its own nature or essence to actualize. . . .

When the idea that development is due to some indwelling end which tends to control the series of changes passed through is abandoned, potentialities must be thought of in terms of consequences of interactions with other things. Hence potentialities cannot be *known* till *after* the interactions have occurred.[41]

Hence, although objective matter contains potentialities that limit the forms it may take, there is no final form that is determined beforehand. There is always an element of uncertainty and contingency. There is always a space in which we are free to create. The limitations do not hinder subjectivity but keep it from devolving into the fantastic or utopian.

The differences between Dewey's and Aristotle's notions of potentiality are paralleled in their theories of knowledge. For Aristotle there are three types of knowledge: theoretical, practical, and productive (art). Dewey, and pragmatism in general, folds Aristotle's notions of theoretical and productive knowledge into his conception of practical knowledge. Thus, for pragmatists, all knowledge is practical. Aristotle conceives of theory as something that exists independently of practice and acts as its guide; art is the craft of realizing the predetermined ends discovered by theory. For Dewey, theories are artifacts (the product of creativity) that are derived from practical experience. Theories are verified, rejected, or altered according to the criteria of practical knowledge: trial and error, intersubjective experience, and so on. Thus, pragmatists see Aristotle's notion of practical knowledge as the only type necessary. Dewey locates creativity in the *process* of discovering ends; Aristotle sees it as a means of achieving predetermined ends. Consider the comments of respected Aristotelian scholar Ernest Barker: "Because his view is teleological, Aristotle emphasizes, not the process of development, but the end. 'Animals are not constructed as they are, because they have developed as they have: they have developed as they have in order to attain the construction which they show.' The end explains the development, and not the development the end . . . [T]eleology thus appears to be the enemy of progress."[42] Aristotle tends to posit the current contingent stage of development as a preset final end or as the essence of a thing. Hence, the current stage of development both of Greek tragedy and the Greek city-state become, for Aristotle, the final end or goal of growth. Dewey explains the effects of fixed ends on the concept of individuality:

Aside from accidental and undesirable variations, each individual has a fixed career to pursue, a fixed path in which to travel. Terms which sound modern, words like potentiality and development abound in Aristotelian thought. . . . But the significance of these words in classic and medieval thought is rigidly determined by their context. . . . Development, evolution, never means, as in modern science, origin of new forms, a mutation from an old species, but only the monotonous traversing of a previously plotted cycle of change. So potentiality never means, as in modern life, the possibility of novelty, of invention, of radical deviation, but only that principle in virtue of which the acorn becomes the oak.[43]

The role of creativity in political deliberation is thus limited, as is the rational character of deliberation itself. For when ends are fixed, deliberation can be over means only. "Deliberation is irrational in the degree in which an end is so fixed, a passion or interest so absorbing, that the foresight of consequences is warped to include only what furthers execution of its predetermined bias. Deliberation is rational in the degree in which forethought flexibly remakes old aims and habits, institutes perception and love of new ends and acts."[44] And so, although Aristotle utilizes both the subjective and objective components in his descriptions of art and growth, his notion of fixed ends to growth drastically limits the space for subjectivity.

Modern organicism. Lewis Hinchman traces the development of the modern concept of individuality to Goethe. Hinchman explains Goethe's belief that "each person has a naturally given, undeveloped potential for harmony that must be elaborated in a unique way." The potential individuals have for harmony is with their natural and social environment. "Goethe saw in human beings an urge toward growth stimulated by their natural and cultural surroundings." Goethe was part of the romantic movement that appeared in response to the Enlightenment's abstract, mechanical, and universal view of existence. Hinchman remarks that the movement "seemed to revive aspects of the older Aristotelian tradition" but "was essentially modern in the postulate of a 'self-unfolding subject' expressing itself in its actions, relationships, and creations," as opposed to a subject with an antecedently determined essence.[45]

In his autobiographical *Poetry and Truth*, Goethe sought to explore the relationship between subjectivity and objectivity in art. One commentator described Goethe's account of the transition of a purely subjective idea into an objective work of art: "[A] poem, for instance, is born in the unconscious, the night; it is raised into the full light of consciousness, but during this process it is worked over, i.e. given artistic form. The beauty of a poem thus owes itself to both worlds, the unconscious, whence it came, and the conscious mind, which has so shaped it that others can take its meaning."[46] The criterion of judgment is cultural, as in Kant's "Critique of Judgment," but unlike Kant's, it is not independent of questions of truth and falsity. Judgment of art is cultural because the symbols used in communication are cultural, and artists are dependent on those symbols as a means of expression. But culture must exist within an objective natural environment and provide for the objectively real needs of its members. The poet must engage "in the difficult task of effecting a synthesis between the differing demands of poetry which stands above life, and truth which is stuck down hard in it."[47]

The similarity to Dewey's conceptions of art and individuality is obvious. Unlike Kant, both Dewey and Goethe saw art (creativity, individuality) as necessarily dealing with questions of objective truth and falsity and as thus requiring the interaction of subjectivity and objectivity. And it is precisely because creativity is more than a mere matter of taste that it is just as necessary for the development of culture as culture is for the development of individuals. Compare Hinchman's account of Goethe's portrayal of the organic relationship between the individual and the community to Dewey's account: "Just as plants draw sustenance through their roots, absorb sunlight, and put oxygen back into the atmosphere, so too individuals strike roots in their culture, absorb experiences and ideas from social contacts, and then return to the environment the creations of their own individuality."[48] And from Dewey: "Human nature exists and operates in an environment. And it is not 'in' that environment as coins are in a box, but as a plant is in the sunlight and soil. It is of them, continuous with their energies, dependent upon their support, capable of increase only as it utilizes them, and as it gradually rebuilds from their crude indifference an environment genially civilized."[49] This is entirely different from the Kantian account, which conceptualizes creativity as important only in the realm of taste, while the important realm of objective political and moral right, being fixed and universal, has no space for the contributions of individuality.

Dewey and Goethe differ, however, in that Dewey did not accept romanticism's almost pantheistic conception of nature. Goethe referred to the "demoniacal"[50] force of nature that controls the destinies of individuals and attributed his "poetic gifts to an indwelling, involuntary natural power."[51] For Goethe, objectivity is derived from some spiritual source of truth, while for Dewey, it is derived from contingent reality. Other romanticists give similar accounts; Ralph Waldo Emerson spoke of the "Oversoul," which takes on unique characteristics as it is reflected through different individuals who tap into its universal natural force through their intuitive faculties. "We lie in the lap of immense intelligence, which makes us receivers of its truth and organs of its activity. When we discern justice, when we discern truth, we do nothing of ourselves, but allow passage of its beams."[52] In this particular aspect of their thought, romanticists are reminiscent of Plato and his conception of the muse and divine inspiration. In this regard, they are still seeking certainty in a transcendent realm, although, unlike Plato, they understand that realm as the source of creative individuality rather than as the source of antecedently fixed ideas.

Still, if one attributes one's insights to a divine force, it lessens the need to subject that insight to practical experience. Dewey warns that "[a] blind creative force is as likely to turn destructive as creative."[53] When warned of this danger by a friend, Emerson claims to have replied, "'They [his intuitions] do not seem to me to be such; but if I am the Devil's child, I will live then from the Devil.' No law can be sacred to me but that of my nature. Good and bad are but names very readily transferable to that or this."[54]

In a certain sense, my discussion of dualist and organic theories has come full circle because it is but a short leap from the preceding statement of Emerson's to the sentiments of contemporary Nietzschean subjectivists like Rorty. Nietzsche's admiration for Emerson is not strange when we consider that once a romanticist does away with such vague notions as the "Oversoul," creativity becomes pure subjectivity. Although I argue that Rorty's particular conception of self-creation depends on the same Platonic/Kantian dualism that he claims to reject, it also has roots in romanticism. Rorty values poetic self-creation just as romanticists do, but he detects no link between poetry and truth, having rejected the objectivist side of the equation altogether. Dewey commented on what he saw to be the extreme subjectivist consequences of romanticism in his own day:

> Romanticism has made the best and the worst of the private and the uncommunicable. It has converted a pervasive and inevitable color and temper of experience into its substance. In conceiving that this inexpungable uniqueness, this ultimate singularity, exhausts the self, it has created a vast and somnambulic egotism out of the fact of subjectivity. For every existence in addition to its qualitative and intrinsic boundaries has affinities and active outreachings for connection and intimate union. . . . Sociability, communication are just as immediate traits of the concrete individual as is the privacy of the closet of consciousness. . . . Here is the ultimate dialectic of the universal and the individual.[55]

Dualism versus organicism. I opened this chapter by claiming that Dewey's definition of creativity as the synthesis of objectivity and subjectivity should be uncontroversial. My argument was that whatever is purely objective cannot, by definition, be the product of creative individuality; and whatever is purely subjective is, by definition, incommunicable and thus meaningless. Human creativity *must*, therefore, *either* be the synthesis of subjectivity and objectivity *or* be impossible. Of the four alternative conceptions of art outlined above, none allows for the possibility that creativity is the synthesis of objectivity and subjectivity. For Plato, objective truth exists in the realm of ideal forms. Humans are capable only of imitating or serving as unconscious mediators of the objective realm—they have nothing new to add. For Aristotle, objectivity exists in the realm of theory. Objective truth is discovered by contemplative reasoning—only the gods create ex nihilo. Humans are capable of striving only for preexisting ends. For Kant, creativity exists only in the realm of taste, not the objective realm of truth and falsity. And finally, for Goethe, subjectivity (intuition) is a conduit through which an impersonal universal intelligence is channeled. Goethe's notion of individuality is therefore merely a democratized notion of Plato's divine poetic inspiration—the romantics encourage everyone to tap into the universal intelligence. For Dewey, creative individuality consists of the interaction of novel ideas (interpretations) and objective reality. Subjectivity is concerned with the imaginative construction of form that simultaneously molds and is molded by the material of objective conditions.

Dewey was, in his early years, a Hegelian, but he replaced the notion of Absolute Spirit (another transcendent source of objectivity) as a controlling agent of historical development with a Darwinist evolutionary conception of nature. He came to see historical as well as personal development as matters of blind cause and effect except when and where there is conscious interference by the creative and controlling efforts of humans. "In art," as Robert Westbrook puts it, "relationships of cause and effect, antecedent and consequent, were converted into bonds of means-ends."[56] However, the Hegelian (and through Hegel the German romanticist) influences are still very evident in Dewey's conception of individuality: the emphasis on process over product, the unfolding of new qualities, and the dialectical interaction between being and nothingness that results in becoming.

Dewey rejected dualist modes of thought because they ultimately confine us to the either/or of Being and nothingness. To accept Plato's theory of the forms, one must accept the notion of a preexisting, existentially real realm of Being independent of the world of time and space. This transcendent realm is our only hope of knowledge. Knowledge is impossible in a physical world characterized by change and contingency. If the notion of a really real nonphysical source of knowledge seems dubious to us, we are left with a world in which we can never get beyond opinion. Art in the lower realm thus has no means of transcending the "is"—it can be imitation only. The poet may transcend to the higher realm, but no subjectivity (individuality) is called for. It is not a unique or creative perspective that the poet can offer but a clearer view of a preexisting and universal truth. But how can we judge this "truth" to determine whether it is real if it is not dependent on experience in the world of time and space?

The same problem presents itself with Kant. The phenomenal world is incapable of providing us with knowledge on any important ethical or political question. It is the realm of aesthetic judgment, the realm of taste: at most, a realm of cultural norms with no relation to truth or falsity; at worst, a realm of personal preference. To attain knowledge on ethical questions, we must transcend the realm of time and space through the universalizing agency of abstract reasoning. If we reject the notion of an abstract and universal rational perspective, then in Kant's dualist philosophy, we are left with only the phenomenal realm of taste or preference.

Rorty thinks he is rejecting the dualism of traditional philosophers like Plato and Kant when he rejects the notion of Being or of a non-contextual rationality, but in reality he is offering us the same either/or between Being and nothingness. Either we accept the notion of absolute truth, or we are incapable of knowing anything. Either we accept the universalizing capacity of reason, or we say that there are no reasons for any of our beliefs, only causes.[57] Either we accept the transcending power of rational argument, or we say that there is nothing but the rhetoric.[58] There can be no subjective perspective on an objective problem because no objective problems exist. There is no way of distinguishing better from worse interpretations of a problem, so all interpretations are arbitrary.[59] It would seem logical to argue that we can at least still have a subjective perspective of an intersubjectively defined problem (even if the intersubjective definition has no relation to knowledge), but Rorty rules even this out by rejecting the metaphor of the tool as applied to individual creations.[60] If the product of a private fantasy should just happen to be found useful and adopted by the community as a whole, he claims, then only coincidence can explain its usefulness. Genius is only a name we give to the coincidence of the intersection of private eccentricity and public need.[61]

The organicist mode of thought that is associated with Aristotle is much more compatible with the notion of human creativity. Because being is seen as existing entirely within the realm of time and space, existence is conceived of as a process of development. Objectivity is gauged by experience rather than viewed as an escape from it. Creativity can be seen as the source of innovation. Imagination can be credited with novelty rather than necessarily limited to imitation. Aristotle's teleological notion of development does, however, profoundly limit the scope of creative freedom. The danger of fixed ends is the tendency to see the current state of development as its fulfillment. Creativity becomes merely a means of achieving preexisting ends in various contingent circumstances. For Dewey, the only end of growth is adaptation. It is the process that is the most important thing, not the particular goods that are relevant to current conditions.

It is hard for organicists to let go of the quest for certainty. Modern organicist thinkers such as Goethe and Hegel felt the need to hold on to notions such as divine nature or Absolute Spirit as directing guides for development within space and time. These notions are a remnant of philosophical and religious dualism. Dewey found an adequate replacement for them in Darwin's theory of evolution. Darwinian evolution is as objective as it is unpredictable. The world is no less real, the consequences of our acts and beliefs are no less objective, just because they are not directed by some presiding spirit or intelligence. The only intelligence we can be sure exists is the intelligence of organic beings. Thus humans may become the directors of their own development by attaining knowledge of the conditions and consequences of alternative social or cultural interactions. Creativity can be the source of real innovations, positing new ends and imagining alternative futures.

Aristotle claims that humans are distinguished from other animals by the ability to reason. Today, many natural scientists claim that this distinction is a matter of degree. Perhaps a clearer distinction between human and nonhuman animals is the capacity for creativity. Animals adapt to changing environments, if they do at all, through the coincidence and subsequent proliferation of a useful individual mutation with a novel need. Humans can adapt through imaginatively constructing and intelligently testing new ways of behaving that are *designed* to deal with specific novel problems.

Thoreau makes much of the fact that animals have a harsher and more precarious existence than do humans and yet show none of the desperation and discouragement that people do; animals do not generally commit suicide, for example.[62] He recommends that people try to emulate this stoic acceptance of things as they are. But the reason the caged bird sings is that it does not have the capacity for imagining things different from the way they are. The fox that has to struggle for its daily existence cannot imagine how much easier life would be *if only* certain conditions of its environment or personal disposition and behavior were to change. It does not look to the future except instinctively (mindlessly). It never frets over the prospect or consequences of its own death. The very capacity that enables humans to adapt and progress is the source of human unhappiness. We can imagine things being different and better than they are now. This capacity to imagine what things might be is the source of both our discontent and our hope; it is the impetus of our activity. Growth stops as soon as we become satisfied with the status quo—with the existing relationship between our institutions, rules, and norms and the natural and social environment.

Aristotle wants us to use our capacity for reason to discover preexisting ends of growth; Dewey wants us to use our capacity for creativity to imagine temporary ends, or ends-in-view, that will serve simultaneously as directions for current growth and as turning points for future growth. Dewey's conception of creative growth implies a narrative conception of life.

Objective self-creation. When Dewey claimed that individuality is derived from the interaction of subjectivity and objectivity, he meant that imagination is free to create within the constraints imposed by objective environmental conditions. Our cultural or social environment is no less real, and the consequences of our interactions with it are no less objective, for its being contingent and changing. Individuality is the virtue of creatively adapting intersubjective (cultural or dialogically determined) institutions, rules, and norms to objective situations. We thus change one aspect of our environment as we are adapting to another.

New economic realities (what Marx would call substructure), for example, may require new social institutions and norms (what Marx would call superstructure). The superstructure necessary to provide for our natural needs can be determined only by the conditions of our particular situation (substructure). While Marx claimed that all superstructures were merely ideological justifications for the current distribution of power, Dewey, along with Talcott Parsons and Max Weber, defines them as meaning-producing cultures that (although they may be and usually are used in the Marxian sense of ideological justifications for the current distribution of power) can and ought to be judged by their capacity to meet the criterion for self-development, that is, equal freedom. Because cultures tend to take on the dogmatic and doctrinaire characteristics of religion and ideology, they also tend to be resistant to change. A culture that is based on the autonomous individual, therefore, is able to circumvent this resistance to change.

It is not a question of whether we should change the environment *or* change ourselves—it is precisely our increased ability to affect our environment that has magnified the necessity of preparing ourselves for adapting to change. In short, as we change our environment, we necessarily change ourselves. Dewey's project was to make this change, or growth, evolutionary rather than revolutionary—to remove the unnecessary social dislocations and ideological battles that occur when cultural norms, institutions, and laws (superstructure) lag behind substructural changes.[63] Thus, while cultural institutions and norms provide context for our reasonings and imaginings, they are, in turn, imaginatively reconstructed when they do not harmonize with the needs imposed by existing conditions. None of our inherited cultural beliefs, therefore, can be seen as fixed and absolute except the virtues.

Dewey regards the individual's life as essentially narrative, meaning simply that who we are, our identity, is determined by the unique quality of the events that make up our personal history. Just as individual cultures develop through time in unique ways, so do individual persons. "Individuality is the uniqueness of the history, of the career, not something given once and for all at the beginning which then proceeds to unroll as a ball of yarn may be unwound."[64] An individual's life can, therefore, be understood in terms of a narrative. And because each of these unique life histories is located within a cultural context of norms and goods, it can further be understood as a narrative within a narrative.

Alasdair MacIntyre tells us that we can understand human behavior only in terms of the intentions, desires, and goals of the actors. In turn, we can grasp the significance of their intentions, desires, and goals only by locating them within the larger cultural context of norms and goods and by understanding their actions as episodes in their particular, personal histories.[65] The ability to reason morally is the ability to give reasons for our behavior. The reasons we give are inseparable from the cultural norms and goods into which we have been socialized and the particular situations in which we have to act. In Dewey's terms, our individuality (or the lack thereof) is a product of the interaction between the norms and goods into which we have been socialized and our imaginative (or unimaginative) responses to the unique and unpredictable experiences that we face as individuals. The narrative direction of an individual's life is thus simultaneously unpredictable (imaginative responses to novel situations) and subject to judgment (of the cultural context in which it is located).

We create ourselves by the way we respond to the unique situations with which we are faced. "Individuality itself is originally a potentiality and is realized only in interaction with surrounding conditions. In this process of intercourse, native capacities, which contain an element of uniqueness, are transformed and become a self. Moreover through resistances encountered, the nature of the self is discovered. The self is both formed and brought to consciousness through interaction with environment."[66] Self-creation does not, therefore, consist merely in constructing an arbitrary and idiosyncratic list of norms and values but by imaginatively reconstructing existing habits in ways that make life more fulfilling. Individuality thus occupies the space between the pure subjectivity of self-expression and the objectivity and self-restraint imposed by cultural habits of thinking, feeling, and acting. Although at a man's death his life may be judged as more or less honorable by the standards of his community, "at critical junctures, his response could not be predicted either from his own past or from the nature of the circumstances, except as possibility." The autonomous person is continually reflecting on and reconstructing his habits of thought, feeling, and behavior in light of present experience. "Our behavior only becomes predictable when we lose our individuality by becoming imprisoned in routine."[67]

Thus, the opportunity for individuality and self-creation does not require the outright rejection of communal norms and goods. In fact, genuine individuality—a nontrivial identity—requires embeddedness in a social context. Observe the similarity to Dewey of MacIntyre's description of the interaction between personal and cultural narratives:

> There is no present which is not informed by some image of some future, and an image of the future that always presents itself in the form of a *telos*—or of a variety of ends and goals—toward which we are moving or failing to move in the present. Unpredictability and teleology therefore coexist as part of our lives; like characters in a fictional narrative we do not know what will happen next, but nonetheless our lives have a certain form which projects itself toward the future. . . . If the narrative of our lives is to continue intelligibly—and either type of narrative may lapse into unintelligibility—it is always the case both that there are constraints on how the story can continue *and* that within those constraints there are indefinitely many ways in which the story can continue.[68]

Consider the last sentence of the preceding quote and compare it to Dewey's theory of art, in which the objectivity of matter is both shaped by and constrains the freedom of the subjective imposition of form. Like all works of art, self-creation is the interaction of objectivity and subjectivity, of the common and the unique.

Perhaps we can better understand a person's life as a product of creativity if we analogize it to a more recognizable work of art. Compare, for instance, Dewey's description of the narrative or biographical character of life in "Time and Individuality" to a musical composition. The essence of both is temporal seriality. In a musical composition, a series of notes, rather than events, occurs in time. A composition heard for the first time can be simultaneously unpredictable and subject to a common criteria of judgment. Just as the act of an individual can be understood and judged only in terms of the unique context in which he acts, the notes of a musical composition can be understood and judged only in terms of the notes that precede and follow it. While there is no single *correct* composition, there are definitely better and worse ones. While there is no single correct life, even within a particular culture, there are definitely more and less worthy ones. The greatest of musical compositions, judged to be so by the aesthetic criteria of a particular culture, not only can be but must be unique, for uniqueness is the essence of creativity. The greatest of human lives, judged to be so by the moral criteria of a particular culture, not only can be but must be unique, for uniqueness is the essence of individuality. No exceptional life or composition can result from mere imitation or conformity. Individuality and originality, however, do not require the rejection of all common criteria of judgment. All great works of art, whether they be musical compositions or the lives of individuals, affect or change to some degree the very criteria by which they are judged, but their imaginative innovations are recognized as such only because they speak to something that is common to all those who do the judging.[69]

Individuality and individualism. The final issue we will address is the relationship between the type of creative individuality that Dewey promoted and the different types of individualism with which we are more familiar. We will by no means exhaust the different meanings given to the term *individualism.* The main concern here is to distinguish individuality from three types of individualism—two philosophical and one political—that have been associated with liberalism.

One type of philosophical individualism, which is for the most part a caricature of the liberal individualist self, can be understood in the sense that what people are, their identities, is purely a matter of free will; that their internal makeup is not, or should not be, influenced by their relationships with others, by their cultural heritage, or by their personal history; and that their relationships with other human beings are purely consensual and matters of individual self-interest. This type of philosophical individualism and Dewey's conception of individuality are completely incompatible. Dewey's conception of individuality assumes that people are naturally social and that personal identity can be understood only in terms of social or cultural context. Because individuality is the product of interaction between the subjectivity of the individual and the objectivity of the community, a doctrine that promotes the noncontextual formation of individual identity, or one that sees membership in a community as optional, is incapable of providing the necessary tools for the achievement of individuality.

Another type of philosophical individualism can be understood in the Kantian sense that all individuals, being ends in themselves, are owed equal respect for their autonomy and are thus protected by certain inviolable rights. Dewey's conception of individuality would be in partial agreement with this type of individualism: seeing individuals as ends in themselves but not understanding this to imply asocial individual rights. For Dewey, the only final end for humans, and thus for human association, is the growth or development of individuals. The individual and the community can be understood only in terms of each other: the individual needing the community in order to realize self-development, and the community existing for the purpose of enabling individuals to develop. Because individual growth and autonomy are inconceivable outside of the community, individual rights must be seen as social rather than as asocial. Also, if individual rights are to be understood as the *means to* the equal liberation for growth of all of a community's members, then the specific content of rights can be determined only by the contingent and changing demands of those members. When rights are understood as asocial and inalienable, there is no necessary relationship between them and the equal liberation of a community's members for growth.

Generally, the notion of asocial rights is connected to the notion of natural rights, and social rights are seen as civil (or of conventional origin). In Dewey's conception, however, contrary to this traditional categorization, rights are both social *and* natural. They are social because they are consequential—specifically, the means to equal liberation for growth within a particular social context. Thus, rights cannot be characterized as claims of the individual *against* the community, as if they existed separately and prior to any particular community or context. Rather, rights are determined by the community in terms of the particular concrete needs of its members. Because, however, the needs of members are objectively real and definable, so are the rights. Thus, while specific rights may change or evolve through time, they are not defined arbitrarily. The individual member of a community has a natural right to a particular good at a particular time. This right is identified, however, by the contingent needs of members, not by a mythical presocial state of nature. Members thus have a natural right to the goods necessary for self-development where these goods are equally available to everyone. The natural right to liberty is thus defined contextually—not as freedom from community but as those negative and positive liberties necessary for individual self-development in this particular social (natural, economic, technological) context.

If, for example, the concrete consequences of a particular presocial individual right is to hinder the liberation for growth of a large segment of a community's population, that right would be suspect from the point of view of a consequential criterion, but it would still be justifiable from the point of view of asocial individual rights. Inalienable prepolitical property rights, for example, may be compatible with equal liberation for growth in a culture prior to the appearance of a corporate economy, but not after. If we see individual rights as prior to the ends of the community, we allow the needs and growth of one portion of society to be sacrificed to protect the mythical asocial rights of another portion. The notion of inviolable asocial rights, therefore, is incompatible with a community that has as its highest end the equal liberation of all individuals for self-development. When equal liberation is the highest end, rights must be justified by a consequential rather than an abstract criterion. By locking rights in before consideration of the needs of the present, the community is making rights in themselves a higher end than the equal liberation of its members (and their current, contingent, needs) for self-development.

The example of property rights is intimately related to the third type of individualism that I want to discuss. Asocial, or economic, individualism can be defined as the view that each of a society's members is responsible to the whole only for doing his or her part in defending the country and for respecting the life, liberty, and property of the other members. This is the conception of individual responsibility that is associated with laissez faire economics or with the "rugged individualism" so popular with economic libertarians. Asocial individualism defined in this way has no direct relation to Dewey's conception of individuality. Whether persons are economic individualists or not has no bearing on whether they can be characterized by conformity, eccentricity, or creative individuality.

There is an indirect relation, however, between economic individualism and Dewey's conception of individuality, and that is the one mentioned above about the incompatibility of economic individualism with the equal liberation for growth of a community's members in a corporate economy. The cultivation of creative individuality is an essential component of the liberation of individuals to pursue their own quest for the good. Its cultivation, however, requires its practice. We develop the habit of expressing our individuality only by actually expressing our individuality. The cultivation of this virtue, therefore, requires the type of social environment that affords opportunities to do so. Some aspects of the combination of a corporate capitalist economy with a minimal (laissez faire) state seem to reduce the opportunities for creative participation for most of the community's members in all aspects of economic production and consumption and in political decision making. In a laissez faire factory economy, for example, the many are consigned to the monotonous and mind-numbing tasks of human machines. Gross economic inequalities deprive the poor of de facto, if not de jure, liberation for growth. The minimization of opportunity for political participation alienates many (especially in the lower economic strata) from involvement in community decision making. The individual tends to be isolated, as if he or she really were an asocial individual locked into a one-sided economic contract.

An adequate discussion of the relationship between economic individualism and the cultivation of individuality is not possible here, but I do want to make the point that if individuals are, indeed, ends in themselves, then only those types of economic, social, and political relations that maximize the opportunity for all individuals to grow are justified.

Conclusion. In this chapter, I have established the following points. First, within the phenomenal world of time and space, in which change and contingency are the recognized norm, human creativity is the only source of innovation (and thus adaptation and harmonization). Second, creativity is the exclusive product of individuality. Third, individuality is incompatible with the notion of fixed and universal ends that are not themselves part of the process of adaptation. Fourth, creativity (individuality) requires the interaction of subjectivity and objectivity. Neither pure subjectivity nor pure objectivity is of value from the point of view of creativity. And fifth, individuality, defined as creativity, is a social product that is opposed to certain forms of individualism usually associated with liberalism.

Individuality is the basis of both cultural and individual growth because it is the only means of transcending the "is" without abstracting from concrete experience. On the contrary, creativity, when defined as the interaction of subjectivity and objectivity, is relevant only to concrete experience. "Unless subjective intents and thoughts are to terminate in picturesque utopias or dogmas irrelevant to constructive action, they are subject to objective requirements and tests. . . . Thinking and desiring, no matter how subjective, are a preliminary, tentative and inchoate mode of action."[70] If we recognize the need for creative individuality, then we must avoid overemphasizing either its objective or its subjective components. If we do not recognize the need for creative individuality, then we do not recognize the need for growth.

Creativity is the realm of freedom.[71] An objective end that has no room for creativity has no room for freedom. A subjectivity that separates itself from objective problems and judgments deprives us of the very ability to create—and thus to work out our own freedom. Freedom is not opposed to objectivity nor can it be defined (as per Plato and Kant) as conformity to it. Freedom is the capacity to create within an objective environment. "Freedom means essentially the part played by thinking—which is personal—in learning: —it means intellectual initiative, independence in observation, judicious invention, foresight of consequences, and ingenuity of adaptation to them."[72] To the degree that these things are done for us by someone else who is supposed to be wiser, we are to that degree less free. The greatest responsibility of paternal authority is to educate the young to perform these tasks for themselves.

Part Two

The Community

4

The Unity of Freedom and Authority: A Deweyan Conception of Social Intelligence

In part one, we looked at the individual. While examining Deweyan notions of autonomy, the self, and individuality, we saw that liberal values such as individual freedom, personal identity, and individuality do not require freedom from the community. On the contrary, we learned in chapter 1 that the virtues of the autonomous individual presuppose the existence of a language community. Liberal values themselves could not survive without the existence of a community of shared liberal values. Many of the problems that have led to the communitarian critique of liberalism are exposed in Dewey's philosophy as pseudoproblems. The real problem comes from supposing that we must choose between individual autonomy and genuine community.

While communitarians and liberals may argue the relative importance of community and individual, Dewey understood the relationship between the two as wholly reciprocal. The end of the community is the self-development of the individual. The community is thus a collective and cooperative enterprise that has as its normative goal the intellectual and moral development of each of its members. Without the community, individual growth is impossible. In chapter 2, we saw that the self, in order to rise above the merely trivial and inauthentic, must be constructed within a context of meanings and valuations that transcend mere personal preferences. Then, in the previous chapter, we came to understand that individuality, in order to escape eccentricity and idiosyncratic fantasy, must operate purposefully in an objective context. All of the differentiating qualities lose their value, not only to the individual but also to the community, unless they are integrated through the power of communication and cooperative inquiry.

Communitarians like Michael Sandel believe that liberalism emphasizes abstract individual rights at the expense of participatory democracy. In part two, we begin our investigation of the community with a look at how Dewey extrapolated the moral and intellectual virtues from scientific method and applied them to the democratic community. Dewey believed that the notion of a community of inquiry (based on the model of the scientific community) is the means of reconciling liberal values (freedom, toleration, and so on) with those of participatory democracy (deliberation, participation, and the like). In addition, he argued that both liberalism and democracy require a particular type of person—one who has cultivated the moral and intellectual virtues—and thus the best place to begin creating a liberal democratic society is in the educational institutions. A reciprocal relationship between individuals (who have been habituated into the moral and intellectual virtues) and the community's social, economic, and political institutions will produce a more democratic culture and a healthier civil society.

Three elements are key to the successful transfer of this model of a community of inquiry to the political community. First, it depends heavily on the concept of communication. Social intelligence will be effective only if there is open communication and publicizing of relevant information. Dewey assigns ultimate responsibility for communication to intellectuals and artists. Second, social intelligence must be understood as a method of dealing with, not escaping from, political conflict. If we assume that there are more or less intelligent ways of handling political conflict, then the Deweyan argument is that the notion of social intelligence is a more intelligent way of dealing with political conflict than the current alternatives. Conflicts of interest are to be deliberated openly and publicly, and conflicts over values are to be minimized by the cultivation of the moral and intellectual virtues—or, in other words, by autonomous citizens. Finally, ideology, like religious fanaticism, must be seen as contrary to the goods, virtues, and principles of liberal democratic society.

Scientific method. Dewey saw that what we today call scientific method is, in its simplest form, nothing more than the practical method of knowledge utilized by the arts and crafts communities since antiquity. The modern scientific community has carried this practical method to the level of an art in itself: the knowledge or study of practical inquiry. The scientific community attains and progresses in knowledge through the communication of trial-and-error experience. Dewey also observed that the disenchantment of the world that resulted from the practice of the scientific method carries with it a death warrant for the notion that morality and politics are informed by a knowledge that does not itself derive from practice. Hence, scientific method, or the method of practical knowledge, is the only source of knowledge available to humanity.

By scientific method, we are not referring here to laboratory or other types of experiments or to the particular skills of professional scientists, but to the mental dispositions or attitudes toward knowledge that are required by scientific inquiry. Those dispositions can be summarized as critical reflection, creative individuality, and communication (or sociability). We have discussed these three dispositions or virtues in the previous chapters. Together, they constitute the method of practical inquiry and the elements of a Deweyan conception of autonomy.

In the political realm, Dewey's conclusions are favorable to participatory democracy. Democracy, like science, institutionalizes the procedures of trial and error. Critical reflection and creative individuality imply intelligence and imagination, while communication implies community. A community that cultivates intelligence and imagination comports well with the republican notion of civic virtue. It relates participatory politics to the cultivation of the intellectual and moral virtues.

When Dewey spoke of practical knowledge informing political practice, he did not mean that the masses must acquire the skills of scientists, nor that they must attain a higher level of intellect than they have now. The fact that the average "mechanic can discourse on ohms and amperes as Sir Isaac Newton could not in his day"[1] does not make the latter any less of a genius, nor does it give us any reason to believe that the former possess a native intelligence greater than the common person of three centuries ago. Contemporary mechanics have more practical knowledge because they are part of a community of inquiry. A body of practical knowledge has evolved through the experience and communication of this particular community of practitioners. They solve practical problems using principles derived from the prior experience of others, ingenuity (by testing imaginative, creative, and experimental hypotheses), and by sharing the results of their experiences with other practitioners.

Two things are necessary to prepare the masses for the practice of democracy. First, they must develop the habit of thinking of politics in the same manner that they think of any other practical enterprise, as problem solving based on experience, imagination, and communication. They must learn to value the political principles and institutions that are necessary to promote and protect the method of practical reasoning: the integrity, courage, impartiality (moral virtues), critical reflection, imaginative creativity, and sociability (or the sharing or public interchange of findings and ideas) of the inquirers.

The sharing or public interchange of findings and ideas is directly related to the second thing that is necessary to prepare the masses for democracy, and that is an environment of communication. Dewey regards communication as the essence of community. It is no coincidence that it is also the essence of social intelligence. As James Gouinlock has argued: "The isolated individual is powerless in scientific and moral situations alike. Only in communication can the deficiencies of the individual intelligence be corrected, its powers developed, fulfilled, and made effective. No one is perfectly good or perfectly wise. Any particular moral conviction is subject to revision, rejection, or expansion."[2]

The practical dispositions that are required of democratic citizens are opposed by those who would tend to limit the value of inquiry. Inquirers will probably exhibit less honesty or integrity when they are reflecting on a practical problem if their motives are ulterior to discovery of the simply best solution—when they are protecting some interest or ideology, for example. When inquirers have ulterior motivations, they are tempted to manipulate their reasonings or experiences to produce preferred conclusions. Inquirers tend to be less courageous when they become overly concerned with the opinions that their fellows may have of their conclusions. Inquirers might be less impartial when the scope of their sympathies is narrow.

Inquirers tend to be dogmatic rather than critically reflective when they are sure that they are in possession of a "Truth" too sacred to be subjected to the test of practical experience. Inquirers will perhaps be conformist rather than imaginative when they have been habituated to believe that there is nothing new that need be contributed to a body of knowledge—that knowledge is complete, fixed. And finally, inquirers may conceal rather than communicate knowledge when they perceive that they are involved with a competitive rather than a cooperative enterprise.

Democratic citizens, therefore, require specific dispositions conducive to cooperative inquiry. This is to say that the method of inquiry put forth by John Stuart Mill in *On Liberty*, which is based solely on negative liberty, is a necessary but not a sufficient condition for genuine freedom of thought. Dewey speaks of the need for a positive conception of liberty.

> He knows little who supposes that freedom of thought is ensured by relaxation of conventions, censorships and intolerant dogmas. The relaxation supplies opportunity. But while it is necessary it is not a sufficient condition. *Freedom* of thought denotes freedom of *thinking*; specific doubting, inquiring, suspense, creating and cultivating of tentative hypothesis, trials or experimentings that are unguaranteed and that involve risk of waste, loss, and error. Let us admit the case of the conservative; if we once start thinking, no one can guarantee where we shall come out, except that many objects, ends and institutions are surely doomed. Every thinker puts

some portion of an apparently stable world in peril and no one can
wholly predict what will emerge in its place.[3]

Although Mill spells out the external conditions necessary for intelligent
thought to take place, he provides for none of the internal requirements.
The attitudes and dispositions necessary for practical reasoning are just
as much a matter of cultural conditioning as are their antithesis.

None of the dispositions that are considered assets to practical inquiry
are beyond the native capacities of the common person. Having said that,
it is also obvious that an entire community of courageous, self-disciplined, and impartial individuals who also are able to overcome the
pitfalls of dogmatism, conformity, and self-absorption is an unrealizable
ideal. Is the vision of a community of practical inquiry thus itself an
impractical ideal? Not necessarily. No more than, for example, Aristotle's eudaimonia. Eudaimonia, or the blessed life, is not something that
the individual achieves and rests in. Rather, it is an ideal that provides
direction for a quest for the good life. It is the quest, and the development of the virtues that are acquired in the process of it, that makes life
blessed. Likewise, the end of the political community is the development
of the dispositions (virtues) of democratic citizenship in its members. The
fact that the quest will never be perfectly achieved does not make the
quest itself any less noble. A political community is more or less worthy according to the degree to which it strives for and maintains institutions and laws that improve the moral and intellectual dispositions
of its citizens.

Many of the "realists" who criticize progressive political theories
apparently fail to understand the instrumental and thus practical nature
of ideals. Ideals are instrumental in that they provide standards of better or worse and thus directions for growth. No individual or state ever
remains static; they are constantly undergoing evolutionary change and
development. Is the evolution an improvement on the previous condition or a regression? How is it possible to tell without an ideal? What
standard of evaluation is otherwise available? Are we indifferent to
whether our prejudices become more or less connected to reality? Are
we indifferent to whether our dispositions become more or less cruel?
Without an ideal to provide a vision of how liberal democratic citizens
ought to think and feel and act, how can we be anything but indifferent to their future development? What is needed is an ideal that is pre-
cise enough to provide direction but broad enough to allow for a plurality of cultural variations.

Dewey's antidemocratic nemeses, at least the more immediate ones,
were thus not Plato and Aristotle, who understood well the function of
ideals, but the realists of his own day: Walter Lippmann, Charles

Merriam, Harold Lasswell, Max Weber, Joseph Schumpeter, and C. Wright Mills. All defined "democracy" in one way or another as a form of competitive elitism. Their criticisms of participatory democracy focused on the public's lack of capacity for rational political action, the impracticability of maximizing participation, the inability of the public to achieve consciousness of actual political realties, and the complexity of the modern industrial state. Surprisingly, Dewey agreed with the findings of the antidemocratic realists in regard to the current inability of the masses to become intelligently involved in politics. He did not, however, agree with them as to its causes and remedies.

The realists argued, in essence, that the masses have always been ruled by uninformed and unintelligent passions. It would be unrealistic to think that they will ever be any different.[4] The masses have always been the slaves of blind passion; they have always been ill-informed about the current state of affairs; they have always been satisfied with bread and circuses. The models of political decision making used by realists were based on their observations of the way things "have always" worked in the past. Reform and improvement were the language of social workers and religious teachers, not serious political analysts. If there are wars, it is not our job to make judgments about war, merely to dispassionately analyze them. If there are elites exploiting the masses, it is not our job to pass judgment on whether this should be so, merely to offer an accurate description of how things are done. If the masses are apathetic and enslaved by unintelligent passions, it is not for us to attempt to change this by theorizing about improved methods of education; we are merely to note the fact and to plan our dealings with them accordingly.

The problem with realist political analysis is that once we stop asking how things ought to work—What is just? What is virtuous? What is possible?—the answers to these questions no longer matter to us. We have no means of judging the worth of a life, a policy, a political institution. Dewey stressed, more than any writer of his time, the gradualness and continuousness of meliorative reform. There was little danger of innocents having to suffer the consequences of rash political optimism when change was planned to proceed at such a slow pace and designed to take into account trial-and-error experience.

Darwinism and modern social psychology had convinced Dewey that the current moral and intellectual dispositions of individuals are the consequences of their environment. Few would argue that dishonesty, cowardice, and egoism are the products of genetics—no more or less so than integrity, courage, and generosity. These dispositions are, to various degrees, encouraged or discouraged by our social environment. Why then should intellectual dispositions (not capacities) be treated any differently? A dogmatic disposition is no more or less a natural disposition than is a healthy skepticism. We are not born conformists any more than we are born self-reliant. All dispositions are habits of thinking and all habits of thinking are learned. Any habit that can be learned can be unlearned, especially by a new generation. To accept as an unchangeable reality the dictum that the masses are motivated by irrational passions, while we are fully cognizant that not all humans are so controlled by their passions, is to imply that some humans are educable while others are not. If so, there would exist a natural hierarchy consisting of the educable ruling over the uneducable. Furthermore, those who are supposedly uneducable could not logically be held responsible for their behavior. It thus seems that realists, and not idealists, remove responsibility from the equation of moral behavior.[5]

Education. In Dewey's theory of education, he is more concerned with how students should be taught than with what they should be taught. He offers no curriculum or canon of literature that would be of interest to the current participants of the "culture wars." When he does speak of the canon of Western classics, for instance, it is only to say that when they are taught the focus should be on the meaning and insight they provide for concrete experience rather than on arcane problems of interpretation that are only of scholarly interest. If I had to put Dewey's theory of education into a nutshell, I would describe it as Socratic. "The undisciplined mind is averse to suspense and intellectual hesitation; it is prone to assertion. It likes things undisturbed, settled, and treats them as such without due warrant. Familiarity, common repute, and congeniality to desire are readily made measuring rods of truth. Ignorance gives way to opinionated and current error,—a greater foe to learning than ignorance itself. A Socrates is thus led to declare that consciousness of ignorance is the beginning of effective love of wisdom, and a Descartes to say that science is born of doubt."[6] The purpose of education is to enable students to think for themselves. Too often, and Dewey was referring to the public schools in his own day, students are treated as mere passive receptacles into which bits of information are fed until their education is pronounced complete and they are released into the "real" world, never to be "educated" again. The information or data that makes up so much of the material that students are taught is the product of thought or inquiry. But it is not so much the *products* of thought and inquiry that students need, Dewey claims (although he does not say that information, per se, is of no value), but rather the *processes* of thought and inquiry.

When teaching science, for example, communication of the fact that water comes to a boil quicker when there is less oxygen in the environment is not so needful as explaining the process by which this fact was discovered. Scientific method itself, and not merely its products, is what is necessary for the education of democratic citizens. Education must be interactive rather than passive because the elements of the method of inquiry can be internalized only when they are practiced. When they are practiced, they become habitual.[7]

Within communities of inquiry, individuals contribute to the proliferation of knowledge by critically evaluating the existing body of knowledge, offering unique and imaginative solutions to empirical or theoretical problems, and carrying on and publicizing this activity within a purposive community of authoritative norms and standards. There is no practical reason why the attitudes and virtues implied by this method of thinking should be the private possession of academics and professional researchers. Dewey argues that only those children who are habituated into the dispositions of reflective criticism, creative individuality, and communication will become adults capable of intelligent and autonomous choices in all facets of their lives.

It is important to understand that Dewey is not merely saying that it would be nice if more people had these virtues, he is saying that the existence of liberalism and genuine democracy (as opposed to mere external forms) requires citizens with these virtues. "If our public-school system merely turns out efficient industrial fodder and citizenship fodder in a state controlled by pecuniary industry, as other schools in other nations have turned our efficient canon fodder, it is . . . only aggravating the problem."[8] In fact, these three virtues, which I refer to collectively as individual autonomy, are the means of dealing with what Rousseau considered to be the problem of modernity: the reconciliation of the "lost community" (participatory and communitarian democracy) with the "long revolution" (liberal freedoms and toleration).[9] The scientific community is a living example of the possibility of reconciling communal authority with individual freedom.

One of the most commonly heard criticisms of Dewey's theory of education is that it is incompatible with liberalism. Liberalism is not concerned, critics claim, with constructing a particular kind of person but with allowing people to choose for themselves what kind of person they want to be. Judith Shklar, in her well-received article "The Liberalism of Fear," makes a point of reminding us that liberalism "began precisely in order to oppose the educative state." However, in the very next paragraph she is careful to add: "To foster well-informed and self-directed adults must be the aim of every effort to educate citizens of a liberal society."[10] What liberalism objects to, Shklar is saying, is the attempt to educate people into a particular comprehensive doctrine. So Dewey's goal of creating autonomous (self-directed) and communicative (well-informed) citizens for democracy is not only compatible with liberalism but demanded by it.

Imagine a society with liberal democratic institutions but in which most members, and most public officials, are dogmatic and fanatical adherents of a particular religious or philosophical doctrine. Could we realistically expect protection for the private sphere in such a society? Are liberal safeguards safe in an illiberal culture? Actually, the only reason liberal societies are free to tolerate dogmatic fanatics is because the fanatics are an unthreatening minority. It is foolish to pretend, however, that liberal democracy does not depend for its success on a particular type of citizen, and school is the "primary practical instrument for transforming and improving society."[11]

Shklar claims that although liberalism is not atheistic, agnostic, relativist, or nihilist, there is "a real psychological connection between" liberalism and skepticism. Skepticism, she points out, "is inclined toward toleration."[12] Likewise, democracy requires citizens who are capable of intelligent choice, or a society is democratic in name only. Real choice requires self-directed and well-informed citizens within a pluralist society. It is just as unrealistic to expect an entire society of Shklar's self-directed and well-informed adults as it is to expect an entire community of Dewey's autonomous citizens. If this were a condition for Shklar's minimal liberalism, it would impose impossible conditions for its realization. But although Shklar has to depend on an ideal conception of the liberal citizen, we know that in practice her theory does not stand or fall with the ideal's complete realization.

Dewey taught that democratic political institutions are more the effect than the cause of democratic culture.[13] The greater the degree to which the citizens of a state have democratic dispositions the greater degree to which democracy will be reflected in political institutions. Political institutions, particularly in a liberal society, make up a relatively small part of the lives of most citizens. A much greater proportion of time and energy is spent in the family, school, business, church, and private association. These nonpolitical institutions have more of an educational effect on persons than do strictly political ones. Shklar warns us that "no system of government, no system of legal procedures, and no system of public education is without psychological effect."[14] Dewey would be quick to agree and to add that if this is true, the same must be said ten-score for the private institutions that occupy so much of our lives. This is why Dewey called democracy "a way of life."[15] If democracy is to be more than an empty formality, it must be the norm in all parts of our lives. "The struggle for democracy has to be maintained on as many fronts as culture has aspects: political, economic, international, educational, scientific and artistic, religious. The problem of social psychology is not how either individual or collective mind forms social groups and customs, but how different customs, established interacting arrangements, form and nurture different minds."[16] The best way to establish and maintain democratic institutions, rules, and norms is to cultivate a community of autonomous citizens. Democratic procedures are of little practical use in a community of dogmatic, conformist, and docile individuals.

Dewey warned Americans concerned about protecting democracy from its foes to concentrate their battle on its most dangerous enemies—attitudes that encourage master/slave relationships in the social and political realms: "The serious threat to our democracy is not the existence of foreign totalitarian states. It is the existence within our own personal attitudes and within our own institutions of conditions similar to those which have given a victory to external authority, discipline, uniformity and dependence upon The Leader in foreign countries. The battlefield is also accordingly here—within ourselves and our institutions."[17] The only way to cultivate democratic attitudes is to habituate them.

Institutions. The relationship between intellectual dispositions and the external influences of social, economic, and political institutions presents a type of chicken and the egg problem. Each helps to determine the other, but where does transformation begin? Dewey believed that the relationship is reciprocal but that the best place to begin is with educational institutions. Dewey realized, as had many before him (Plato, Aristotle, Rousseau, and others) that children are more susceptible than adults to habituation into new norms. If educational institutions begin to produce a greater proportion of autonomous dispositions, eventually there is likely to be a proportionately greater demand for participation in other types of institutions (economic, religious, political, and familial institutions, for example).[18]

Because, as Shklar reminds us, these now more participatory institutions will have a psychological effect on the people whose lives they touch, they will have an educative effect on other, less autonomous members. Dewey's hope was that once the ball gets rolling, recognition of the need for the habituation of autonomous citizens in the educational system will increase proportionately, producing more autonomous citizens who will, in turn, demand more participatory or democratic institutions, which will produce even more autonomous citizens. The influence should be equally strong, regardless of the direction. As Dewey said, "society and individuals are correlative, organic, to one another."[19]

Dewey did not devise an antecedently fixed picture of what this more democratic society will look like. He had no preconceived utopian visionary scheme to impose on society, producing who knows what unpredictable consequences.[20] Rather, he believed that a more autonomous citizen-body, and the more autonomous members of families, churches, businesses, and civic associations, will demand and gradually work out more participatory modes of organization through the process of trial and error, experience, and communication. Leaders of institutions, faced with the demand for more participation, must work out agreements with members, employees, and the like or risk losing these people as affiliates. Any enterprise that values energy, imagination, and intelligence in its ranks will not opt to alienate them. Any association that does not value these virtues among its members will have to compete with those that do. If the enemies of democracy are correct, and the institutions that prefer unthinking and unimaginative members outperform those who value autonomous participants, then Dewey's vision will fail, but in its failure it will not have imposed any irremediable harm on society.[21] If Dewey is correct, and meliorative progress in regard to more autonomous and thus democratic citizens is practical, then the increased degree of energy, imagination, and intelligence will be a priceless boon to every aspect of society.

Democracy as a way of life has important consequences if the notion that self-development depends on self-rule has any truth to it. By conceptualizing democracy as applicable to every aspect of society, Dewey opened up the opportunity for self-development to a much greater body of citizens. If political participation by the masses "enlarges their spirit, ennobles their thoughts, and establishes among them a kind of intellectual equality which forms the glory and power of a people,"[22] then by enlarging the scope of the political to include decision making in all social and economic institutions, we create an almost unlimited sphere of opportunity for all citizens to realize their moral and intellectual potentials. If democratic participation were limited to strictly political institutions, there would not be sufficient opportunity for most citizens of a liberal state, characterized as it would be by a large private sphere and representative democracy. But Dewey realized that the decisions made where we live, work, and worship have as much or probably more effect on our daily lives as do the laws made in the state capital and in Washington, D.C.

Dewey stressed the fact that opportunity for democratic participation in a liberal society depends to a large extent on the existence of a healthy civic community. Let me briefly summarize Dewey's conceptions of pluralism, the public, and the state. People naturally involve themselves in activity—economic, religious, recreational, and the like. Activity of any sort generally produces consequences. When the consequences of activity affect only those who are voluntarily involved, then the activity is private. When the consequences affect those who are not voluntarily involved, then the activity becomes public. Business and religion, for example, become public to the extent that their actions have public consequences.[23] All of those affected by the consequences of an activity together make up a public which, to facilitate its claims, must form an association. There will, therefore, be many associations, and most members of a large industrial society will probably belong to more than one. The purpose of the state, according to Dewey, is to regulate the relationships between the actors and associations and between different associations.[24] Civil society is essentially pluralist, therefore, and the state plays the role of a symphony conductor whose task it is to maintain harmony among the instruments.[25]

Unlike many pluralist theories, however, Dewey's does not include a neutral state. To maintain harmony requires the state to ensure that publics that are injured by the activities of others are justly recompensed.[26] The market alone is not an adequate mechanism for insuring either a just society or equal opportunity for participation.[27] Advocating the cause of legitimate publics will in itself encourage the organization of associations.

In addition, Dewey argues that the state should be biased in favor of a particular type of association. He gives two criteria for distinguishing the types of association worthy of being promoted by the larger community, both of which have to do with communication and thus with participatory democratic community. The first criterion is in regard to the internal constitution of an association, that is, the number of dimensions or ties by which an association's members are held together. Associations that are able to accommodate a large degree of differentiation or diversity in their membership, some participatory citizens' groups, for example, enable the free and open communication of ideas, points of view, and lifestyles. Associations that have only a single dimension of commonality and hence a not very diverse membership, corporate political action committees, for example, provide little opportunity for such enriching communication, and are hence less valuable from the point of view of promoting a democratic culture.[28]

The second criterion is external and concerns a group's relationships with other groups, that is, the number of dimensions of commonality to other groups in the community. Once again, a group that is preoccupied with a single narrow interest has little or no role to play in the formation and attainment of the public good. On the other hand, a group that is open and is able to find common ground with the goals and ways of life of other associations is a valuable asset in the quest for reasonable and just public policy.[29] Like all fixed principles in Dewey's philosophy, these two criteria are methods of inquiry. They are the necessary conditions for democratic forms internal to groups and for democratic deliberation and communication external to, or between, associations.

Thus, the state should encourage (through tax, spending, and regulatory policies) those associations that are internally and externally democratic. Associations that are nondemocratic and predatory should be discouraged by the same means; and those associations that are nondemocratic but nonpredatory (an Amish community or a monastery, for example) should be neither encouraged nor discouraged by the liberal democratic state.

While Dewey does not specifically detail the means and extent of state intervention in regard to civic associations, he does tell us that the means of state protection of legitimate publics will take the form of government agencies. A state is "good" to the degree that its publics are organized and to the degree in which its offices perform the function of caring for the interests of publics.[30] Dewey also informs us that associations such as political machines and business corporations whose members associate for the sole purpose of exploiting others for profit may by his criteria be considered unworthy (undemocratic, uncooperative) associations. Dewey's views in regard to economics can probably best be described as syndicalist, except that Dewey placed less emphasis on labor unions (which he believed to be as narrow and undemocratic as their corporate opponents) and more on internally democratic relationships between workers and management. Dewey wanted corporations to see themselves as members of the community with responsibilities as well as rights; he foresaw the attitude of multinational corporations that are quick to claim their constitutional rights as "persons," on the one hand, but are just as quick to forswear their loyalty or responsibility to any particular nation or community, on the other.

Dewey did not see his democratic views as contrary to the demands of economic growth that publics have come to expect. On the contrary, Dewey persisted in believing that the greatness of a state is directly tied to the liberation of the capacities of its citizens. All the economic growth and advancement that the United States had seen in the nineteenth and twentieth centuries was not caused by egoistic individualism, Dewey insisted, but by the technological advances of science: advances that were the result of a collective mode of inquiry. Agricultural output, for example, did not quadruple from the early nineteenth to the early twentieth centuries because farmers now had four times the incentive to produce, but because of technological advances in equipment, fertilization, and so on.

The virtues of autonomy are encouraged to a certain degree in the United States today but usually only in the scientific and professional communities. The productive results of these collective inquiries are then appropriated by private interests for pecuniary motives. Only when the energy, imagination, and intelligence of all of the community's members are freed in all of their relationships, and when the results are shared by the community as a whole, will we reach the height of our possibilities. Dewey's conception of civil society thus combines the virtues of the small deliberative community with the ostensibly "private" associations of the economic realm. But as Dewey pointed out, there is nothing particularly individual or private about modern economic relationships.[31]

Once again, we arrive at an ideal (a civil society characterized by internally and externally cooperative associations) that, for Dewey, was no less valuable for being unattainable in its ideal form. Once again, the ideal provides society with a direction for growth. When we compare free and open states to those that are closed and paranoid of change, we see evidence that some states can have healthier civil societies than others. Is it likely that Western institutions have become as participatory as they could ever hope to be? Or could they stand to experience some meliorative growth in this regard as well? The main obstacle we face is our inability to stop thinking of the masses as a passionate mob that needs to be controlled, and to start thinking of them as a potential that needs to be realized.

Communication. I said above that two things are necessary in order to realize a Deweyan vision of democracy: the first is a more autonomous or self-directed citizenry; the second is improved communication. Communication is the only way to have the well-informed citizens that even minimalist liberals such as Judith Shklar insist are necessary. Critical and imaginative intelligence is limited by the amount and veracity of information that it has to work with. The less information that citizens have about the environment in which they live, the more vulnerable they are to manipulation.[32]

Walter Lippmann, in *Public Opinion,* wrote of "the insertion between man and his environment of a pseudo-environment."[33] Individual citizens cannot experience the entire social environment directly and thus depend on others for information. The "others" who supply information (newspapers, politicians, public relations experts, ideological or interest groups) have private interests that motivate them to manipulate rather than inform their audience. Lippmann was saying essentially the same thing as Joseph Schumpeter and later Edward Herman and Noam Chomsky—that public opinion is "manufactured."[34] Dewey agreed with the diagnosis: "Sentiment can be manufactured by mass methods for almost any person or any cause."[35] Dewey saw ideology as the principal means of enforcing mass conformity, but with the introduction of new technologies, manipulation became easier. Practical people, Dewey warns, concerned with private interests, have long known the connection between habits and thought and have grown expert at manipulating them for their own advantage.[36]

Although Dewey agreed with the diagnosis of the realists, once again he charted a different course in regard to a remedy. If the argument put forth by antidemocratic realists is true— that public opinion is produced by ideology and false information—then this necessarily implies that the unworthy aspects of public opinion are social products. Once it is accepted that the beliefs and political behavior of the people are socially conditioned, logically we should be able to trace these thoughts and actions to the conditions that produced them. We should also be able to create new conditions that are conducive to new ways of thinking and acting that reflect self-directed and well-informed intelligence.

Dewey saw the education of autonomous individuals to be the first line of defense against manipulation. People who are habituated to think for themselves are less likely to accept uncritically a picture of the world created for them by others.

> The spread of literacy, the immense extension of the influence of the press in books, newspapers, periodicals, make the issue peculiarly urgent for a democracy. The very agencies that a century and a half ago were looked upon as those that were sure to advance the cause of democratic freedom, are those which now make it possible to create pseudo-public opinion and to undermine democracy from within. Callousness due to continuous reiteration may produce a certain immunity to the grosser kinds of propaganda. But in the long run negative measures afford no assurance. While it would be absurd to believe it desirable or possible for everyone to become a scientist when science is defined from the side of subject matter, the future of democracy is allied with spread of the scientific attitude. It is the sole guarantee against wholesale misleading by propaganda. More important still, it is the only assurance of the possibility of a public opinion intelligent enough to meet present social problems.[37]

Dewey pointed out the simple-mindedness of the belief that individuals are either controlled by their passions or by their reason, as if our minds are divided into two separate, warring faculties—like the little angel who stands on one shoulder competing with the little devil on the other. All humans are motivated by passions and ideas, and many times the passions that motivate us are defined by ideas. The difference between intelligent and unintelligent action is equivalent to the difference between intelligent and unintelligent passions or desires. Immediate or unreflective desires are, by definition, unintelligent. Desires that are the result of reflection on conditions and consequences are intelligent. Critical reflection does not guarantee that we will always make the right decisions, but it does guarantee that we will learn.

Are the majority of people in the world incapable of being habituated to reflect on the possible consequences of their immediate desires and impulses? If we believe this, then we relegate the great majority of humanity to the status of cattle that need to be controlled for their own good. If we do not believe it, then we must accept the logical consequence of our belief, that is, that the multitude possesses the capacity of becoming autonomous choosers.

Being able to critically review information that is intended to manipulate does not, however, guarantee the availability of honest information. Earlier I explained that Dewey's conception of a public is of a group of people who are affected by the activities of other actors. The formation of such a public is inhibited by the lack of information (communication). Sometimes a group of people may not know that they are being affected by an activity (victims of asbestos use, for example) or, if they are aware, they are unable to trace the source (or cause) of the effect. They may not be aware that others besides themselves are suffering from the same effects. The lack of such information prevents the formation of a public, thus the lack of communication serves the private interests of those whose activities are responsible for the adverse effects. Thus, "the outstanding problem of the public is discovery and identification of itself."[38] When the only sources of information are politicians who represent private interests and newspapers that depend on private interests for operating revenue and profit margins, then honest communication will be the exception rather than the rule. Dewey believed that the responsibility for communication lies with the state and with intellectuals.

That the state has a responsibility to protect the interests of legitimate publics who suffer adverse consequences as a result of the activities of one-dimensional associations is an essential element of any concept of political justice. The state has a responsibility to ensure that, for example, the findings of physical and social science research (in regard to the effects of asbestos, to continue the previous example) are available to the public.[39] Because government is not immune to the influence of private interests, however, it cannot be the final bulwark against false information or the lack of communication altogether. Dewey gives this responsibility to intellectuals. They are the ones who, in the final analysis, always have been and always will be responsible for whether the public has access to factual information. This is no less true for open societies than for closed.

Those whose interests are served by minimizing communication are happiest with intellectuals when they focus their research on arcane or abstract subjects that have little or no relation to the problems of contemporary society. Kenneth Wain, commenting on Dewey's conception of the social function of philosophy, which deals with the "conflicts and difficulties of social life," explains that this pragmatic aspect of philosophy is "disguised because philosophers become a specialized class which uses technical language" indecipherable by the general public.[40]

Artists, according to Dewey, have an equally heavy responsibility to communicate information to the public.[41] Art, he argues, is probably the most efficient means of communicating with the general public, for three reasons. First, it is more likely to be digested (novels, films, and photographs, for example, are more attractive than research papers).[42] Some will scoff at the notion that the general public represents a potential audience for the works of socially minded artists. But consider the fact that the enemies of open society, from Plato's imaginary *Republic*[43] to twentieth-century totalitarian states, have censored the products of artists. Censorship in a closed society is by no means limited to the types of materials that only intellectuals are expected to read or view. Thus, the enemies of open society tend to understand the power of art more than its friends. The point is that art (from children's books to the great treasures of literary history) is useful for purposes of communication of ideas.

The second reason artists are effective at communicating to the wider public is the fact that they appeal to the feelings of their audience. Research usually deals with cold facts. Feelings are more likely to induce action. Statistics about the adverse effects of child labor provided those who sought to eradicate it with useful ammunition. But many of those who became involved in the movement were initially motivated by viewing the photographs of child laborers. The same might be said for the public that has formed around environmental concerns. Statistics and hard research can be frightening, but how many became involved because of the love of nature induced by poets like Robert Frost or photographers like Ansel Adams?[44] Feelings combined with reason result in *will*. Facts devoid of feelings are impotent; feelings without knowledge are blind.

The third advantage of artistic communication is that it is capable of simultaneously providing a critique of existing norms and beliefs and creating an imaginative vision of alternative meanings. Films and novels may be the only opportunity many will have of seeing the world from an alternative perspective. The film *Philadelphia,* for example, tried to do for sufferers from AIDS what Steinbeck's *The Grapes of Wrath* did for the victims of the "dust bowl"; both raised awareness of current conditions and their consequences. A film from India, *The Bandit Queen,* examined openly and honestly cultural norms that relegate women and the members of lower castes to a subhuman existence. The consequences of traditional ways of thinking, both on individuals and on the energy of the nation as a whole, are more efficiently brought home to people through this kind of art. Speaking of the responsibility of intellectuals in the United States, Dewey argued that it "is the work of sociologists, psychologists, novelists, dramatists and poets to exhibit the consequences of our present economic regime upon taste, desire, satisfaction and standards of value." Intellectuals (philosophers, critics, writers) can wield an immense influence if not intellectually dispersed and divided. The enemies of open society are correct to fear this kind of communication, because it is the instigator of change.[45]

Political conflict. Critics of Dewey's analogy of the scientific community with the political community point out that scientists are, on the whole, genuinely motivated by the desire for knowledge, whereas political actors are generally motivated by private or group interests or by conflicting moral values. As a result, critics like C. Wright Mills argue, Dewey has a vision of politics that is "a set of images out of a fairy tale: they are not adequate even as an approximate model of how the American system of power works."[46] Mills accuses Dewey of wanting to replace political conflict with cooperative inquiry.

Such critics write as though Dewey had proposed a utopian structure of political institutions that are designed to eliminate political conflict by providing a mechanism of foolproof consensus making. Let's look at what Dewey actually proposes. First, staying true to his belief that all institutions are tools for liberating individuals for growth in specific contexts, he leaves the construction of political institutions to the public, whose experiences are constrained by those contexts. Correct institutions are not derived from an antecedent model but from the intelligent desires of a self-directed and well-informed public. The fact that this public in its ideal manifestation would probably never be realized did not mean that the public could not be better informed and more self-directed than it is today and thus demand more participatory institutions.

Second, Dewey did not promote social intelligence as a solution or alternative to political conflict. On the contrary, he saw political conflict as a necessary condition for social intelligence. If there were no conflict, a method of dealing with it would be unnecessary. Dewey does not provide a method for arriving at a Rousseauian "general will." In fact, he thought the general will was a recipe for totalitarianism because the individual is only free when his or her will meshes with the collective will.[47] He did not urge us to rely, then, on some method of discovering the correct answer behind conflicting opinions, nor did he ask us to submit to the will of current consensus. Dewey simply argued that to the degree the public is organized, autonomous, and well informed, and political conflicts are conducted openly and publicly, political decisions are *more likely* to be based on intelligence than on power relations.

Conflicts over legitimate but conflicting interests can be settled in a number of ways. The two ways that are at issue in the debate between realists and participatory democrats is between might and right: either we resort to a method in which the stronger or more powerful interest wins or to a method in which the interests of all citizens are considered more or less equally in the final resolution. Political realists believe that because the former type of method describes politics as it is currently practiced, then it must describe political reality, as opposed to fantasy. This viewpoint apparently assumes that if things could have been done better or more fairly in the past, then they would have been. But if this assumption is true, slavery would still exist and women would still be denied access to the voting both. To believe that, while a perfect world is beyond our reach, we may nonetheless be able to improve on "reality," is not ipso facto utopian. When Aristotle advised that the formation of a middle class would result in less conflict of interest than the current grossly unequal division of wealth, was he making a utopian suggestion? Was he not suggesting a change that would make conflict less likely than before?

Dewey simply made the rather obvious point that improved communication and more autonomous citizens will result in a more organized and aware public. The more conscious the public is of conditions and consequences, the more able it is to deal with conflict intelligently. "[D]emocratic method is persuasion through public discussion carried on not only in legislative halls but in the press, private conversations and public assemblies." In regard to the progress democracy had already made since the Revolutionary War, Dewey pointed out that "with all its defects and partialities in determination of political decisions, it has worked to keep factional disputes within bounds, to an extent that was incredible a century or more ago." He saw no logical reason meliorative progress could not continue. He added: "While Carlyle could bring his gift of satire into play in ridiculing the notion that men talking to and at each other in an assembly hall can settle what is true in social affairs any more than they can settle what is true in the multiplication table, he failed to see that if men had been using clubs to maim and kill one another to decide the product of 7 times 7, there would have been sound reasons for appealing to discussion and persuasion even in the latter case."[48] Although face-to-face political deliberation within and between associations is important, deliberation can also be carried on in newspapers, periodicals, books, films, private conversations, and so on.

The goal of deliberation is not the discovery of some metaphysically existing common good or will, but an agreement that comes as close as possible to representing the interests of all sides of a conflict. Advocates of a particular interest should be made to give reasons for their advocacy—and to give them publicly. Interests that are narrow and damaging to others are more likely to be found out when debate is public, when advocates of private interests must present coherent and legitimate arguments for their positions. The motivation for their arguments is irrelevant. As Martin Diamond reminds us, it is the function of political thought to distinguish genuine reasons from facile;[49] that is why it is important that intellectuals focus their efforts on problems and events in current affairs.

When there are two equally legitimate and conflicting interests (environmentalists and working-class loggers in the Pacific Northwest, for instance), the public interest, Dewey argued, is not discovered by transcending our sympathies, as one would find in a method of Kantian universalism, but by expanding their scope. This is done by becoming conscious of more and various perspectives, not by abstracting from all sympathies as such.[50]

> [T]here are as many associations as there are goods which are enhanced by being mutually communicated and participated in. And these are literally indefinite in number. Indeed, capacity to endure publicity and communication is the test by which it is decided whether a pretended good is genuine or spurious. Moralists have always insisted upon the fact that good is universal, objective, not just private, particular. But too often, like Plato, they have been content with a metaphysical universality or, like Kant, with a logical universality. Communication, sharing, joint participation are the only actual ways of universalizing the moral law and end.[51]

Methods are needed that allow the political actors to become familiar with the legitimate needs of the other side. Artistic communication plays an important role in this respect. The same function can be extended to deliberation.

Let's look at another type of political conflict: conflict over values. Conflicting values are more likely in a society with a plurality of cultures. Ideally, in a liberal society, controversial religious, philosophical, and cultural values will be confined to a private realm. The notion of toleration for different religious values is the basis of classical liberalism. As I pointed out above, however, it is foolish for liberals to pretend that liberalism is indifferent to the kind of citizens it produces. A liberal society of dogmatic fanatics is a contradiction in terms.[52] The combination of autonomous citizens and free communication will not result in the discovery of "true" moral values, but it may increase the propensity of citizens to believe that when deliberating over value conflicts, "pompous moral indignation is less admirable then patient analysis."[53] Dogmatism does exist, however, and it is the main cause of the most controversial value conflicts in the United States. The less fanatical citizens are, the more likely they are to arrive at compromises.

How should society deal with religious or ideological fanatics? Dewey had no magical solution for dealing with such people in the current political environment. He does ask us, however, to consider why such people exist within our social environment at all. Dewey thinks that it should be of interest to us to discover precisely what conditions are responsible for the creation of various types of citizens. If we understand the social causes of criminals or fanatics, for example, perhaps we could arrange to produce fewer of them in the future. Fanatical attitudes are both antiliberal and antidemocratic. A liberal democratic society should have a collective interest in minimizing the social conditions that lead to their construction. Dewey argues that by stressing the educational and institutional conditions described above for the cultivation of a more autonomous public, the degree to which society is characterized by dogmatism and fanaticism will be minimized.

Contrary to what many of his critics contend, Dewey does not attempt to avoid political conflict but rather to develop a public that is capable of dealing with conflict more intelligently. The creation of social intelligence is the gradual habituation of a more critically reflective, imaginative, and communicative public. "Intolerance, abuse, calling of names because of differences of opinion about religion or politics or business, as well as because of differences of race, color, wealth, or degree of culture, are treason to the democratic way of life. For everything which bars freedom and fullness of communication sets up barriers that divide human beings into sets and cliques, into antagonistic sects and factions, and thereby undermines the democratic way of life."[54] The concept of loyal opposition is essential to democracy. It also exists within the scientific and scholarly communities. "[A]micable cooperation—which may include, as in sport, rivalry and competition—is itself a priceless addition to life. To take as far as possible every conflict which arises— and they are bound to arise—out of the atmosphere and medium of force . . . into that of discussion and intelligence, is to treat those who disagree—even profoundly . . . as friends." Furthermore: "A genuinely democratic faith in peace is faith in the possibility of conducting disputes, controversies, and conflicts as cooperative undertakings in which both parties learn by giving the other a chance to express itself, instead of having one party conquer by forceful suppression of the other—a suppression that is none the less one of violence when it takes place by psychological means of ridicule, abuse, intimidation, instead of by overt imprisonment or in concentration camps."[55] Critics may object in the following way: "Sure, if the public is more self-directing and well informed, it will be able to deal with political conflict more intelligently than it does now. Tell us something we don't know. Optimistic democrats have been saying that since the time of Pericles; the problem is that the public never becomes any more self-directed or well informed. Saying that it can be done and doing it are two different things."

First, there is no doubt that modern liberal society has access to more means of communication of facts and ideas than it had in the past, when values, beliefs, and interests were more completely communal and local, and means of communication were at a comparative minimum. Second, if the public is not more self-directed and well informed than it is, what is the cause? Is it because all of the attempts to improve the public have failed? What attempts, specifically? Never has a society attempted the method of social intelligence. Why has there been so much opposition to Dewey's theory of education? Surely those who are pessimistic about the capacities of the public believe that their own children are capable of becoming autonomous and of being well informed. Why not the children of others? Perhaps it is the passions—that is, interests—of the *elite*, rather than of the masses, that present the greatest obstacle to the creation of a more autonomous public. People who are informed and used to thinking for themselves are, after all, much harder to control than are the uninformed and passion-driven. Consider the following analysis of the issue from Dewey's *Freedom and Culture:* "The simple fact is that all the deliberately liberal and progressive movements of modern times have based themselves on the idea that actions are determined by ideas, up to the time when Hume said that reason was and should be the 'slave of the passions.' . . . The classic economic school made wants [or passions] the prime motors of human action, reducing reason to a power of calculating the means best fitted to satisfy the wants [or passions]." Furthermore: "Denial that they [passions] can be influenced by knowledge points emphatically to the non-rational and anti-rational forces that will form them. . . . [A]ll that is left is competition on the part of various bodies and interests to decide which shall come out ahead in a struggle, carried on by intimidation, coercion, bribery, and all sorts of propaganda, to shape the desires which shall predominantly control the ends of human action." And further: "[T]he fact which is decisive . . . is whether the desires that are effective in settling the course of action are innate and fixed, or are themselves the product of a certain culture. If the latter is the case, the practical issue reduces itself to this: Is it possible for the scientific attitude to become such a weighty and widespread constituent of culture that, through the medium of culture, it may shape human desires and purposes?"[56] In short, if it is easier to control the masses by manipulating their passions than by persuading their intellects, then there is reason for the resistance to Dewey's call for the cultivation of social intelligence.

Public policy. One of the most common sources of conflict when deciding public policy issues is ideology. Of course we all suspect that some people use ideological arguments to mask their interests, but we can be just as certain that many people are truly directed in their political thinking by a framework of ideas that explains the world in a particular way. One of the main ideological divisions in the United States is between libertarian-leaning liberals and egalitarian-leaning liberals. (I say "leaning" because most people do not carry their views to the most extreme end of the ideological spectrum.) Libertarians stress the values of liberty and economic efficiency in public policy issues, and egalitarians stress the values of equality and social justice.

I said above that Dewey does not offer social intelligence as an alternative to political conflict but rather as the best method for carrying out conflict in a peaceful and intelligent manner. Dewey's pragmatism, however, can be seen as an alternative to ideological thinking. The problem with ideological thinking, according to Dewey, is that it justifies positions on policy questions independent of experience. Usually some abstract principle takes precedence over observation of the actual consequences of policy. Ideology, like religion, becomes a matter of faith. When actual practice does not accord with theory, we tend to look for excuses rather than for alternative policies.[57] Dewey anticipated the failure of Soviet communism and the lesson to be learned from it, which was "the importance of. . . a plurality of ideas employed in experimental activity as working hypotheses."[58]

Dewey interprets the libertarian/egalitarian distinction as the division within liberalism of two factions that have carried particular liberal values to extreme positions at the expense of other liberal values. According to Dewey, the original values of liberalism are those contained within the motto of the French revolution—liberty, equality, and fraternity.[59] Libertarians have focused on liberty at the expense of the latter two. Egalitarians have focused on equality at the expense of liberty. Egalitarians value fraternity, but only on economic issues; they have left fraternity on norms and beliefs to conservatives. For Dewey, any of the three without the others, carried to its logical extreme, will have monstrous consequences.

Liberty is necessary for self-fulfillment and is required in both its negative and positive forms. Fulfillment of personal potentialities requires that each person be afforded an opportunity to offer an individualized contribution to a common enterprise. In *Democracy and Education,* Dewey explains that "the essence of the demand for freedom is the need of conditions which will enable an individual to make his own special contribution to a group interest, and to partake of its activities in such ways that social guidance shall be a matter of his own mental attitude, and not a mere authoritative dictation of his acts."[60] It also requires a sphere of freedom in which autonomous choice is available.

The two types of freedom are not incompatible. They may seem so, but that is only because negative freedom is so often characterized as a tenet of individualism that many assume that it presupposes an opposition between the individual and the community. But such an opposition is entirely fictional. Involvement in a purposive association does not require that one surrender his or her private life. On the other hand, autonomous choices do not require separation from community but the opposite; social influences prevent our private choices from collapsing into fantasy or eccentricity.

Dewey interprets equality to be the just distribution of the consequences of associated action as measured by need and capacity to utilize. Dewey observed that far from limiting economic efficiency, associated activity (of the scientific community) was responsible for most technological advances and that all major industrial productive activities are cooperative. None of the high-tech innovations and none of the major productive activity that accounts for the great wealth of the West is carried on according to the tenets of economic individualism. Individualism is applicable only when the rewards of technological innovation and productive activity are distributed. The individuals who actually do the innovating and producing get meager shares. Equality, in its essence, also means an equal opportunity to realize one's potential, to make meaningful contributions as well as to reap a fair share of the rewards for associated activity. In this sense, equality and liberty cannot be distinguished. A certain level of economic equality is necessary to liberate individuals to develop their capacities.[61]

Dewey's was not a "bleeding-heart" egalitarianism. He expected a just distribution based on the fact that wealth is a cooperative rather than an individual product. He also stressed that no economic aid program should be used that did not require those receiving benefits to act on their own behalf. This was as much in the interest of those receiving benefits as it was in the interests of society in general. "What is sometimes called a benevolent interest in others may be but an unwitting mask for an attempt to dictate to them what their good shall be, instead of an endeavor to free them so that they may seek and find the good of their own choice."[62] The main determinant of redistributive economic policy should be the consequences the policy has on the self-development of the persons being helped. Dewey urged that "social conditions should be such that all individuals can exercise their own initiative in a social medium which will develop their personal capacities and reward their efforts. That is, it is concerned with providing the objective political, economic, and social conditions which will enable the greatest possible number because of their *own* endeavors to have a full and generous share in the values of living" (my emphasis).[63]

Needless to say, neither liberty nor equality, as Dewey defines them, is possible outside of a genuine community. Fraternity is a necessary condition of both. Dewey's theory of a public (discussed above) is his theory of fraternity or community. "'We' and 'our' exist only when consequences of combined action are perceived and become an object of desire."[64] Advocates of individualism base their arguments on the notion that humans are naturally self-regarding. While Dewey dismisses the notion that self-regarding habits are any more or less the product of nature than other-regarding habits, he stresses the fact that fraternity does not require regard for the community as an alternative to regard for self: "regard for self and regard for others are both of them secondary phases of a more normal and complete interest: regard for the welfare and integrity of the social groups of which we form a part."[65]

Regard for the group requires self-discipline, not self-sacrifice. Acting collectively for the good of the group is the means to self-development. "In a justly organized social order, the very relations which persons bear to one another demand of the one carrying on a line of business the kind of conduct which meets the needs of others, while they also enable him to express and fulfill the capacities of his own being."[66] Thus, the democratic community requires individuals to contribute to a collective welfare that is itself the means for individual self-development. The strength and energy of the community and that of the individuals that constitute it are inseparable. "Society is strong, forceful, stable against accident only when all of its members can function to the limit of their capacity." The lack of political involvement encouraged by the state, "in its hostility to the free experimentation and power of choice of the individual in determining social affairs, . . . limits the capacity of many or most individuals to share effectively in social operations, and thereby deprives society of the full contribution of all its members."[67]

The "Great Community" will come into being when society as a whole attains awareness of the conditions and consequences that make up its environment. This is another way of saying that the great community exists to the degree that it achieves self-consciousness. The ideal of complete self-consciousness will probably never be realized but, like all ideals, it provides direction and can be measured in degrees of more and less, better and worse. The need for community is thus left to the many smaller communities or publics that make up civil society. They are the associations that should provide us with equal liberty to realize our individual capacities.

Liberty, equality, and fraternity, therefore, cannot be achieved independently of each other. In Dewey's conception of pragmatic liberalism, the end of society is the equal liberation of individuals for self-realization.[68] The end, therefore, of any particular policy question must be determined by the needs of the present situation when seen in terms of society's ultimate goal of individual growth. One particular policy problem may call for equality as the dominant end (educational opportunity, perhaps), another may call for efficiency (city services), a third for social justice (health care), and a fourth for liberty (conscience). "Instruction in what to do next can never come from an infinite goal, which for us is bound to be empty. It can be derived only from study of the deficiencies, irregularities and possibilities of the actual situation."[69] Ideologies are oblivious to particular conditions and subsequent consequences; libertarians see a market solution for every problem, radical egalitarians some type of imposed numerical equality. Pragmatic liberals believe that concrete conditions combined with the ultimate end of liberalism (self-development) dictate the policy approach and that consequences are the test of the policy's utility for realizing the desired end. If market solutions work in one area, then they should be used. Social justice and equality may work better to promote individual growth in other areas of public policy. This approach is not about trade-offs between competing values. It is based on the notion that the liberal values of liberty, equality, and fraternity relate to each other harmoniously when seen in terms of each other. As Charles Anderson points out, if any of the values is abstracted from the others and carried to its extreme conclusion, the results will be hideous. Each of the liberal policy values provides a natural boundary to the others so that they produce a kind of Aristotelian just proportion of each.[70]

Pragmatic liberalism requires pragmatic citizens. The citizens of a liberal state will grow more pragmatic (as opposed to ideological) to the degree that education, institutions, and communication succeed in producing more autonomous individuals. Ideologies are, after all, just alternatives to genuine thought. To the degree that individuals learn to think for themselves, they will not need to depend on such shortcuts in order to make decisions. Anderson provides four categories of reasons to explain the workings of pragmatic political deliberation. All thinking must start within a particular context, and pragmatic political deliberation is no exception: it starts with the customs, precedents, and common usages of the liberal community. Anderson refers to this as "reasons of trusteeship." "Critical reason" is useful for protest or critiques of these existing meanings and usages. "Entrepreneurial reason" proposes new undertakings, policies, and so on and attempts to fashion coalitions, or new publics. "Meliorative reason" focuses on specific problems and strives for agreement on solutions.[71] The virtues contained in Dewey's conception of autonomy (critical reflection, creative individuality, and sociability—for intersubjective verification) are essential to this type of political deliberation.

Conclusion. I have tried to make the following points in this chapter. First, the democratic ideal of a purposive community of inquiry is capable of providing direction to meliorative growth.[72] The establishment of such a community begins with culturally habituated ways of thinking and acting and not with political institutions. Second, education is a practical means of initiating this cultural transformation and the education of autonomous individuals requires no major social dislocations.[73] Third, the interaction between individuals and institutional associations can have the effect of gradually creating a more participatory society. Civic associations and more democratic economic institutions can provide the opportunities that individuals in a populous society need to exercise their capacities for self-governance. Fourth, the communication needed to ensure that we have well-informed citizens requires a commitment by intellectuals in the scientific, academic, and artistic communities. Fifth, although interest and value conflicts are inevitable, the way that a society deals with them is not. Currently existing societies deal with conflict in a variety of ways (suppression in totalitarian systems, competition in pluralist systems, cooperation in consociational systems); Dewey is merely offering a method to deal with conflict that utilizes social intelligence. Methods that rely entirely on power politics to deal with conflict cannot, except by accident, arrive at intelligent solutions. And finally, social intelligence, being pragmatic rather than ideological, focuses on solving particular problems rather than on pushing an ideological agenda. This is preferable because it is a more efficient way of dealing with policy problems and because it minimizes the waste of energy used on unnecessary conflict.

Collective authority and freedom are reconciled by the method of social intelligence. "Science has made its way by releasing, not by suppressing, the elements of variation, of invention and innovation, of novel creation of individuals." And yet, "[i]n spite of science's dependence upon the free initiative, invention and enterprise of individual inquirers, the authority of science issues from and is based upon collective activity, cooperatively organized." Thus, "the operation of cooperative intelligence as displayed in science is a working model of the union of freedom and authority."[74]

> There is no need to dwell upon the enormous obstacles that stand in the way of extending from its limited field to the larger field of human relations the control of organized intelligence, operating through the release of individual powers and capacities. There is the weight of past history on the side of those who are pessimistic about the possibility of achieving this humanly desirable and humanly necessary task. I do not predict that the extension will ever

be effectively actualized. But I do claim that the problem of the relation of authority and freedom, of stability and change, if it can be solved, will be solved in this way.[75]

In the New Testament, there is a parable attributed to Jesus about a Pharisee and a publican. While both are in the temple, the Pharisee thanks God for making him such a righteous soul compared to the miserable publican in the back of the temple. According to the parable, this Pharisee goes away cursed. The publican, on the other hand, compares himself to an ideal (in this case, Jesus), thus magnifying his own inadequacies, and asks God to forgive him for being such a worthless sinner. The publican goes away saved. The moral is that the Pharisee compared himself to someone who was a worse sinner than himself and thus felt satisfaction. He was doomed never to strive to improve. The publican compared himself to an ideal that he knew he would never be able to attain. He left the temple saved because he was conscious of where he stood in comparison to the ideal and was thus destined to grow. Realists are like the Pharisee. They compare the existing attainments of liberalism to what they perceive to be the lesser achievements of other types of regimes and pronounce themselves satisfied while ridiculing progressives as foolish for looking to ideals. Like the publican, Dewey urges us to strive patiently but persistently toward an ideal that may be unattainable.[76] Growth, however, need not be measured in terms of success or failure, but rather in terms of better or worse. This is because no distinction of better and worse is possible without the existence of an ideal standard to measure the gradations against. Perhaps this is what Socrates meant when he said that the unexamined life is not worth living—that we should reflect critically on ourselves and judge ourselves in terms of an imaginable better life. Dewey is asking us to reflect critically on our selves, our culture, and our political institutions and to judge them in terms of the ultimate end of individuals and community alike: individual self-development.

5

The Unity of Freedom and the Good:
A Deweyan Justification of Liberalism

In the preceding chapters, we have been confronted with an argument that the pragmatic principles of inquiry—critical reflection, creative individuality, and intersubjective verification—are necessary for both individual and cultural growth. In this chapter, we examine the political and social implications for a culture that is based on the three pragmatic principles of inquiry. My assertion is that Dewey's method of inquiry provides a defense for liberal democracy that avoids both Kantian transcendentalism and postmodern multiculturalism and subjectivism.

The defense that Dewey's pragmatism provides for liberalism can be generalized to various cultural contexts because it is a method for the intelligent and moral evolution of institutions, laws, and norms within a contingent and changing social, economic, and technological environment. Unlike Kantian absolutes, which require us to abstract from experience, Dewey's principles of inquiry are generalizable *because* of the changing and contingent nature of experience. They are not historical artifacts because they are the principles of a method that can work within any particular historical narrative. They go beyond subjectivity, not only because the method is generalizable but also because the method assumes the existence of better and worse answers to all of the moral and political questions we ask—even if the answers we come up with sometimes apply only to qualitatively individualized questions.

Dewey assumed, first, that the end of any political community ought to be the growth, or self-development, of its members. Second, he assumed that the environment in which this self-development must take place is precarious. The community needs, therefore, a correct method of determining the best institutions, laws, and norms for liberating its members for self-development in any particular social, economic, and technological environment.

By community, Dewey means much more than what liberals have come to see as the public realm:

> Government, business, art, religion, all social institutions have a meaning, a purpose. The purpose is to set free and to develop the capacities of human individuals without respect to race, sex, class or economic status. And all this is one with saying that the test of their value is the extent to which they educate every individual into the full stature of his possibility. Democracy has many meanings, but if it has a moral meaning, it is found in resolving that the supreme test of all political institutions and industrial arrangements shall be the contribution they make to the all-around growth of every member of society.[1]

Thus, the end of Dewey's liberal society is the good of the individual. Ultimately, this is the strength of Dewey's defense of liberalism. It justifies liberal principles such as negative freedom, individual rights, toleration, and pluralism because they are components of the method for discovering and realizing one's good, not because they are neutral between competing conceptions of the good. And because the good, in a contingent and changing environment, can never be settled and fixed, it is the process itself that is the final end. The developed self is thus the self that has attained the intellectual and moral virtues of the autonomous individual. Dewey's liberal democracy is, in turn, the best social environment for cultivating the intellectual virtues of critical reflection, creative individuality, and intersubjective verification.

This chapter begins by drawing out the consequences for a society that wishes to promote the principles of critical reflection, creative individuality, and intersubjective verification. We see that their actualization requires a liberal society. Next, Dewey's organic defense of liberalism is compared to John Rawls's Kantian defense. Whereas Rawls values liberalism because he sees it as distinct from the private realm of comprehensive goods, Dewey sees a liberal culture as valuable precisely because it is able to cultivate the virtues necessary for self-development. Finally, Dewey's defense of liberalism is compared to Richard Rorty's postmodern defense. Rorty's strict division of public justice and private perfection is revealed to be untenable. Liberal justice totters on an uncertain base when it is grounded solely on habit (that is, liberal principles are good because they are "ours"), and when principles of right are abstracted from the need of individuals to find meaning and purpose in their lives. Also, Rorty proposes an untenable subjective notion of individual perfection that devalues not only the intellectual and moral virtues that have transcended cultural boundaries but also the need for a cultural horizon of norms in the construction of personal identity.

The necessity of negative freedom. In the preceding chapters, we discussed the fact that for Dewey, growth (in the sense of adapting harmoniously to the environment) is the only final end. We have also seen that genuine growth, as opposed to merely change per se, requires certain generalizable principles that constitute the method of practical inquiry. The moral principles include persistence, wholeheartedness, and impartiality, and the intellectual principles are reflective criticism, individuality, and intersubjective verification. Growth provides the telos for both moral and political inquiry.

Humans are cultural animals precisely because it is only within culture that individuals are able to realize the virtues that are necessary for personal growth. Culture, therefore, may be seen as a functional concept. Its function is to develop the institutions, laws, and norms that are necessary to ensure the continued moral and intellectual development of its members in a contingent and changing world. Because culture is a functional concept, it is thus subject to evaluation.

In chapter 1, we saw that one of the principles necessary for autonomous choice is the intellectual virtue of critical reflection. We also saw that the attitude called out by the necessity of critical reflection occupied a sort of Aristotelian "just proportion" between two opposing extremes. On one side is the extreme of dogmatism. To hold dogmatically to a particular set of institutions, laws, and norms is to halt moral and political inquiry. Not only does dogmatism prevent the realization of what may be a superior set of institutions, laws, and norms for dealing with a community's particular problems but it also does not admit the possibility that changing environmental circumstances (national or global economic transformations, for example) could render particular traditional institutions obsolete. Thus, Dewey insisted, philosophy's "chief function is to free men's minds from bias and prejudice and to enlarge their perception of the world about them."[2] The function of philosophy within a culture is, therefore, to offer a reflective critique and an imaginative reconstruction of existing meanings, thereby providing the alternative perspectives necessary for intelligent inquiry. Like Socrates, we must reflect critically to avoid unthinking bias and prejudice. A culture that is characterized by dogmatic adherence to existing norms has no means of judging the worth of either existing or alternative ideas.

The opposing extreme that the virtue of reflective criticism is meant to avoid is a kind of moral skepticism—the belief that in regard to moral and cultural norms and institutions all judgments of value are subjective because there are no adequate grounds for determining truth or knowledge. A skeptical culture would be one that believes that the social consequence of philosophical fallibility is a privatism in regard to all questions of the good. Individual perfection is thus an affair of the private sphere, and there is little or no room for interaction between culture and politics. In other words, because we cannot be sure of finding a fixed and absolute Truth in regard to the good, questions of the good must be a matter of personal preference. A skeptical society may have some shared political values but will only hold them because they are necessary for social peace between various subcultures. Thus, no set of institutions, laws, or norms will be developed specifically for the purpose of liberating individuals to realize their moral and intellectual capacities.[3]

Because socialization is a fact—and not an option—institutions, laws, and norms can never be neutral in regard to questions about the good. The attitudes that individuals have are largely determined by their immediate environment. An individual born into a social environment that holds dogmatically to a fixed set of institutions and norms is likely to end up with a dogmatic disposition. An individual born into an environment of moral skepticism, where institutions and norms are designed to be indifferent to competing conceptions of the good, is likely to end up with a morally skeptical disposition. In a skeptical society, no goods are promoted by the larger culture as being more conducive to growth than others; thus, the body of values that *is* cultivated is incoherent and conflicting.

Individuals may be socialized by their immediate environment to desire, for example, personal pleasure, material wealth, power, celebrity, eternal salvation, or comfort as their ultimate goal. Or they may be socialized to have a plurality of goals that are equally desired yet rationally incompatible. Conversely, they may be socialized to have no ultimate goal in life, but rather to exist from moment to moment, being led first this way and then that by various amusements and tentative interests, like the rich aesthetes that MacIntyre uses as one of his character types of modernity. The emotive theory of ethics, originating with Hume, says that our passions provide our ends. MacIntyre, in *After Virtue,* defines emotivism as the "doctrine that all evaluative judgments and more specifically all moral judgments are *nothing but* expressions of preference, expressions of attitude or feeling."[4] Individuals in such a culture would be deprived of the moral context in which to judge some activities as more or less worthy than others.

In addition, members of a skeptical society, not being habituated into a set of intellectual and moral virtues as a method of self-development, may see their particular ends as justifying whatever means—that is, attitudes resulting in behavior—necessary to achieve their ends. If Dewey was correct in asserting that the function of culture is to enable the growth of each of its members, then this would be a very poor method of doing so. It may be argued that moral and intellectual growth is solely the function of subcultures within a pluralist society; but what guarantee have we that such subcultures are available to all or even most members of a modern liberal society? It is precisely the collapse of such traditional cultures, prompted by the urbanization and disenchantment of modernity, that makes habituation into the virtues of autonomy more necessary than ever.

A critically reflective culture occupies the middle ground between the two extremes of dogmatism and skepticism. While not habituating its members to blindly accept its existing institutions, laws, and norms as dogma, it is not indifferent to the influences these have on the moral life of society. It encourages social criticism as an inherent good because of its interest in providing the best institutions, laws, and norms for its members. It is concerned with replacing flawed ones (racism, Jim Crow laws, and intolerance, for example) with better ones, not only to protect the rights of certain individuals and minorities but because of the effect those institutions, laws, and norms have on the moral life of society as a whole.

If a society genuinely wishes to promote intelligent reflection on and criticism of existing institutions, laws, and norms, then it must guarantee certain liberal rights and freedoms. These rights and freedoms are not justified just because individuals are naturally rights and freedom-bearing units prior to the artificial construction of society. They are justified because of their consequences in regard to individual growth within any particular culture. The liberal rights and freedoms necessary to promote intelligent critical reflection on existing institutions, laws, and norms are those freedoms of expression contained within the First Amendment of the United States Constitution. Thus: For the principle of critical reflection to be a genuine element of any society, that society must be characterized by the negative freedoms of expression (speech, press, association, and so on).

The necessity of toleration and pluralism. In chapter 1, we saw that individuality, like critical reflection, takes the form of a just proportion between two extremes. In this case, the extremes are conformism and eccentricity. As Tocqueville pointed out, negative freedom does nothing to prevent the existence of a conformist culture.[5] When the social pressure to accept and follow the beliefs of the group is strong, conformity of thought and action becomes the rule. Conformity, unlike dogmatism, does not require adherence to a fixed doctrine. The beliefs of the group may be as fleeting as the wind, but in a conformist culture individuals will bend whichever way the wind is blowing. If, after reflecting critically on an existing cultural belief, a culture has found that particular belief no longer results in desirable consequences, it must look for an alternative. But where to look? "Every *new* idea, every conception of things differing from that authorized by current belief, must have its origin in an individual."[6] When individuals conform to the beliefs of the group to which they belong, however, they are a poor source of original ideas.

If a society wants to encourage imaginative innovation, it must, at a minimum, promote toleration of difference. Dewey wrote that a "progressive society counts individual variations as precious since it finds in them the means of its own growth. Hence a democratic society must, in consistency with its ideal, allow for intellectual freedom and the play of diverse gifts and interests."[7] Individuality, as Dewey insisted, is a potential quality of all persons, but it is not cultivated merely by leaving them alone. Society must take positive measures to cultivate creative and imaginative innovation among its members. Totalitarian societies are notorious for taking positive action to inhibit individuality because innovation and creative vision are seen as destabilizing. Such positive action takes the form of censorship in art, the promotion of conformity in education, and discouragement of innovation in business or government. A society that wants to encourage individuality should invert the totalitarian strategy by opposing censorship in art, rewarding individuality in education, and encouraging experimental innovation in business and politics. A look at American society in the early twentieth century, Dewey assures us, reveals a society still characterized by mass suggestibility and homogeneity of thought.[8]

The opposing extreme of conformity is eccentricity. A culture that is characterized by eccentricity is one in which the free play of subjectivity is the highest good. In Dewey's theory of art, you will remember, subjectivity becomes creative only when it is harnessed to an objective purpose and forced into a form or medium by which it may be communicated to others. To promote the free play of subjectivity, therefore, is to neglect both objective purposes and communication. Without objective purpose and communication, there can be no cooperative inquiry. Cooperative inquiry is the basis of the purposive community. "Society is the *process* of associating in such ways that experiences, ideas, emotions, values are transmitted and made common."[9] In a culture characterized by eccentricity, there can be neither community nor inquiry.

To prevent members from falling into eccentric subjectivity, therefore, a culture must promote purposeful community. In a culture where dogmatism is discouraged, however, the promotion of community must necessarily take the form of pluralism. A homogeneous communitarianism discourages diversity. Not the state, Dewey argues, but "[g]roupings for promoting the diversity of goods that men share have became the real social units. They occupy the place which traditional theory has claimed either for mere isolated individuals or for the supreme and single political organization."[10] Unlike MacIntyre, who describes a plurality of interests and perspectives as moral chaos, Dewey sees such pluralism as necessary for cultural progress. "Reflective morals uses all particular codes as data."[11] If community is purposive, as opposed to merely regional, then community takes the form of civil society: of churches, unions, social and political associations, and the like. Thus: A society that wants to promote individuality must be characterized by the liberal institutions of toleration and pluralism in the form of a healthy and diverse civil society.

The necessity of communication and democracy. In chapter 1, we saw that sociability, the virtue necessary for intersubjective verification, is the just proportion between the extremes of docility and rebelliousness. A culture that is characterized by docility is one in which individuals are socialized in such a way that they become too slavish to stand up for their own rights and too complacent to demand a voice in the construction of the institutions, laws, and norms that wholly govern their lives. A traditional Confucian society is an example of a culture characterized by docile members.[12] A rebellious culture, on the other hand, is one in which members are socialized to be so self-centered and self-willed that they will not consider waiving an individual right—either for a moral obligation or for the good of the community as a whole. Members of such cultures are isolated individuals who shun cooperation and deliberation in exchange for individual quests for purely personal goals. A rights-based society in which the moral good, and even the safety, of the community is subordinated to the sacred rights of the individual is an example of the rebellious, or self-willed, culture. As Feinberg notes: "A person who never presses his claims or stands on his rights is servile, but the person who never waives a right, never releases others from their correlative obligations, or never does another a favor when he has a right to refuse to do so is a bloodless moral automaton."[13] Neither the docile nor the rebellious character types are useful from the point of view of a culture that wants to not only allow but encourage reflective criticism and individuality.

Dewey's method of inquiry, while encouraging criticism and individuality, is necessarily cooperative. Both criticism and creativity require intersubjective verification. A cooperative effort to critique and reconstruct cultural institutions, laws, and norms requires more than the freedom to be left alone and the right to vote. Participation in political dialogue must be actively encouraged by society. Democracy, as we saw in chapter 4, is the method of cultivating social intelligence. Rather than a community of docile subjects or a society of isolated individuals, social intelligence requires a community of autonomous participants. Thus,

the best way for a culture to promote sociability is to educate or socialize its citizens to be autonomous. In other words, a liberal culture must
actively cultivate the liberal virtues of reflective criticism, individuality,
and sociability.

Dewey warned us that democratic political structures are the effect,
not the cause, of democratic culture. Only when reflective and democratic attitudes are the norm among economic, social, and religious associations and institutions can we realistically expect people to exhibit
them politically.[14] Thus, while negative freedom and toleration are necessary for any culture that wants to cultivate reflective criticism and
individuality, they are not sufficient. Direct participation in cooperative
problem solving (which is how Dewey thought of democracy) must be
encouraged at all levels of society (in school, at work, in the community, church, or association). As with other aspects of democracy, if citizens cultivate the habit of communicative problem solving at the social
and cultural level, they will not be frightened or put off by the prospect
of participating at the political level. Thus: A culture that wants to promote intersubjective verification must promote communicative (deliberative, participatory) democracy. In previous chapters, we saw that the
principles necessary for a correct method of inquiry in a world characterized by the generic traits of nature are critical reflection, creative individuality, and intersubjective verification. When these principles are
applied to the study of nature, we have scientific method. When applied
to personal morality as virtues, we have a Deweyan conception of autonomy. Now we can see that when these principles are applied to culture, we have a Deweyan defense of liberal democracy—of freedoms of
expression, toleration, pluralism, and participatory institutions. We can
now compare Dewey's defense of liberal democracy to the theories of
Rawls and Rorty.

Rawls's neutrality-based justification. John Rawls describes his "political liberalism" as neutral in aim, not in procedure. By neutral in aim,
Rawls means that his principles of justice do not "intentionally favor
or promote any particular" religious, philosophical, or moral doctrine.
Political liberalism is not procedurally neutral, however, because it appeals to certain liberal principles such as "fair social cooperation," "ci-
vility," "tolerance," "reasonableness," and "fairness" that may be con-
strued as disadvantageous to certain illiberal doctrines. It appeals to these
principles, however, not to promote liberal doctrines but to create a
neutral political framework within which a plurality of different doctrines may interact peacefully. Despite its intentions, the consequence
of appealing to these liberal principles is that illiberal conceptions of the
good may be adversely affected; namely those intolerant and repressive
doctrines that are incompatible with Rawls's theory of liberalism.[15]

In appealing to these principles, Rawls is, I believe, appealing to the liberal conception of the good. In this Rawls and Dewey would be in agreement. But Rawls wants to insist that questions of fairness, toleration, reasonableness, and so on are concepts *only* of the right (because they are political) and not concepts of the good (which are private). This is why he gives priority to the right over the good. This prevents him from putting forth a liberal conception of the good life as the life of the autonomous chooser.

As I mentioned in the introduction, Rawls's theory can be described as a minimalist justification of liberalism. Macedo describes Rawls's minimalist justification as asking, "What is the least that must be asserted; and if it must be asserted, what is its least controversial form?"[16] He intentionally limits his theory to the political realm and explicitly rejects any connection between liberalism and a philosophy of humanity or nature.[17] The conclusion one might be tempted to draw from this insistence is that the primary goal of liberalism is peace between conflicting religious, philosophical, and moral doctrines.

Rawls's conception of liberalism goes beyond this, however, when he includes within his notion of the right the concept of primary goods. Rawls argues that there is an objectively identifiable list of goods that all people need in their quest for self-development, regardless of what their particular conception of the good life is. While we may never agree on what we should prefer, want, value, or believe, we can agree, or arrive at an "overlapping consensus," on what primary goods are necessary and due to all of us. The primary goods Rawls settles on are (1) equal basic rights, liberties, and opportunities; (2) a minimum level of income or wealth; and (3) a social basis for self-respect.[18]

When Rawls says that "the right and the good are complimentary,"[19] I interpret him to mean that he accepts the Aristotelian view that the right consists of those rules that must be followed if the good is to be achieved. If this is so, the existence of primary goods within Rawls's conception of the right implies that the purpose of liberalism is not merely to keep peace between competing conceptions of the good but to promote individual realization of the good whatever one's particular conception of it may be, as long as it does not infringe on the right of others.

There is strong similarity between Rawls's theory so defined and the portrait of a skeptical culture that I sketched above. As long as our life plans do not conflict with the political conception of right, they are a private concern. Other than this restriction, the state is not involved in promoting the notion that some conceptions of the good may be more or less worthy than others nor in promoting any particular virtues as being conducive to self-development. Thus, the principles of fascism are discouraged by Rawls's political conception of right as being less worthy because this is the least that must be insisted upon by a liberal state. Thus, it is not the direction in which Rawls's theory would lead us that Dewey would object to but the fact that he does not travel nearly far enough down the road.

In the previous chapter, I expressed Dewey's insistence that democratic political procedures were of little value without a democratic culture— that political democracy is, in fact, the *consequence* of a democratic culture. The same holds true for the principles of liberalism. Toleration, fairness, openness, reasonableness, and cooperation in the political realm are the consequence of a liberal culture, and a liberal culture is the consequence of liberal attitudes and dispositions in individuals. It is not enough to discourage fascism and outward displays of intolerance. For a culture to be genuinely grounded in liberal principles, it must actively promote liberal attitudes and dispositions (what I call intellectual and moral virtues) as more worthy than illiberal attitudes and dispositions. Liberal principles are not neutral between conceptions of the good life— they clearly favor the life of the autonomous chooser.

Theories, such as Dewey's, that require the state to promote certain virtues (attitudes and dispositions) over others are called perfectionist. Rawls gives three reasons for rejecting perfectionist political theories. First, because perfectionist doctrines want to impose a particular conception of the good on persons, thus depriving them of choice. Rawls believes that when a state takes on the responsibility of teaching its citizens what constitutes a virtuous life, its citizens are no longer free to choose their own conceptions of the good life. This is harmful because, Rawls believes, it is in the essential interest of individuals to have the capacity and opportunity to examine and revise their own conceptions of the good.[20]

The second and third reasons are closely related. Rawls believes that perfectionist theories are necessarily teleological, and that teleological theories define the good independently of the right. The right, or justice, becomes merely a means for maximizing the good. Rawls claims that the distribution of goods within a society is a concept of right, not of the good. Therefore, the second objection that Rawls has to perfectionism is that justice—which in Rawls's case refers to the equal distribution of primary goods—is subordinated to maximization of the good. If the good can be maximized only by violating the rule of equal distribution, then its subordination can be justified when the good is given priority over the right. If a theory wants to assure that primary goods such as liberty, opportunity, and respect are always distributed equally, then it must give priority to the right. Rawls calls all such theories deontological as opposed to teleological.[21]

The third objection that Rawls has to perfectionism is derived directly from this distinction between teleological and deontological theories. Teleological theories, because they subordinate justice to the ultimate goal of maximizing the good, necessarily treat some individuals as merely the means to achieve the good of others. They fail to take into account the separateness of persons. Deontological theories, on the other hand, treat all individuals as ends in themselves. This can be done, Rawls argues, only by giving priority to the right—that is, principles of justice—over particular conceptions of the good.

In response to Rawls's objections to perfectionism, Dewey would argue that Rawls has set up a pseudoproblem by imagining a dualistic relationship between the right and the good. It is no more acceptable to define the right independently of the good than it is to define the good independently of the right. Moreover, there is no reason why we should have to choose between one or the other. Neither the right nor the good can be understood independently of the other. The right does indeed consist of those virtues and principles that are a means to the good. In fact, Dewey claims that we determine the right by generalizing the particular demands of citizens in their quest for the good life. But, by the same token, the good consists of nothing other than the principles and virtues that are contained in the right, for the good is not a separate thing that is more noble or superior to the right; rather, it is the consequence of doing what is right. For the individual, the good life is the consequence of living virtuously; for the state, the maximization of the good is a consequence of just laws and institutions.[22]

Rawls's claim that treating persons as ends in themselves is an exclusive property of deontological theories does not stand up to reason. When we ask *why* it is important to treat persons as ends in themselves, we are led back to questions of the good life. One must have a particular conception of the good life in order to conclude that being used as a means (slave) for the ends of someone else (master) prevents those persons who are being used from attaining their good. Dewey's perfectionist theory sees the end or good of the state, community, society, or culture as the fulfillment of the capacities of its members.

As Will Kymlicka points out in his discussion of Rawls, there is no "real issue about which of the right and the good is prior": "To define the right as maximization of the good, and to view people simply as means to the promotion of that good, is not to present an unusual interpretation of the moral point of view. It is to abandon the moral point of view entirely, to take up a non-moral ideal instead."[23] The notion that all individuals are ends in themselves is a presupposition, not a product, of deontological theory. Rawls's original position was constructed as it was because equal respect for each person's good was an intuitive starting point. I admitted as much in regard to Dewey at the beginning of chapter 1. Once it is accepted that each person's good matters equally, a perfectionist theory must necessarily be concerned with equal liberation for self-fulfillment. Equal distribution of primary goods is thus not the result of giving priority to the right over the good but of accepting a functional conception of both the individual and the community. The function of the individual is to strive for perfection, and the function of the community is to meet the needs of its members.

In regard to Rawls's objection that perfectionist theories deprive individuals of the ability and opportunity to examine and revise their conceptions of the good, this can hardly be the case with Dewey's perfectionism, which consists of the realization of the capacities of critical reflection, individuality, and communication. In fact, having called his "just society" (which is, after all, a liberal society) a good,[24] Rawls is unable to take the step to advancing a liberal conception of the good life for individuals only because of the false dualism he has posited between the right and the good. If the capacity to examine and revise our conceptions of the good is, as Rawls believes, an essential interest of all individuals, then Dewey's conception of individual perfection (autonomy) is an essential interest of all individuals in their quest for the good, and its realization is in itself the good life.

Prioritizing the right thus creates a couple of unnecessary problems for Rawls's conception of liberalism. First, the importance of the good is minimized. If some choices are, in fact, more worthy than others, then the good is not being promoted by simply leaving individuals alone. The function of culture is to lend meaning and significance to the lives of its members—to enable them to make moral and intelligent choices. The only way to do this, and simultaneously avoid dogmatism, is to socialize individuals to be moral and intelligent choosers. Dewey writes: "[S]ocial arrangements, laws, institutions, are . . . not means for obtaining something for individuals, not even happiness. They are means of *creating* individuals."[25] What kind of institutions, laws, and norms create moral and intelligent choosers?

If a society is indifferent to whether the individual quest for the good is carried on by means of the moral and intellectual virtues, when it does not promote courage as more worthy than timidity, wholeheartedness as more worthy than duplicity, impartiality as more worthy than prejudice, critical reflection as more worthy than dogmatism, individuality as more worthy than conformity, or sociability as more worthy than atomized individualism, then it is basically indifferent as to whether its members achieve the good life or not. Giving them negative freedom and a minimum level of wealth is similar to what convicts receive when they are released from prison. To promote justice without virtue is merely to try to regulate outward activity without affecting attitudes and dispositions.

If the function of culture is to create certain kinds of individuals, then how can we evaluate a liberal culture that insists on neutrality in regard to what kind of individuals are created by its institutions, laws, and norms, with the exception that they not be fascists or racists? Rights-based liberals will probably object that liberalism is based on opposition to the educative state—that liberalism prefers members who are capable of autonomously choosing their own conceptions of the good. Dewey would reply that all social arrangements, laws, and institutions are educative, regardless of whether they are planned to be so or not—and that autonomous choosers are just as much the product of social habituation as are blind conformists. A society that educates its members to be autonomous, that is, moral and intelligent choosers, is not neutral between conceptions of the good; it is biased in favor of the liberal conception of the good.

It does not matter that Rawls does not want to create a certain type of individual. Certain types of people will be created by the social environment regardless of what it is. What matters is that we understand the causal connection between alternative social conditions and their consequences. The entire history of theories and practices in education, sociology, and anthropology is a meaningless blowing into the wind if there is no causal connection between social conditions and individual attitudes and dispositions. Questioning their relationship is like questioning the relationship between the flame by my elbow and the pain in my arm.

The second problem that prioritizing the right creates for Rawls is that it does not provide any concrete or practical connection between the subjectively defined good of its individual members and Rawls's particular conception of the right (which implies a form of welfare state). The importance of the fact that the Aristotelian notion of right consists of the principles and/or virtues that are needed to achieve the good is that the principles and virtues contained within the concept of the right derive their authority from the ends they serve.[26] Rawls, as I quoted him above, also says that he believes that the good and the right are complementary. But if the good I choose is, for example, to maximize my personal wealth, and I feel that I can achieve this good without the aid of the community as a whole, why should I feel obligated to limit my quest by a respect for the needs of others? Why should I see society as a co-operative venture if I can achieve my good independently?

The principles of justice may make sense to me in the original position because they then seem to be in my interest. But if no ends or virtues are promoted as being more worthy than others, and I can obtain the primary goods that I need without the aid of the state (in other words, I am not disadvantaged), then there is no connection between Rawls's notion of the right and my personal conception of the good. Because Rawls bases his principles of justice on individual self-interest (what self-interested individuals would agree to in the "original position") rather than on a particular liberal conception of the good, the only reason I have for allowing the political right to hinder my personal quest is state coercion. Unless the right is justified as a means to a particular conception of the good, it can derive no authority from the ends it serves. To say that the just society is a good is only true if it is concretely related to the good of its individual members. A correspondence between the good promoted by a Rawlsian conception of the just society and the good of any particular individual should not be left to chance—it should be the end of society itself as well as the justification of its institutions, norms, and rules.

The fact that the right derives its authority from the good has been a central problem for liberal theory. One of the major tenets of liberalism is toleration for diverse notions of the good. But, as MacIntyre points out, if society cannot agree on a definition of the good, how can it justify a shared conception of justice (which is the means to the good)? If Rawls's conception of justice implies a conception of the good, then it is not neutral between competing conceptions of the good life. Like Dewey, Rawls must defend a liberal conception of the good life—the autonomous life—as the best way to live.

While Dewey's conception of autonomous choice allows us to distinguish the desired from the desirable and the valued from the valuable, it does not provide a fixed substantive definition of either. Because the value or desirability of a good is eventually determined by experience, our choices must always in some sense be hypothetical. The method of intelligent choice is the best way to proceed in a world of qualitatively individuated situations. For example, a good that is the product of unthinking habit, immediate desire, blind conformity, or radical choice may eventually be judged valuable but, if so, the correctness of the choice can be explained only by coincidence. On the other hand, a good that is chosen after critical reflection of existing and alternative (perhaps innovative) beliefs and that is the result of a choice made within the context of a cultural horizon of meanings is more likely to earn the distinction of a valuable and desirable choice because it takes into consideration the possible consequences of the choice. Dewey's method allows for a plurality of worthy goods but also provides a means of distinguishing better from worse goods. If the right consists of the means necessary for obtaining the liberal conception of the good, then we must ask what social arrangements, institutions, and laws are necessary to create the kinds of individuals who can intelligently and morally choose what is valuable and desirable.[27]

The distinction between Rawls and Dewey therefore begins with Rawls's assumptions that either individuals already possess the ability to make intelligent and moral choices prior to being socialized, or that they have already been socialized to be autonomous choosers prior to the creation of his just society. In Rawls's discussion of the two moral powers, he describes the characteristics of a "reasonable and rational citizen." "[T]here are a) the two moral powers, the capacity for a sense of justice and a capacity for a conception of the good. As necessary for the exercise of the moral powers we add b) the intellectual powers of judgment, thought, and inference. Citizens are also assumed c) to have at any given time a determinate conception of the good interpreted in the light of a (reasonable) comprehensive view."[28] Making these assumptions allows Rawls to derive what he calls the "social division of responsibility." According to Rawls, the external primary goods constitute objective needs and as such are the responsibility of society. Particular comprehensive conceptions of the good, on the other hand, being subjective or intersubjective desires, are the responsibility of individuals and private associations.[29]

Assuming that individuals have these moral and intellectual powers and their own conception of the good at the outset, prior to a particular theory of justice, is a prime example of what distinguishes liberal individualist theories from the theories of their communitarian critics. Assuming that individuals have these powers before considering the basic structure of society necessarily implies one of two things: either that the ability to exercise the two moral powers is possible prior to membership in a society or culture (in other words, that humans have some innate nonsocialized ability and propensity to reflect morally and intelligently on the norms, values, and beliefs into which they are socialized); or Rawls is assuming that all individuals have already been habituated into the two moral powers by some subculture.

If the latter is true, then because the two moral powers consist of the ability to exercise "judgment, thought and inference" in regard to both the right and the good, the assumed subcultures must *already* be liberal in a Deweyan sense. Thus, Rawls's liberal community depends on the preexistence of individuals who have already been socialized to be good liberals—that is, intelligent and moral choosers. If we are to accept the former assumption, then we would also have to assume that such tasks as child rearing and nonvocational education are unnecessary because individuals already possess the intellectual and moral virtues as innate instincts. If this were the case, then we would have to attribute only nonmoral and unintelligent dispositions to socialization. Dogmatism, nihilism, narcissism, conformity, impulsiveness, selfishness, and the like would not, therefore, be significant problems for a liberal individualist society. The problem is that by assuming the two moral powers are already functional in citizens, prior to his theory, Rawls does not feel the need to cultivate them.

Dewey does not assume that individuals already possess the virtues of autonomy. Instead, he argues that the virtues necessary to exercise the moral and intellectual powers, like all virtues, are the product of education. If individuals do not learn to reflect critically on their existing cultural values[30] or to exercise their creative individuality within that cultural context, then these virtues will never just magically appear. If we want individuals to have the moral and intellectual virtues and the healthy liberal civil society within which to exercise them, then these things must be promoted by a liberal culture.

In other words, negative freedom plus a minimum amount of income or wealth will seldom be sufficient to produce a developed self, unless a culture also provides the necessary internal skills and participatory social environment. Dewey argued that a concrete, as opposed to abstract, conception of freedom must be quantifiable.[31] Concrete freedom consists of the power to do specific things. The power to do more things is equivalent to the availability of more valuable choices. More valuable choices are equivalent to more freedom.

Genuine freedom requires the distinction between valuable choice from choice per se. A slave does not lack freedom merely because he lacks choice. He may be given the choice between working in the fields or being whipped. We would not therefore consider him to be free. His choices may even be multiplied indefinitely to include such options as working in the fields, being whipped, hanged, beaten, starved, separated from his family, and so on, but regardless of the number of choices, we still consider him to be a slave as long as he must choose between the lesser of various evils. It is only when the value, or quality, of the options improves that we begin to see the distinction between freedom and slavery. When he can choose between working in the fields of this or that employer, or working in a factory, or going to school, or becoming a sailor, we can begin to speak of him as being *more* free than a slave, but still less free than the individual who has the options of going to Harvard or Yale, or buying his own farm, or starting his own business.

Certain external goods (wealth or income, for example) allow more choices, but so do certain intellectual and moral virtues. Autonomous choosers have access to more valuable choices than the person who blindly follows tradition, authority, or passion because they are not limited to the choices suggested by tradition, authority, and passion. So while negative freedom and external goods are necessary, they are not a sufficient means to the liberal conception of the good—they do not provide the internal liberty to make intelligent and moral life choices.

Let's reformulate Rawls's social division of responsibility to fit Dewey's theory of liberalism. Because Dewey's justification of liberalism requires negative liberty, toleration, and the existence of a diverse civil society, we can say that he agrees with Rawls's first primary good of equal basic liberties.

As for Rawls's second primary good, in his essay "Liberty and Social Control," Dewey disputes the notion that liberty and equality are at odds by arguing that the real issue is whether there is equal liberty. Liberty, as I pointed out above, means the power to act or the availability of valuable choices. The power to act is in direct relation to one's economic resources. From this, he concludes that the effort by non-Marxist egalitarians to make American society more equal economically is in no way a threat to individual liberty. Rather, it is a threat only to the unequal amount of liberty possessed by a few. A roughly equal opportunity for each individual to realize the good will require at least the assurance of a minimum of resources. If the end of liberalism is "the liberation of individuals so that realization of their capacities may be law of their life,"[32] then Rawls's second primary good (the difference principle) seems entirely reasonable from the perspective of Dewey's theory.

The third primary good is the social basis of self-respect which, in Rawls's theory, is derived from the first two primary goods. If society affords everyone the same basic liberties and opportunities, and if it shows an equal concern for the economic well-being of all its members, then every individual has the social basis for self-respect. To respect oneself is, according to Rawls, another good that is necessary for all particular conceptions of the good. Rawls also says, however, that if citizens are afforded equal liberty and opportunity to develop and exercise their moral powers and to pursue a conception of the good and yet fail to do so, that "they show a lack of self-respect and weakness of character."[33]

Because Dewey does not assume that individuals are capable of exercising the two moral powers without being educated to do so, he does not locate the social basis for self-respect solely in the first two primary goods; he also includes the achievement of some measure of autonomy.[34] Although autonomy requires individual effort, it is unlikely to be achieved outside of a culture that values and cultivates the virtues that make autonomy possible. Because the virtues of autonomy are necessary for any individual's quest for the good and the achievement of autonomy is in part a social product, then we can say that autonomy is an objective need and is thus the responsibility of society.

The reformulation of Rawls's primary goods in terms of Dewey's justification of liberalism, therefore, looks like this:

1. Equal basic liberties, rights, and opportunities.
2. Minimum level of income or wealth.
3. Cultivation of the intellectual and moral virtues of autonomous choosers.

Rawls justifies his three kinds of primary goods based on what self-interested individuals would choose in the original position. A Deweyan perspective defends the above principles as necessary to liberate individuals equally to realize their good, and thus as being obligatory for any community that exists for the good of its members. Equal rights and liberties are necessary to liberate individuals from external coercion. Negative liberty makes communication of critical reflection and innovative vision possible. A minimum level of wealth or income is necessary for liberty from economic coercion or, in other words, for the availability of valuable choices. Habituation into the moral and intellectual virtues is necessary for liberty from internal constraints. Autonomy is merely an empty and formal concept unless it includes the internal capacities to overcome moral and intellectual limitations.

The addition of intellectual and moral virtues to Rawls's list of external goods is surely in line with Dewey's admonition that negative liberty is necessary but not sufficient. Despite some of the better-known expositions on the relative merits of positive and negative freedom,[35] the two are not necessarily mutually exclusive. Dewey argues convincingly that autonomy is a good that is absolutely essential for a fulfilled life. But he argues that achievement of this good is possible only in a particular kind of social environment—that is, a liberal one. Far from being incompatible with negative freedom, the intellectual virtues of autonomy can be exercised only within an open society. On the other hand, an open society rests on a precarious foundation if its members consist of few genuinely autonomous choosers. Thus, the virtues of critical reflection, individuality, and sociability are such that, when individuals grow in them, they benefit the whole community.

Rorty's ironic justification of liberalism. In *Contingency, Irony, and Solidarity,* Rorty gives Dewey credit for being one of the philosophers who "undermined the notion that liberalism depends on trans-historical 'absolutely valid' foundations."[36] Rorty claims that Dewey was one of those who provided the ground for rejecting philosophical foundations because he pointed out the contingent nature of language, self, and culture. But, as we have seen, Dewey saw the contingent nature of language, self, and culture as providing a groundmap for a method of inquiry on which a philosophical foundation for liberalism is based.

Rorty argues that when we ask a question that presupposes a universal answer, for example: "What is it to be human?", we are attempting to escape from time and chance. But time and chance, according to Rorty, cannot be escaped. They condition everything.[37] It would seem, therefore, that time and chance, change and contingency, are universal, and all attempts to escape them are futile. But this makes Rorty's argument self-refuting because the only motive metaphysicians have for escaping time and chance is to establish universals. Rorty himself praises Wittgenstein and Heidegger, who wrote "philosophy in order to exhibit the *universality and necessity of the individual and contingent*"(my emphasis).[38] Dewey recognized, unlike Rorty, that the universality of contingency has metaphysical consequences.

Dewey understood that because change is a necessary consequence of time and space—and all of nature is located within time and space—then change must be a generic trait of nature. The fact that time and chance cannot be escaped provides a solid foundation or, as Dewey preferred to call it, a groundmap for a method of inquiry. That method of inquiry is, as we have seen, the basis for Dewey's conception of autonomy and for his philosophical defense of liberalism. He turns Rorty's objection around and asks: If time and chance cannot be escaped, what are the consequences for humans? The answers he comes up with provide the principles for his defense of liberalism.

Although Rorty does not believe that liberalism can be philosophically justified, he prefers it to the available alternatives.[39] He seems to offer conflicting reasons for this. First, in Rawlsian fashion, he explains that we need to agree on some public conception of justice, and our traditions are our only available source of agreement. He thus suggests that we keep liberalism because it represents our beliefs.[40] If we ever feel the need to argue in favor of liberal goods, Rorty recommends that we use the vocabulary of rhetoric to describe it (liberalism) in ways that make it sound better than its alternatives. For those who fear that this provides too little protection for liberal rights and freedoms and too little legitimation for liberal conceptions of justice, Rorty offers the notion of "ironic commitment." He falls back on Berlin's quote of Schumpeter, who said: "To realize the relative validity of one's convictions and yet stand for them unflinchingly, is what distinguishes a civilized man from a barbarian."[41]

The second reason that Rorty gives for preferring liberalism to its alternatives, here following Judith Shklar, is that it is less cruel. Although this seems to be a transcultural standard, Rorty attempts to satisfy the criterion of noncontradiction by stating that for "liberal ironists, there is no answer to the question 'Why not be cruel?' —no noncircular theoretical backup for the belief that cruelty is horrible."[42] This would seem to imply that liberals abhor cruelty only because they are socialized to feel that way. In his final chapter on "Solidarity," however, Rorty argues for "a moral obligation to feel a sense of solidarity with *all other* human beings" (my emphasis) based on the notion that pain and humiliation are more "salient" similarities between persons than are more traditional similarities such as "tribe, religion, race, customs, and the like."[43] A tension thus appears between the Rawlsian justification, which assumes no transcultural validity, and the Shklarian justification, which does.[44] This tension in Rorty's thought begins to take on the character of a contradiction even in his own text. Thus, at one place he argues that to "accept the claim that there is no standpoint outside the particular historically conditioned and temporary vocabulary we are presently using [in this case, the vocabulary of liberalism] . . . is to give up on the idea that there can be reasons for using languages as well as reasons within languages for believing statements. This amounts to giving up the idea that intellectual or political progress is rational, in any sense of 'rational' which is neutral between vocabularies."[45] But the ability to empathize with the pain and humiliation of other human beings seems to be a reason and a reason that is "neutral between vocabularies." Thus, in another place Rorty confides that the "view that I am offering says that there is such a thing as moral progress, and that this progress is indeed in the direction of greater human solidarity."[46]

The third reason Rorty gives for preferring liberalism to its alternatives has to do with his belief that the quest for individual perfection is "necessarily private, unshared, [and] unsuited to argument." It is the product of private fantasy, which can have no relevance to the needs of the community unless by coincidence. The attempt by "strong poets" (those who are able to transcend the common cultural identity by re-creating themselves) to give cultural relevancy to their private fantasies is at best futile, and at worst dangerous.[47] To attempt to impose a common identity upon these strong poets, however, would be to hinder the cause of personal growth as well as to deprive society of a possible source of innovation. What is needed, then, is a culture that allows the free play of subjectivity in the private realm while it maintains a system of shared rules in the public realm. Thus, Rorty prefers a liberal culture with its strict distinction between the public and private spheres. Liberals, for the sake of solidarity, commit themselves to a framework of rules called justice at the public level, which is tolerant of the free play of subjectivity (or difference) at the private level. Thus, Rorty presents what seems to be another transcultural reason for why he prefers liberalism to its alternatives—because it is tolerant of the free play of subjectivity that is necessary for private perfection.

Thus we can see that, for Rorty, public solidarity is based on a common desire to privatize. Privatization is necessary because the cruelty that liberals despise is caused by a "political attitude which will lead you to think that there is some social goal more important than avoiding cruelty."[48] To guard against cruelty, therefore, we must minimize our social goals to the provision of social conditions that allow individuals to conduct private quests for perfection. Rorty's hope is that this aversion to cruelty, which is apparently peculiar to liberals, will eventually be adopted by the rest of humanity.

There are three core differences between Dewey's philosophy and the theory of liberalism put forth by Rorty that help to explain why Dewey's justification of liberalism works, and Rorty's ironic justification offers no valuable alternative. The first concerns human nature, the second the relationship between the right and the good, and the third the concept of creativity.

Human nature. Rorty claims that theories of human nature are futile attempts to escape from time and chance. He argues that rather than ask, "What is it to be human?", we should ask, "What is it to be a citizen of a twentieth-century liberal society?" We are all the products of socialization, not nature, and socialization "goes all the way down."[49] Dewey, on the other hand, believes that all humans have the same basic natural instincts and needs. Although he believes that different cultures can satisfy these needs in different ways and can channel the instincts in radically different directions, the same needs and instincts must be accounted for in any theory of self-development: thus, the fixed nature of Dewey's moral and intellectual virtues. Rather than say that there is no human nature, therefore, Dewey would say that human nature is malleable.[50]

Now, if socialization "goes all the way down," as Rorty claims, it would follow that the goal of any quest for individual perfection would necessarily be a contingent social product. To be socialized "all the way down" is, after all, about as socialized as you can get. If certain persons can find their perfection *only* in the free play of subjectivity, therefore, they must have been socialized to be that way. But Rorty is making the argument that the quest for perfection *must* be the product of the free play of subjectivity. If this is his argument, however, he must be assuming a particular theory of human nature. He must be arguing that part of what it is to be human requires us to seek our perfection in the private world of idiosyncratic fantasy. He must accept as fact the belief he attributes to Heidegger and Foucault that "socialization is antithetical to something deep inside us."[51] Thus, Rorty must be assuming some aspect of human nature that transcends time and space. Otherwise, he cannot make the claim that individual perfection is *necessarily* a private affair.

Is Rorty saying that perfection is necessarily a private affair only for those socialized into a twentieth-century liberal democracy? I do not believe that he is, for Rorty ponders the question of whether "a more comprehensive philosophical outlook would let us hold self-creation and justice, private perfection and human solidarity, in a single vision" and concludes that: "There is *no way* in which philosophy, *or any other* theoretical discipline, will *ever* let us do that. The closest we will come to joining these two quests is to see the aim of a just and free society as letting its citizens be as privatistic, 'irrationalist,' and aestheticist as they please so long as they do it on their own time. . . . But there is *no way* to bring self-creation together with justice at the level of theory. The vocabulary of self-creation is *necessarily* private, unshared, unsuited to argument. The vocabulary of justice is necessarily public and shared, a medium for argumentative exchange" (my emphasis).[52] Thus, the private nature of the good is not, according to Rorty, a product of socialization. It is, using Dewey's terms, a generic trait of nature.

Public right and private good. Rorty's confusion concerning human nature leads him to propose an untenable dualistic relationship between the right (public justice) and the good (individual perfection). Rorty claims that we can distinguish two opposing types of philosophers: those, such as Dewey and Marx, "for whom the desire for a free and just society dominates," and those, such as Heidegger and Foucault, "for whom the desire for private perfection dominates." He goes on to claim that those for whom the desire for a more free and just society is dominant see the desire for private perfection as being "infected by irrationalism and aestheticism."[53]

Rorty's characterization of theorists such as Dewey and Marx, however, shows a fundamental misunderstanding of what these men were about. Dewey's defense of liberalism based on self-development argues for freedom and justice solely as means to individual perfection. Thus, when we hear that Dewey desired a free and just society, we must ask, "Free and just in what sense?" What criteria, in other words, did Dewey use to distinguish free and just societies from unfree and unjust ones? Without a consideration of Dewey's conception of individual perfection, we cannot answer that question. As I have pointed out previously, the right (freedom and justice) is defined and derives its authority from the good (individual perfection). We can understand what Dewey meant by a free and just society only when we realize that for him the final good of society is the equal liberation of individuals to seek their perfection or fulfillment. To distinguish theorists who are more concerned with a free and just society from those who are more concerned with individual perfection is to mistakenly assume that the two concepts have no relation.

When Rorty says that theorists such as Dewey see the desire for private perfection as infected by irrationalism and aestheticism, he should be sure to distinguish between his notion of private perfection and individual perfection per se. It is true that Dewey would see the type of perfectionism advocated by Heidegger and Foucault as infected by irrationalism and aestheticism, but the quest for individual perfection did not begin with the postmodernists. It is probably the oldest theme in philosophy. It is also at the core of Dewey's entire philosophy. There is no incompatibility between the desire for a free and just society and the desire for individual perfection unless individual perfection is conceived of as being necessarily a private affair.

Poetic creativity. This brings us to the third difference between Dewey's and Rorty's theories. Rorty sees individual perfection as self-creation and, in turn, views creativity as the free play of subjectivity. "By seeing every human being as consciously or unconsciously acting out an idiosyncratic fantasy, we can see the distinctively human, as opposed to animal, portion of each human life as the use for symbolic purposes of every particular person, object, situation, event, and word encountered in later life. This process amounts to redescribing them, thereby saying of them all, 'Thus I willed it.'"[54] In Rorty's world, if private fantasy has any relevance to society at all, it is only coincidental. Thus, "poetic, artistic, philosophical, scientific, or political progress results from the accidental coincidence of a private obsession with a public need."[55] For Rorty, therefore, self-creation must be a solely private affair. If, on the other hand, creation of selves or, in other words, identity, *is* a social affair, then creativity plays no role, because creativity is necessarily idiosyncratic. From Rorty's point of view, social construction of identity requires the suppression of individuality, and individuality requires the suppression of social influence. If individuality, or authenticity in the Heideggerian sense, is to be saved, identity must be wholly the creation of subjectivity.

In chapter 3, when I discussed Dewey's theory of art, we saw that he defined creativity as the synthesis of subjectivity and objectivity—that is, a subjective perspective of an objective situation communicated through an intersubjective medium. Creativity can thus be of relevance to society as the source of a solution to a shared problem. Being innovative, the solution must have at least partially originated ex nihilo from the imagination of an individual; it is therefore the product of subjectivity. Being the solution to a common problem, the subjective innovation must (1) have an objective purpose; (2) be communicable; and (3) be subject to intersubjective verification. It is, therefore, a product of the interaction between subjectivity and objectivity. It cannot be pure subjectivity, which is necessarily without objective purpose, incommunicable, and not subject to argumentation. An idiosyncratic fantasy must then be objectified through both a common purpose and a means of communication in order to be genuinely creative.

Deweyan creativity is a functional concept that can be judged according to its ability to be communicated and to fulfill a public function—whether that function is to predict thunderstorms, heighten aesthetic awareness of the human condition, or more efficiently trap mice. Dewey can thus distinguish genius from mere eccentricity. Rorty, on the other hand, must argue that "when some private obsession produces a metaphor which we can find a use for, we speak of genius rather than of eccentricity or perversity. The difference between genius and fantasy is not the difference between impresses which lock on to something universal, some antecedent reality out there in the world or deep within the self, and those which do not. Rather, it is the difference between idiosyncrasies which *just happen* to catch on with other people" (my emphasis).[56] Must we conclude, therefore, that Western culture has labeled as genius the creations of Shakespeare, Mozart, and van Gogh for no other reason than that their particular idiosyncrasies just happened to catch on? If we take Rorty's definition seriously, there is no standard for judging the works of these artists as better or worse than the creations of any others.

By contrast, Dewey believed that Beethoven, had he been raised from infancy in a primitive tribal society, would still have been a musical genius even though he would not have composed symphonies.[57] Beethoven's particular private fantasy did not "just happen to catch on" because it met a contingent public need. Rather, Beethoven's genius lies in his ability to express a subjective vision in a way that can be understood and that can be meaningful to others in his language community. The manifestation of genius may be channeled in a variety of different directions by cultural influences, but the capacity is objective. Otherwise we would have to conclude that the only reason Beethoven's musical abilities have been judged as higher than yours or mine is blind chance. Dewey would argue that expressing one's personal vision in a way that is profoundly meaningful to one's cultural fellows is itself the greatest evidence of genius. The genius of van Gogh, molded by Japanese culture, would have expressed itself in a way that Japanese culture finds meaningful. Rorty's supposed elevation of creativity is in reality a devaluation of it.

We saw above that Dewey's conception of individuality is the just proportion between the opposite extremes of conformity and eccentricity. He would thus characterize Rorty's conception of creativity as an overreaction to conformity. He would see it as the replacement of one extreme by another, the result of yet another false dichotomy. The free play of subjectivity, when it is not organized or channeled by any objective purpose, results in eccentricity, not creativity. The authentic self, according to Dewey's definition of creativity, is the result of the interaction between the subjectivity of the individual and the objectivity of the community. As Charles Taylor points out in *The Ethics of Authenticity,* an identity that is purely the product of subjectivity is trivial and insignificant, for all meaning and significance are derived from a particular moral community.[58]

Rorty's conception of creativity as pure subjectivity fails even for his own purposes. For example, when he speaks of the need for solidarity at the public level, he dismisses the role previously played in this endeavor by philosophy and recommends to us the poet, particularly the novelist. Because solidarity in Rorty's liberal utopia is based on the common repudiation of cruelty, one function of the poet is to increase our sensitivity to the pain of others.[59] But this advice is incompatible with Rorty's conception of creativity as the free play of subjectivity. As we have just seen, when subjectivity is channeled by an objective purpose, it is no longer idiosyncratic free play. In this case, Rorty has proposed an objective function for poets—the sensitization of the public to the pain of others. Not only does creativity become a functional concept that we can judge objectively as better or worse but it requires poets to channel their unique perspectives in such a way that it touches a common nerve with the public at large. If we wish to sensitize others, we must communicate. Communication requires reference to a common language. The type of creativity that Rorty is demanding from poets in his liberal utopia, therefore, can be delivered only by poets who are creative according to Dewey's conception of it, not Rorty's.

Rorty's reference to revolutionaries and prophets as strong poets also fails to fit with his notion of creativity as purely subjective.[60] The vision of the revolutionary and the prophet must (1) be communicated by a common medium; (2) be continuous with at least some of the community's existing norms if it is to be accepted; and (3) attempt to deal with some objectively existing problem (or at least with what has been intersubjectively agreed upon to be a problem by a certain proportion of a community's population). The visions of Marx and Moses, for example, meet all three of these criteria. But it does not follow that either Marx or Moses was, by consequence of meeting these three criteria, motivated by a private and idiosyncratic fantasy. The vision of neither was accepted by a large number of people merely because it just happened by coincidence to meet their contingent needs. Both were tools designed specifically to communicate a concrete solution to an actually existing problem. In both cases, the problems (economic exploitation and slavery) were deemed to be so by the preexisting norms of the communities. Thus, if poetic creativity is defined as eccentric and idiosyncratic fantasy, then neither Moses nor Marx can be considered strong poets.

Rorty explicitly rejects the analogy between a new metaphor and a tool because the "craftsman typically knows what job he needs to do before picking or inventing tools with which to do it. By contrast, someone like Galileo, Yeats, or Hegel (a 'poet' in my wide sense of the term—the sense of 'one who makes things new') is typically unable to make clear exactly what it is he wants to do before developing the language in which he succeeds in doing it."[61] Dewey would describe Rorty's strong poets as the makers of conceptual tools. When creativity is defined according to Dewey's conception of it, we see that the achievement of genuine creative genius requires interaction between subjectivity and objectivity. Individual perfection, per se, cannot be seen as a purely private endeavor. Rather, it requires a particular type of society, one in which all individuals are afforded the opportunity of exercising their creative potential. Thus, a free and just society is one in which the liberation of individuals (freedom) to realize their potential is achieved impartially (justice).

Rorty's ironic defense of liberalism fails, therefore, at all three points of contention with Dewey's philosophical defense. In regard to human nature, Rorty cannot say that we are socialized all the way down at the same time that he claims that individual perfection is necessarily private. If we are socialized all the way down, then we can be socialized to be the kind of persons who find their greatest good, or happiness, in a public manner. To say that individual perfection *must* be private is to assume a particular conception of human nature. Dewey's conception of human nature is of beings who must satisfy fixed and universal needs and instincts in changing and contingent environments. Individual perfection thus requires a generalizable method of determining the value of temporal goods rather than a body of fixed and universal goods. The method, as we have seen, requires the virtues and principles that provide the basis for both individual autonomy and cultural liberalism.

In regard to the relationship between the right and the good, Rorty cannot say that certain theorists, such as Dewey and Marx, are concerned with public justice and freedom while others are concerned with individual perfection because the justification of the particular conceptions of justice and freedom offered by Dewey and Marx cannot be understood in isolation from their goals in regard to individual perfection. Unless we have a particular conception of individual perfection, we cannot provide a nonarbitrary justification for a public conception of right. Even Rorty must have a particular conception of the good—a *private* and thus idiosyncratic construction of the self—in order to justify his particular conception of the right, which is concerned primarily with preserving a large sphere of privacy and toleration for the private fantasies and eccentricities involved in individual perfectionism.[62]

Finally, Rorty cannot simultaneously define creativity as idiosyncratic fantasy and say that it is the means of creating solidarity against cruelty in the public sphere. If creativity is private fantasy, then it cannot be prescribed, as a tool, for anything. Tools are functional and purposive. They are designed for specific objective purposes; their designs are usually not, therefore, the product of arbitrary and fantastical play. Creating tools requires the application of a subjective solution to an objective problem. For such an enterprise, idiosyncratic fantasy is trivial and insignificant.

Conclusion. The generic traits of nature—which include change, contingency, continuity, and qualitative individuality—provide a groundmap for a correct method of inquiry. This method includes the basic intellectual principles of critical reflection, creative individuality, and intersubjective verification. Any culture that wants to embody these principles must be characterized by such liberal institutions as negative freedom, individual rights, toleration, and pluralism. It must also promote such communitarian institutions as participatory democracy and public promotion of the moral and intellectual virtues of the autonomous chooser.

The principles of liberalism can thus be defended philosophically without having to assume the myth of a presocial, isolated individual. If Kantian rights-based justifications of liberalism assume this presocial, isolated, rights-bearing individual, then they must necessarily ground their justifications of freedom and equality on enlightened self-interest. In such theories, all justification of socioeconomic equality is necessarily suspect. The myth of the presocial individual was constructed specifically to liberate individuals from communal responsibility. It thus makes a poor base from which to justify a procedure of redistribution. Likewise, a conception of freedom that is defended solely on the grounds of enlightened self-interest must necessarily be limited to the absence of external physical coercion, providing no measure of protection whatsoever against economic coercion that inhibits valuable choice or against the types of internal constraints that prevent individuals from making autonomous decisions.

Recognizing such shortcomings, some liberal theorists have decided to co-opt much of the communitarian critique. Rawls, for example, has declared that his theory of justice is political, not metaphysical, because it is supposedly based on the intuitions of Western liberal democratic culture.[63] But the fact that many liberal theorists have chosen to concede to such communitarian claims as the contingency of rights or the social and historically contingent nature of the self creates a problem of justification. If liberalism is merely a cultural artifact, then what justification for liberal values can it rely on other than Rorty's ironic commitment? And as we have seen, Rorty's ironic commitment provides no justification at all. Where can liberals look to distinguish the "ought" from the "is" if the only guide we have is where we have been in the past?[64]

Dewey's philosophical defense of liberalism provides a way out of this quandary. It defends liberal freedoms and toleration without forcing us to neglect the importance of community or to deny the social and historically contingent nature of culture and the self. We are not saddled with a mythical justification that overemphasizes individual rights at the expense of the community, nor must we deprive individuals of the genuine freedom that comes from economic opportunity. Most important of all, we can see that educating people into the intellectual and moral virtues of the autonomous chooser, far from being a threat to liberal freedom and toleration, is necessary for their protection.

6

Cultural Evolution

We should not misunderstand Dewey's notion of cultural progress to mean that there exists an "end of history" or some other such ideal toward which a culture—or all cultures—is progressing. Rather, Dewey interpreted cultural progress in the same way he did all growth, as a series of ends in view and consummations, a continuous cycle of problematics: "problem, inquiry, solution" or "tension, movement, harmony" as we saw in the introduction. As always for Dewey, harmony (in the prescriptive sense) is defined as a social environment in which all individuals are liberated to realize to the utmost their intellectual and moral capacities.[1] Thus, in this sense of growth, Dewey saw cultural progress as cyclical rather than linear, desirable rather than inevitable.

There is another sense, however, in which Dewey was able to conceive of cultural progress as moving on a linear path toward a fixed goal, as when a culture realizes internally the principles that are necessary for a correct method of growth in the cyclical sense. The method of critical reflection, creative individuality, and intersubjective verification is necessary for cultural growth as it is for personal. While these principles can never be perfectly realized, Dewey believed that meliorative growth in the direction they provide is always possible. Thus, if a culture wants to be able to respond to problematics by devising new ends in view to reestablish a harmonious relationship with its environment, it must act to avoid the vices we spoke of in earlier chapters as representing the extremes Dewey's method of inquiry is meant to avoid. In other words, a culture must guard against falling into dogmatism, conformity, and docility, on the one hand, or skepticism, eccentricity, and rebelliousness, on the other.

In this chapter, Dewey's theory of cultural growth is compared to MacIntyre's and Rorty's theories. Although the fit is not perfect, Mac-

Intyre's theory is a type that tends toward the extremes of dogmatism, conformity, and docility, and Rorty's toward skepticism, eccentricity, and rebelliousness. The argument proceeds in the following manner. First, culture is defined; second, we discuss the question of why cultures need to grow; third, we look at how cultural growth is measured; and finally, we examine the internal dynamics of cultural growth—or, in other words, who and/or what causes cultures to evolve. The weaknesses inherent in MacIntyre's and Rorty's notions of cultural growth are used to show that Dewey's naturalistic conception of cultural growth provides the best available method.

What is culture? The *American Heritage Dictionary* definition of culture is: "The totality of socially transmitted behavior patterns, arts, beliefs, institutions, and all other products of human work and thought characteristic of a community or population." Culture embodies customary and traditional ways of thinking, doing, and feeling, ways that are passed from generation to generation through conscious and unconscious processes of socialization. Any particular culture's ways of thinking, doing, and feeling are necessarily unique. This follows from the fact that the origin and development of a specific culture is contingent on countless random factors. A unique climate and geography lead to certain economic possibilities. The economic mode of the community determines, to a large extent, the political and social relations. Events such as natural disasters and internal or external conflicts may be turning points in the development of a culture. Its current character is a result of countless reactions to natural and social experiences. It has become what it is by the way it has responded to the events in its unique history.

Each culture's ways of thinking, doing, and feeling have consequences, and the people who hold these cultural meanings have natural needs. When certain ways of thinking, doing, and feeling are found to produce consequences that satisfy people's needs better than others, these ways become the habitual ways of the culture. Dewey refers to these unique ways of thinking, doing, and feeling as cultural biases. Modern anthropologists refer to them as memes.[2] A culture's memes are habituated into its members through socialization. When we speak of "raising" our children, or of "bringing them up right," we are referring to this practice of habituating them into the memes of our culture. Culture continues to exist only through the intergenerational communication of memes.

> The continuity of any experience, through renewing of the social group, is a literal fact. Education, in its broadest sense [beyond merely formal education], is the means of this social continuity of life. . . . Each individual, each unit who is the carrier of the life experiences of his group, in time passes away. Yet the life of the group goes on. . . . Transmission occurs by means of communica-

tion of habits of doing, thinking and feeling from the older to the younger. . . . Yet this renewal is not automatic. Unless pains are taken to see that genuine and thorough transmission takes place, the most civilized group will relapse into barbarism and savagery.[3]

"[I]n time these ideas filter into the average consciousness, and their truth becomes, wholly unawares to the average consciousness, a part of the ordinary insight into life."[4] Thus, if we are successful when raising our children, they will intuitively recognize, for example, the distinction between polite and rude behavior, respectable and disrespectable behavior. They will have been habituated to do so. The specific cause-effect relationships that led to the development of the habit will not be available to immediate awareness. The memes of the culture will be experienced aesthetically. Our children are habituated to *feel* the difference between polite and rude behavior, the former evoking feelings of satisfaction and the latter feelings of indignation.

The aesthetic standard[5] by which we judge polite/rude, right/wrong, good/bad, and so on is provided by the whole body of memes into which we are socialized. We learn to distinguish the polite/right/good ways of thinking, doing, and feeling from the impolite/wrong/bad ways. These cultural habits necessarily take the form of generalizations. After we have been socialized into a particular culture, we have a whole mind full of generalizations that allow us to pass judgment on particular thoughts, actions, and feelings. We have already seen that this body of cultural generalizations is what Dewey refers to as context or background. It is the body of unspoken assumptions that makes understanding, and thus rational thought, possible. "When we think, there are some things which we are immediately thinking *of*, considerations . . . with which we are wrestling, trying to overcome its difficulties and to reduce to order. Surrounding, bathing, saturating, the things of which we are explicitly aware is some inclusive situation which does not enter into the direct material of reflection. It does not come into question; it is taken for granted. . . . It has a solidity and stability not found in the focal material of thinking."[6] Furthermore, "the vague and extensive background is present in every conscious experience. . . . It represents that which is being used and taken for granted, while the focal phase is that which is imminent and critical. . . . The larger system of meanings suffuses, interpenetrates, colors what is now and here uppermost; it gives them sense, feeling."[7] The perspective our immediate consciousness has of any particular event or object is influenced by cultural context. When we speak of reason or rationality, we are alluding to the capacity of humans to justify, or *give reasons for,* their thoughts, actions, and feelings. Because this ability is dependent on culture, Dewey concludes that all rationality is contextual even though the method of thinking itself is general.

I believe that the above description of culture is similar to, though not identical with, Alasdair MacIntyre's conception of "tradition" in his works *After Virtue* and *Whose Justice? Which Rationality?* What relation does MacIntyre's notion of tradition have to Dewey's notion of culture? MacIntyre writes: "Every tradition is embodied in some particular set of utterances and actions and thereby in all the particulars of some specific language and culture." Each consists of an "inherited moral language." MacIntyre concludes that: "What the good life is for a fifth-century Athenian general will not be the same as what it was for a medieval nun or a seventeenth-century farmer. . . . For all reasoning takes place within the context of some traditional mode of thought, transcending through criticism and invention the limitations of what had hitherto been reasoned in that tradition."[8] If "all reasoning takes place within the context of some traditional mode of thought," then I see no essential difference between MacIntyre's conception of tradition as spelled out here and Dewey's conception of culture as providing a dynamic context for moral reasoning.

I believe that the same can be said for Richard Rorty's conception of "vocabulary" in his work *Contingency, Irony, and Solidarity.* When Rorty uses the word "vocabulary," he refers to a comprehensive scheme of meanings that provides context to a specific area of knowledge. To provide context is to provide a particular way of thinking, feeling, and acting within a specific domain. A certain vocabulary dominates discussion among physicists, for example. A body of cultural meanings is the source of its member's habits of thinking, doing, and feeling, and thus fits into Rorty's definition of vocabulary.[9]

Why cultures need to grow. As we saw above, memes are biases. They are the accepted ways of thinking, doing, and feeling that become the basis for the norms, rules, and institutions of a culture. Memes can be both objective and relative in that while as humans we have objective natural needs, satisfaction of these needs is relative to the contingent social and natural environments in which we live. The particular set of norms, rules, and institutions that best serves to meet our needs is thus determined by the interaction of necessity and contingency. All humans need food, but the particular kind of food a culture grows used to, and the manner in which it is appropriated, is contingent on the natural environment. Different manners of meeting physical needs lead to different economic, social, and political norms and institutions, and these become part of a culture's environment. In other words, all attempts to adapt ourselves to our environment result in a changed environment. Determination of the best memes is thus a matter of discovering the best way to satisfy natural needs in a contingent social and natural environment. Thus, for Dewey, "all conduct is *interaction* between elements of human nature and the environment, natural and social."[10]

The evolutionary growth of capitalism in seventeenth- and eighteenth-century Great Britain provides an example of the necessity of cultural change. If the spirit of capitalism originated with the Puritans, as Max Weber argues, then the original capitalists did not know that they were, in fact, capitalists. The theory that defined capitalism came along subsequently to provide an economic, as opposed to religious, way of speaking about the creation of wealth. Along with the changes in the economic system, capitalism inevitably led to a demand for political change. Eventually, theories were devised to provide ways of speaking about these political changes as well—the natural rights and natural equality of classical liberalism. Institutions, rules, and norms had to be reconstructed so that the consciousness of the people was in tune with concrete economic, political, and thus, social realities. This reconstruction began with classical liberal political theory. Resistance to cultural innovation meant that much of the concrete change was accompanied by revolutionary violence.

Dewey envisions a liberal culture in which a method of adapting to historical contingency is built into the culture's memes. In this culture, one set of institutions, rules, and norms would be for the most part fixed: those individual virtues and political principles that encourage criticism, creativity, and intersubjective verification. This fixed set of memes would provide a cultural method of cooperative and evolutionary adaptation to change and contingency. All of the culture's remaining institutions, rules, and norms would constitute the other set of cultural memes that are subject to the deconstructing and reconstructing method created by the first set.

Our memes supply the necessary context for all of our reasoning. In other words, when our consciousness is focused on particular events and objects, the collective experience of our culture furnishes them with meaning. But if the particular events and objects that are the focus of our consciousness belong to a changed environment, the context provided by former experiences will not always serve us well. Dewey believed that this was especially relevant to modernity because of the rapid pace of technological and thus economic and social change. A "gap" existed between the needs of individuals in modern technological society and the habits of thinking, doing, and feeling that developed in a pretechnological era. "There is always a gap between the here and now of direct interaction and the past interactions whose funded result constitutes the meanings with which we grasp and understand what is now occurring. Because of this gap, all conscious perception involves a risk. . . . When past and present fit exactly into one another . . . the resulting experience is routine and mechanical."[11] Also, "the present time is one which is in peculiar need of reflective morals and of a working theory of morals. . . . Methods of industry, of the production, and distribution of goods have been completely transformed. The basic conditions on which men meet and associate . . . have been altered. . . . A multitude of such relationships have brought to the fore new moral problems with which neither old customs nor beliefs are competent to cope."[12] We cannot, and need not, reflect critically on all of our existing institutions, laws, and norms all of the time. But when certain ways of thinking, feeling, and doing become problematic in regard to current realities, critical reflection and creative reconstruction are called for. "As a society becomes more enlightened," explains Dewey, "it realizes that it is responsible *not* to transmit and conserve the whole of its existing achievements [or memes], but only such as make for a better future society."[13] Once again, the natural cycle of tension, movement, and harmony (problem, inquiry, and solution) is implicated.

Like Dewey, MacIntyre recognizes that the contingent character of the technological, economic, and social environment may result in the need to adjust cultural institutions, rules, and norms to novel conditions. When MacIntyre speaks of "tradition," he refers to the rationalization and dialectical transcendence of a particular body of cultural habits. "For it is central to the conception of such a tradition that the past is never something merely to be discarded, but rather that the present is intelligible only as a commentary upon and response to the past in which the past, if necessary and if possible, is corrected and transcended, yet corrected and transcended in a way that leaves the present open to being in turn corrected and transcended by some yet more adequate future point of view." Furthermore, "[a] tradition which reaches this point of development will have become to greater or lesser degree a form of enquiry and will have had to institutionalize and regulate to some extent at least its methods of enquiry."[14] Are only such rationalized cultures labeled as traditions? Apparently not, for MacIntyre writes: "Not all traditions, of course, have embodied rational enquiry as a constitutive part of themselves."[15] The goal of such rationalization, MacIntyre argues, is to develop a "fully adequate and rationally defensible conception of the good and the best. . . . The more nearly complete [a rational system of moral thought becomes], the greater the range of political and moral phenomena—actions, judgments, dispositions, forms of political organization—which prove susceptible of explanation."[16] MacIntyre recognizes that although these comprehensive rational schemes of thought are designed to provide answers to all of a culture's moral questions, they are limited by the contingent and changing nature of reality. He warns that "new situations, engendering new questions, may reveal within established practices and beliefs a lack of resources for offering or for justifying answers to these new questions." A culture's ability to respond to this challenge "will depend not only on a stock of reasons . . . and reasoning abilities they already possess, but also upon their inventiveness." These statements demonstrate that MacIntyre recognizes the necessity both of adapting cultural meanings to change and of utilizing "inventiveness" for that purpose.[17]

Like Dewey and MacIntyre, Rorty conceives of a cultural "vocabulary" as a body of meanings that slowly evolves to reflect the needs of the people who use it within a changing environment. One major difference is that Rorty does not understand cultural evolution to be a conscious process. To understand this difference, we will have to digress for a moment and return to a subject that we covered in the introduction. You will recall the argument that Darwinian natural selection was an accidental, cause-and-effect type of evolution rather than an intelligent, means-and-end process of growth. It was not until after the development of mind in humans that we were able to create tools, or memes, that served the same adaptative purposes as the accidental organic mutations in Darwin's theory. Hence, humans became intelligent creatures able to adapt themselves to their environment through the use of material and conceptual tools. To quote Jacob Bronowski in *The Ascent of Man*: "Nature—that is, biological evolution—has not fitted man to any specific environment. . . . Among the multitude of animals which scamper, fly, burrow, and swim around us, man is the only one who is not locked into his environment. His imagination, his reason, his emotional subtlety and toughness, make it possible for him not to accept the environment but to change it. And that series of inventions by which man from age to age has remade his environment is a different kind of evolution—not biological, but cultural evolution."[18] According to Rorty's description of the process of cultural evolution, we have never truly reached the point described by Bronowski at which we are able to purposefully, and thus intelligently, adapt ourselves to our environment. While vocabularies do, in fact, develop through time to meet our changing needs, the method is not intelligent choice but still a variation of Darwin's accidental selection.

Persons involved in their own private fantasies and projects create idiosyncratic conceptual artifacts. Some of these artifacts may, by coincidence, be of use to the culture as a whole. A culture does not consciously decide to begin utilizing the artifact, however; rather, it unconsciously and gradually loses the habit of using existing memes and develops the habit of using new ones.[19] Thus Rorty, as we saw in the previous chapter, explicitly rejects the analogy of ideas to tools. "[T]he person who designs a new tool can usually explain what it will be useful for—why she wants it—in advance; by contrast the creation of a new form of cultural life, a new vocabulary, will have its utility explained retrospectively. We cannot see Christianity or Newtonianism or the Romantic movement or political liberalism as a tool while we are still in the course of figuring out how to use it. . . . Christianity did not know that its purpose was the alleviation of cruelty, Newton did not know that his purpose was modern technology."[20] Thus, for Rorty, there can be no "criterion of choice between alternative metaphors."[21] Nor can there be any way of controlling the direction in which a culture grows. Without the ability to value some metaphors over others because of their use in achieving some overriding purpose, all change must be a kind of pointless drifting. According to Rorty, we cannot know the purpose of a conceptual tool until after it has done its work. Thus: "Nietzschean history of culture, and Davidsonian philosophy of language, see language as we now see evolution, as new forms of life constantly killing off old forms—not to accomplish a higher purpose, but blindly. Whereas the positivists see Galileo making a discovery . . . , the Davidsonian sees him as having hit upon a tool which happened to work better for certain purposes than any previous tool."[22] For Rorty, therefore, cultural evolution is not just a reaction to contingency but a product of it as well.

How to measure cultural growth. I have already addressed the fact that not all growth is necessarily progress. Cancer grows, fascism develops. How then do we determine desirable directions of growth from undesirable ones? If we have a substantive definition of the good, then growth is good when it moves closer to the telos provided by this ideal. In Dewey's philosophy, a life distinguished by autonomous choice and action is not only the means to but partially constitutes the good life. Thus, all cultural growth in the direction of a social environment that will produce autonomous citizens is good. All change that creates the type of social environment that discourages the virtues of autonomy is bad. In terms of process or method, therefore, we can speak of a good direction of growth.

But there is a second criterion for measuring cultural growth. If the first criterion calls for cultural conditions that nurture autonomous choosers, then it is instrumental to the second criterion, which is adaptation to change—the degree to which a culture is able to adapt its institutions, rules, and norms to meet the needs of its members. Pragmatists such as Dewey believe that the degree to which a culture is able to cultivate the virtues of critical reflection, individuality, and sociability in its members— in other words, the degree to which it cultivates autonomous choosers— it will be able to adapt to change and contingency successfully.

MacIntyre also recognizes that cultural institutions, rules, and norms will need to adapt to change and contingency. He writes that there are "three stages in the initial development of a tradition: a first in which the relevant beliefs, texts, and authorities have not yet been put in question; a second in which inadequacies of various types have been identified, but not yet remedied; and a third in which response to those inadequacies has resulted in a set of reformulations, reevaluations, and new formulations and evaluations, designed to remedy inadequacies and overcome limitations." And, to repeat and expand the quote from above, a

> tradition which reaches this point of development will have become to greater or lesser degree a form of enquiry and will have had to institutionalize and regulate to some extent at least its methods of enquiry. . . . [To] some degree, insofar as a tradition of enquiry is such, it will tend to recognize what it shares as such with other traditions, and in the development of such traditions common characteristic, if not universal, patterns will appear. . . . To claim truth for one's present mindset and the judgments which are its expression is to claim that this kind of inadequacy, this kind of discrepancy, will never appear in any possible future situation, no matter how searching the enquiry, no matter how much evidence is provided, no matter what developments in rational enquiry may occur.[23]

What are these "common characteristic, if not universal, patterns"? They are the "methods of enquiry" that MacIntyre claims a tradition will need to "institutionalize and regulate." For Dewey, these methods are critical reflection, creative innovation, and intersubjective verification, and they are institutionalized in a liberal democratic political culture. They are the principles of inquiry that need to be institutionalized and regulated in every culture that expects to grow in the sense of adapting to contingency and change. These liberal cultural principles will negate the need, which is admitted as a possibility by MacIntyre, of trashing an entire cultural tradition in favor of another because the established tradition is unable to provide the concepts and principles necessary to meet the needs of members should they encounter "hitherto unrecognized incoherences, and new problems for the solution of which there seems to be insufficient or no resources within the established fabric of belief."[24] When a tradition encounters what he calls an "epistemological crisis," it may need to be replaced by a tradition that has, internal to it, the concepts and principles necessary to overcome the problems that stumped the tradition in crisis. This seems to admit into his scheme of things the existence of a neutral standard for evaluating traditions. The standard seems quite clearly to be the utility, or effectiveness, of a tradition when it functions as a method of inquiry for adapting its members to change and contingency.

Dewey made recognition of this fact the keystone of his theory of cultural evolution. He defended his conception of liberalism on the basis that it provides the best available method of cultural inquiry. MacIntyre, while he refers to culture as a tradition of inquiry, denies that this fact imposes any transcultural evaluative criterion of what a tradition ought to look like, other than it ought to be internally coherent. But internal coherence does not assure external efficacy at meeting human needs in a precarious environment. Although he believes that the test of a tradition is its ability to adapt to "new situations, engendering new questions," he provides no universal method for doing so. A tradition, like a theory, can be entirely rational in regard to its internal coherence and simultaneously totally inadequate in regard to its external relations, that is, its ability to meet the practical needs of its members.

MacIntyre concludes that "to claim truth for one's present mindset . . . is to claim that this kind of inadequacy . . . will never appear in any possible future situation."[25] The method of cultural enquiry provided by Dewey, however, will cultivate a mindset of critical reflection and imaginative reconstruction of existing institutions, rules, and norms— plus intersubjective verification of the changes. Dewey can thus claim that his conception of liberal culture is not subject to "this kind of inadequacy" because it *presupposes* that "the appearance of new situations, engendering new questions" will show current norms, rules, and institutions to be inadequate at regulating social, economic, and political relations. While we can certainly never claim the truth for the particular set of institutions, rules, and norms that has been derived and rationalized from a historically contingent tradition, we can claim the validity of a process of inquiry and growth that is derived precisely from the historically contingent nature of existence itself.

Rorty, similarly, sees cultural growth as the gradual evolution of concepts within a cultural "vocabulary." It involves "a contest between an entrenched vocabulary which has become a nuisance and a half-formed new vocabulary which vaguely promises better things. . . . The method is to describe lots and lots of things in new ways, until you have created a pattern of linguistic behavior which will tempt the rising generation to adopt it. . . . [A] recognition of . . . contingency leads to a recognition of the contingency of conscience, and . . . both recognitions lead to a picture of intellectual and moral progress as a history of increasingly useful metaphors rather than of increasing understanding of how things really are."[26] But what does Rorty mean by "useful?" Dewey understands the social and natural world as providing an objective environment to which we must adapt; thus, one set of institutions, rules, and norms can be judged as more or less useful than another. Rorty, however, rejects both the "tool analogy" and the notion that there is any set of criteria outside of a particular vocabulary by which to evaluate the usefulness of one compared to another. The telos for Dewey's theory of cultural growth is adaptation to a contingent and changing, and yet objectively real, set of problems and goals. Rorty's conception of cultural growth is nonteleological.

> A nonteleological view of intellectual history, including the history of science, does for the theory of culture what the Mendelian, mechanistic, account of natural selection did for evolutionary theory. Mendel let us see mind as something which just happened rather than as something which was the point of the whole process. Davidson lets us think of the history of language, and thus of culture, as Darwin taught us to think of the history of a coral reef. Old metaphors are constantly dying off into literalness, and then serving as a platform and foil for new metaphors. This analogy lets us think of "our language" . . . as something that took shape as the result of a great number of sheer contingencies. . . . [O]f thousands of small mutations finding niches (and millions of others finding no niches). . . . [N]ew forms of life constantly killing off old forms—not to accomplish a higher purpose, but blindly. . . . [Thus,] the world does not provide us with any criterion of choice between alternative metaphors . . . with something beyond language called "fact."[27]

Rorty's theory of cultural evolution explicitly denies that there is any standard or method for evaluating vocabularies or the metaphors that cause vocabularies to change. The adoption of new metaphors is unconscious and accidental. We can know the use to which the new metaphor is put only in retrospect.[28]

While Rorty argues that there is no way of judging between metaphors or vocabularies, he simultaneously claims that aversion to cruelty and humiliation provides a potential basis for solidarity among all cultural vocabularies.[29] Rorty claims that the defining characteristic of liberals is the belief that cruelty is the worst thing we do;[30] why does this not provide liberal cultures with a telos and thus a criterion for evaluating competing metaphors? Are not certain metaphors—racist, homophobic, and so on—more cruel, and thus less acceptable to a liberal culture, than others? Rorty seems to be expressing an "ought" for liberal culture in the same way that he wants to extend this aversion to cruelty to humans in general. But if Rorty were saying this, he would be arguing for a criterion for both evaluating metaphors internal to liberalism and for evaluating cultures per se, that is, the less cruel a culture the better.

Can Rorty say that all cultural development is the product of unconscious drift at the same time he tries to argue that the criterion of aversion to cruelty and humiliation is the only possibility of a transcultural source of human solidarity? "The view I am offering says that there is such a thing as moral progress, and that this progress is indeed in the direction of greater human solidarity. But that solidarity is not thought of as recognition of a core self, the human essence, in all human beings. Rather, it is thought of as the ability to see more and more traditional differences (of tribe, religion, race, customs, and the like) as unimportant when compared with similarities with respect to pain and humiliation—the ability to think of people wildly different from ourselves as included in the range of us."[31] Are not the "similarities with respect to pain and humiliation" that all humans share somehow related to "the human essence, in all human beings?"

In addition, Rorty claims that the liberal aversion to cruelty and humiliation is good because it allows private space for individual quests for perfection which, as we have seen, he claims are necessarily private. Once again, why does this not provide a criterion by which cultural vocabularies can be judged—according to their compatibility with individual perfection? If all cultural vocabularies are blindly evolving, then why should the current liberal aversion to cruelty not change also? How can Rorty justify absolutizing it?[32] If the aversion to cruelty "arose," as Rorty states, "rather late in the history of humanity and is still a rather local phenomenon,"[33] why should we liberals expect it, or even want it, to remain unless it has some kind of transcultural and transhistorical value? If so, then we should be able to order cultures as more or less cruel and within liberal culture, evaluate new metaphors according to their ability to make society less cruel and humiliating. But this implies a neutral standard for evaluating cultural vocabularies, something that Rorty assures us does not exist. If the aversion to cruelty is merely a cultural preference, then there is no reason to think that it contains the potential to be a transcultural basis for human solidarity. If no standard for evaluating cultures exists, we must conclude that a culture with an aversion to cruelty is neither more nor less valuable than a culture with the tendency to be cruel. Rorty simply wants to have his cake and eat it too.

Rorty rejects Dewey's generic traits of nature as an attempt to make valuations "simultaneously naturalistic and transcendental."[34] Yet if *all* thought, and thus every belief, is historically or culturally conditioned, then this fact transcends culture. That is what Wittgenstein and Heidegger also understood. Rorty recognizes that "[p]ost-Nietzschean philosophers like Wittgenstein and Heidegger write philosophy in order to exhibit the universality and necessity of the individual and the contingent. Both philosophers become caught up in the quarrel between philosophy and poetry which Plato began, and both ended by trying to work out honorable terms on which philosophy may surrender to poetry."[35]

Rorty claims that the attempt to universalize any condition of nature is an effort to continue the quest of the priests and philosophers, but the universalization of time and chance cannot be portrayed as an attempt to escape from time and chance. Such a portrayal is a logical contradiction. Rorty may, if he wishes, try to claim that all attempts to use pure logic to discover the really real have failed and thus reject logic as a means of transcending socialization. But he cannot reject logic as it pertains to his own reasoning. He cannot say, for example, that it is impossible to escape from time and chance and yet maintain that there are no traits of nature, including time and chance, that are universal.

Dewey realized that if contingency and change are universal, then it is a logical necessity that we ask what the consequence is for humans. He concluded that although the products of moral inquiry must be contingent, the method itself is not. He saw no need to oppose the scientist and philosopher to the poet. Rather, he recognized that poetry, or making, was a large part of what scientists and philosophers did. We need not reject objectivity in order to recognize that the objective context in which we find ourselves is not fixed nor that there are various culturally determined perspectives from which a single objective context can be seen. "Instruction in what to do next can never come from an infinite goal, which for us is bound to be empty," but "[i]t can be derived . . . from study of the deficiencies, irregularities and possibilities of the actual situation."[36]

Despite his supposed rejection of traditional philosophy, Rorty still allows traditional philosophical dualisms to define his worldview. He sees the world as presenting us with a set of radical either/ors. Either we are capable of discovering a universal and absolutely fixed hierarchy of goods, or the good is purely a matter of opinion. Either we are capable of discovering humanity's naturally true essence, or the only authentic identities are those that are a product of "thus I willed it" subjectivity.[37] Dogmatic absolutism or skepticism. Conformity or eccentricity.

Dewey refers to such dichotomous choices as pseudochoices. He rejects unchallengeable absolutes because they "have no locus in time, a fact naively stated in calling them eternal. They belong neither here nor there. In applying to everything, they apply to nothing in particular." But he is equally adamant in his rejection of what is now called postmodern skepticism, which he describes as: "a denial that criticism in the sense of judgment is possible, and an assertion that judgment should be replaced by . . . the responses of feeling . . ., [which is] to reduce all experience to a shifting kaleidoscope of meaningless incidents. . . . Because . . . [absolutists] set up false notions of objective values and objective standards, it was made easy . . . to deny there are objective values at all."[38] We can measure a culture's growth by the degree to which it is able to adapt its fundamental end, which is the equal liberation of individuals to realize their moral and intellectual capacities, to a contingent and continually evolving economic, technological, and thus social environment. In other words, culture, as a method of inquiry, must be able to determine what set of social and political institutions, rules, and norms are best able to cultivate and enhance the individual virtues of critical reflection, individuality, and sociability. That this culture must be democratic and comprehensively liberal is a given. How democracy and liberalism are manifested in a particular culture is dependent on the state of its economic, technological, and social environment.

MacIntyre seems to agree with Dewey that the criterion for growth is the ability to answer questions and solve problems that arise as a result of economic, technological, and social change. Unlike Dewey, however, he does not provide a method of evolution that transcends cultural traditions and thus provides no telos other than adaptation itself. Rorty, on the other hand, rejects the notion that cultural growth can be measured at all. According to Rorty, all cultural development is blind. This seems to me to be a rather strange interpretation of Darwinistic evolution which, although not provided with a preexisting final state, did have a criterion of selection: namely, physical survival within an objective environment. Humans did not evolve the way they did because the changes were arbitrary but because some alternative ways of changing worked better than others in respect to survival. Cultural evolution is about more than survival—it is about self-development and about providing meaning and purpose to individual lives. I would agree with Dewey that some cultural memes work better than others at performing this function.

How cultures grow. Although both Rorty and MacIntyre, like Dewey, accept the historically and culturally contingent nature of institutions, rules, and norms, they do not make a logical connection between this contingency and the necessary method of cultural inquiry that seems to follow. For example, when trying to determine which is the best method of inquiry, it would seem to be entirely logical to say that the best method is theoretical contemplation if we proceed from the initial premise that the answers we seek are derived from universal and fixed essences, or that romantic poetry is the best method if we proceed from the initial premise that the answers we seek are purely matters of feeling. By the same token, it is also entirely logical to say with Dewey that critical reflection, creative reconstruction, and intersubjective verification follow from the initial premise that institutions and norms are historically contingent—the result of interaction between fixed human needs and a changing, but objectively real, environment. We must wonder, therefore, why MacIntyre focuses so exclusively on the internally coherent rationality and homogeneity of traditions even though he believes that traditions must enable a people to deal with their objectively real external environment and why Rorty focuses so exclusively on subjectivity even though he believes that vocabularies are cultural artifacts that, of necessity, are the product of intersubjective experience.

While Dewey recognizes the value of poetry, his conception of it differs significantly from that of Rorty. Dewey looks to the creative imagination of individuals as the only source of technological or conceptual innovation, but the free play of subjectivity is channeled and given meaning by objective purpose. Too much emphasis on objectivity results in a formal, uninspired, and unimaginative product. Too much emphasis on subjectivity results in an eccentric, fantastic, and incommunicable one.[39]

Objectivity is supplied by facts and by the cultural habits (or memes) that provide context for our reasonings. Immediate awareness is colored by the body of memes into which we are socialized. Subjectivity is the product of a unique life history. The interaction within our minds between memes and the series of experiences that make up our personal histories produces a self that is at once unique and situated within a common frame of reference. Thus, there is a constant interaction within our minds between the influences of our culture and the experiences of perception. While cultural prejudices color all of our perceptions, our perceptions just as surely lead to adjustments in the way we think, act, and feel as individuals. Consequently, while being socialized into a shared body of memes gives members some salient commonalities, it does not necessarily hinder the formation of individuality.[40] Sandra Rosenthal explains that freedom in Dewey's philosophy is not the result of liberation from memes but "the proper dynamic relationship between the two poles of the self:" one pole being the "conformity of group perspective" and the other the "creativity of its unique individual perspective."[41]

Just as there is a constant interaction between memes and particular perceptions in the mind of the individual, there is a continual interaction at the cultural level between memes and the perspectives of individual members. Through all forms of cultural interaction—science, philosophy, art, literature, film, pop culture, casual conversation—there is a give and take between cultural bias and individual perspective. A culture's memes may, in fact, be characterized as a set of generalizations of the various individual perspectives of its members. If this is not the case, if a culture's memes originated in an earlier era and are no longer reflective of the perspectives of its members, then the culture is failing to adapt to the changes of its environment.

In a culture characterized by Deweyan liberalism, the mutual adjustment between individual perspectives and cultural generalizations would be more free-flowing. He wants to avoid the social disintegration that results from revolutionary change—and the violence that would be unnecessary if we tended to cling less blindly to the memes of an earlier era. "The oscillation between impulse arrested and frozen in rigid custom and impulse isolated and undirected is seen most conspicuously when epochs of conservatism and revolutionary ardor alternate. But the same phenomenon is repeated on a smaller scale in individuals. And in society the two tendencies and philosophies exist simultaneously; they waste in controversial strife the energy that is needed for specific criticism and specific reconstruction."[42] Dewey's notion of cultural growth is considered "progressive." The word progressive connotes, for most people, an opposition to conservatism or tradition. But, in reality, Dewey's theory emphasizes tradition as much, if not more than, change. We are more likely to retain the stability of the past—of tradition—if we change gradually rather than by violent jerks and stops. If particular memes no longer prove useful at helping us to understand our world or to achieve our shared goal of individual growth, they should be reconstructed.

To a great extent, but to varying degrees, the gradual adjustment of memes is already a constant in all cultures because of the infusion of unique individual perspectives. Although most unique perspectives will not become a part of or have much influence on the common perspective, a few that are found useful will find their way into the culture's language. As Dewey writes, "individual variations of thought remain private reveries or are soon translated into objective established institutions through gradual accumulation of imperceptible variations."[43] The difference between Dewey's and Rorty's theories is that Dewey believes we can intelligently control the process of cultural evolution while Rorty believes that it is, and always will be, an unconscious and accidental process. Dewey's "private reveries" must become purposive and communicable before they can be adopted by the community as a whole. Rorty's "private fantasies" are adopted even though they are idiosyncratic and purposeless.

Dewey argues that if a culture socializes its members into the habits of critical reflection, individuality, and sociability, it will make the process of mutual adjustment between collective and individual more free-flowing. The community will provide itself with more sources of creative innovation for practical problem solving. To the degree that creativity is promoted by a culture, the presence of cultural gaps will be proportionately lessened.

Cultural evolution according to Rorty. Like Dewey, Rorty suggests that culture evolves through the creative contributions of its members, but the method—or in Rorty's case, the lack of method—differs. Dewey argues that negative freedom is a necessary but not sufficient condition for the development of a participatory and innovative public. In addition to negative freedom, a culture must also actively promote critical reflection of existing institutions, laws, and norms; creative individuality; and genuine participation at all levels of society. Otherwise, he argues, a culture is unlikely to avoid conformity and various forms of elite manipulation.

Rorty, on the other hand, believes that negative liberty is sufficient. He calls for a strict division of the public and private spheres. The public sphere will enforce a Rawlsian conception of political justice, while the private sphere provides a realm of negative freedom for private perfection. Supposedly, some of the private fantasies involved in individual quests for perfection will "just happen" to meet evolving public needs. Rorty does not suggest any measures for encouraging such "creativity" nor for providing a communicative linkage between these private ideas and the public. Apparently, it will be sufficient just to leave individuals alone. Rorty does not explain, however, why, if they are "socialized all the way down," simply leaving individuals alone will not produce conformists rather than "strong poets" nor why individuals are likely to become authentic and autonomous choosers as opposed to docile fodder for media manipulation.[44]

Rorty rejects Dewey's conception of creativity because he rejects Dewey's conception of experience. For Dewey, experience is what ties us to the objective aspects of our world: it is interaction between memes (or interpretation) and objective environment. The adoption of new memes is not arbitrary for a community that bases its decisions on experience. Experience becomes the key to determining better from worse. We criticize existing memes and test innovative memes on the basis of intersubjective experience—reasons can thus be given. For Rorty, there is no objective experience, only interpretation. No reasons can therefore be given, only more or less rhetorically attractive interpretations.

Rorty's interpretation of creativity, and thus individuality, is that of pure subjectivity. The purpose of the private sphere is thus to allow for the free play of subjectivity, which is the means to individual self-creation. Self-creation is thus incompatible with the virtue of sociability as I have defined it here, that is, as a means for a dialogical construction of identity. While subjectivity is, for Rorty, the source of the innovative metaphors that are necessary for the gradual transformation of cultural memes, the usefulness of these metaphors is purely coincidental. New ideas cannot be interpreted as purposeful attempts to meet objective public needs. They are no more a matter of conscious design than are the Darwinian mutations that are the source of novelty in the process of natural selection. We can conclude that these private fantasies, being idiosyncratic and lacking purpose,necessarily lack meaning. A critic could perceive Rorty's ideal liberal citizen as an eccentric who whiles away the hours in meaningless private fantasy. If the meaningless musings are somehow subsequently found to be of some use to the community as a whole, the community will respond by pinning the label "genius" on the fantasizer, mistaking the meaningless musings for the product of a purposeful project.[45]

Because Rorty defines creativity as pure subjectivity, he subsequently emphasizes the private, or nonsocial, nature of individual perfection. A culture must depend on luck, therefore, and not conscious effort to provide solutions to current conceptual inadequacies in a shared vocabulary. This seems to be at odds with other parts of Rorty's project. Once again, consider the example of Rorty's claim that the core goal of liberalism (although he admits that he has no noncircular argument for justifying it) is to make society less cruel. When he says that an aversion to cruelty is the core liberal value, he claims to be expressing a contingent feature of liberal culture. But as we have seen, he assigns to novelists the task of increasing our scope of sympathy.[46] Does this not elevate the aversion to cruelty to an "ought" that should be inculcated into the population of the culture? And if Rorty is positing an "ought," is he not positing a cultural criterion for distinguishing better from worse metaphors? A cultural criterion of better and worse provides us with a reason for judging one potential metaphor as more desirable than another. Rorty claims, however, that there are no reasons to act one way rather than another—there are only *causes*.[47] Why must the adoption of new metaphors be a blind process if a criterion of better and worse exists?

Novels, for example, are supposed to *cause* us to be less cruel without giving us *reasons* for being less cruel, but how can this be? The only answer is that they must manipulate us. The talents of the authors must focus on effecting the emotional rather than the cognitive function of our minds. But even this is possible only because a culture has some form of common emotional or aesthetic standard—some habitual way of feeling—so that many members can be touched in the same way by the same story. If this is not the case, then the aversion to cruelty must be a universal trait of humans. In either case, the author's private musings must be communicated in such a way that they speak to common feelings—of the culture in one case, of humanity in the other. All of this just goes to say that the artist must have a purpose in mind when beginning such a project that will serve to channel his or her subjective creativity. The artist's idiosyncratic fantasy, in order to be communicated to others, must be given meaning by being channeled through a common vocabulary. The necessity of this is recognized by Rorty, who admits that there are no private languages.[48] But he never tells us why this fact does not provide a bridge between private perfection and public justice, between subjectivity and intersubjectivity, or why the metaphors provided by individuality cannot be considered purposeful tools. Nor does he explain how being "caused" to be less cruel is compatible with a conception of private perfection that depends on *self*-creation.

We have seen how Rorty devalues the label "genius" by claiming that we bestow it on people whose private fantasies only coincidentally meet a public need. He then reelevates these same individuals under the labels "strong poet" and "utopian revolutionary" and claims that they are society's heroes and the ideal citizens of his liberal utopia.[49] But when Rorty claims that strong poets and utopian revolutionaries who seek social reform "are protesting in the name of the society itself against those aspects of the society which are unfaithful to its own self-image,"[50] he is contradicting his claim that the adoption of new metaphors is accidental—that no reasons can be given for choosing one metaphor over another. Rorty is not claiming merely that no reasons *outside* of our vocabulary can be given for believing one thing rather than another, but that no reasons *within* languages can be given.[51] When Rorty says that in his utopian liberal society ideals can be fulfilled by persuasion, once again he contradicts his argument that only causes, not reasons, can be given, for persuasion (as opposed to manipulation, for which rhetoric works just fine) depends on reasons.

If Rorty wants to argue that his strong poets can persuade society to be less cruel, then he cannot argue that the new metaphors they introduce are useful only by coincidence. When Rorty writes, for example: "A liberal society is one whose ideals can be fulfilled by persuasion rather than by force, by reform rather than revolution, by the free and open encounters of present linguistic and other practices with suggestions for new practices," he sounds like Dewey. But he concludes that "this is to say that an ideal liberal society is one which has no purpose except . . . to make life easier for poets and revolutionaries," who help society evolve through "accidentally produced metaphors."[52] I have already shown that Rorty defines the poet as one who produces idiosyncratic fantasies and that he denies that there can be any criteria within a vocabulary for distinguishing better from worse metaphors (a metaphor, by definition, being outside of the vocabulary to which it is introduced). Dewey would argue that less idiosyncratic conceptions of creativity and identity formation and a more purposive conception of metaphor will be necessary if such a liberal society is to be practical.

Dewey's interpretation of creativity as the synthesis of objectivity and subjectivity allows for the possibility of reform, as opposed to revolution, and for persuasion based on shared beliefs. It also allows for the possibility that some people may have more capacity than others for formulating creative solutions to public problems, or that some people may be better able to heighten our awareness of the emotional content of immediate experience than others. In other words, some people may be better poets than others. We say that these people have genius. But the eventual verification of creative genius is always the intersubjective acclaim of the audience. Genius can thus be judged as a capacity, not a contingent event.

Why is it important to Rorty that he reject the label "genius"? It may be part of a quest for a more egalitarian society. Perhaps Rorty believes that if we simply fail to acknowledge the fact that natural or acquired abilities differ, it will result in improved self-respect for those with less ability. The larger reason, I suspect, is that the admission of genius would work contrary to Rorty's project. If some people's creations are simply better than others, perhaps because they have more insight into the emotional content of everyday experience or are better able to adapt their private visions to the objective needs of the community, but not because they just got lucky, he would have to admit to the existence of a standard of better and worse. We would then have reasons for preferring one metaphor over another.

By interpreting creativity as pure subjectivity and treating all subjective creations as of equal value, Rorty encourages only eccentricity, not self-perfection.[53] Charles Taylor's rebuttal to this postmodern tendency is similar to Dewey's. Taylor argues that human life is fundamentally dialogical. All of the important issues in our lives—including self-identity—are defined in dialogue with others. In order for our self-definition to have significance, it must be located within some context—it must have a background of intelligibility. He writes: "Unless some options are more significant than others, the very idea of self-choice falls into triviality and hence incoherence." Taylor insists that we are not limited to a dichotomous choice between self-creation or conformity because "self-choice as an ideal makes sense only because some *issues* are more significant than others." And worth, or significance, can only be determined within a dialogical context. Authenticity, therefore, is a nontrivial identity—a free choice of what is worthy to be chosen.[54]

Since Rorty admits that the reasons we give for our beliefs are the product of our particular vocabularies, it would seem to follow that the *meanings* that we apply to events and objects, because they derive from our vocabularies, must be the product of intersubjective verification. Self-creation interpreted as the free play of subjectivity—and thus not dependent on reasons or meanings provided by a shared vocabulary[55]—must necessarily be *meaningless*. Yet, Rorty maintains that the quest for private perfection is "necessarily private, unshared, unsuited to argument," or, in other words, nondialogical.[56] But Rorty's insistence seems entirely unnecessary. Why must the quest for self-perfection be accomplished by meaningless fantasy when we have the option of autonomous choosers within a meaningful social context? Rorty's subjective creativity is the worst imaginable means of developing a meaningful personal identity or of harnessing individual creativity for the mutual benefit of society. Recognition of this fact verifies Dewey's warning that genuine inquiry is hindered just as completely by skepticism and eccentricity as it is by dogmatism and conformity.

Rorty speaks of a shared vocabulary only in respect to a liberal conception of justice that says, essentially, that we should all be free to indulge in our private fantasies as long as we do not hurt anyone else. This shared vocabulary is a contingent product of historical cultural evolution and thus has no transcultural justification. Our commitment to this contingent vocabulary is merely ironic. What if, however, the liberal conception of justice had not evolved historically in our culture? Wouldn't private perfection, as Rorty defines it, require us to transcend our cultural vocabulary in order to import liberal freedoms from an external source? If private perfection depends on the freedoms provided by liberalism, then in what sense is our commitment to them ironic? Wouldn't liberalism be justified as the means to the end of private perfection? Dewey believes that liberal freedoms are, in fact, justified because they are a means to individual self-development. The threat to these liberal freedoms does not arise from those who seek to create a liberal culture as the "best way" to achieve this end.

Cultural evolution according to MacIntyre. MacIntyre rejects liberalism because he believes that persons within pluralist societies are unable to justify their beliefs. He recommends an internally coherent tradition within which moral reasoning can take place. According to MacIntyre, traditions progress through an internal dialectic. Who takes part in this process? The historical examples that are given in *After Virtue* and *Whose Justice? Which Rationality?* lead one to understand that the process is confined to, or at least dominated by, philosophers. MacIntyre makes no mention of the need for an inclusive intersubjective dialogue, nor does he give us any reason to believe that this dialectic involves any experiential verification. Experience rears its ugly head only when a tradition finds itself in the midst of what MacIntyre calls an "epistemological crisis": the tradition simply meets with practical problems its principles are unable to solve.

MacIntyre mentions that, should such a crisis occur, a society must fall back on inventiveness, but he does not tell us its source. Socialization into a nonpluralist hierarchy of shared values is probably not an ideal breeding ground for creative individuality. The cultivation of creative imagination implies the cultivation of reflective criticism of existing institutions, rules, and norms. Is this compatible with a system that has as its primary concern a body of shared values? The answer would seem to be no, unless the body of shared values included critical reflection and creative individuality. Perhaps the few philosophers who are capable of comprehending the internal logic of the tradition are the source of innovative change. But if this is so, does it mean that individual perfection (that is, the cultivation of the critical and creative capacities) is limited to a few philosophers? These questions concerning the method of progress in MacIntyre's conception of tradition remain unanswered.

Dewey argues that we should focus on a method for solving a hierarchy of problems facing our society rather than on formulating an abstract hierarchy of goods that may or may not prove adequate to our needs. Particular problems define their own hierarchy of goods. Some problems point to health as the most important good, while others point to efficiency or equity. The only good in itself is individual development. Growth is defined as the overcoming of problems (institutions, laws, and norms) that hinder this final end—for example, institutions, laws, and norms relating to the subordination of women have hindered their ability to achieve self-development by minimizing their participation in social, economic, and political enterprises.

The hierarchy of goods in Dewey's conception of liberalism is justified by a general need for self-development. In MacIntyre's conception of tradition, on the other hand, the necessity of a hierarchy of goods, internal to a particular tradition, implies the need of a final good that has no rational justification. This must be the case because, first, the final good serves as the rational justification for all of the efficient goods within a tradition and, second, MacIntyre assures us that there is no nontraditional rationality with which to secure the final good independently of the tradition.[57] The final good of any tradition must therefore be the arbitrary product of historical contingency. It follows that the good life for individuals is not the end of all cultures; otherwise, a transcultural standard for evaluating particular cultures would exist.

According to MacIntyre's theory, a radical change in the direction of a tradition, made necessary by an epistemological crisis, requires a new final end. One final end must be trashed in favor of another for the sake of constructing a new internally coherent hierarchy of goods. MacIntyre's rationally coherent traditions must grow or change when they are forced to invent new answers by the existence of new problems. In between times of crisis, society can practice a form of Kuhnian "normal" inquiry, or in this case, normal social problem solving. An epistemological crisis would require, as in Kuhn's philosophy of science, revolutionary rather than evolutionary change. Thus, it would seem that when a change of traditions becomes absolutely necessary, the criterion for determining between better and worse traditions must be similar to the pragmatic instrumentalism that is built into the continuing process of Deweyan liberalism.

For memes to be considered instruments, however, they must have a purpose. The ahistorical final end of individual self-realization provides a purpose or end for evaluating memes in Dewey's theory. The lack of a transcultural or ahistorical final end would seem to leave memes in MacIntyre's traditions without a purpose external to the tradition in which they originated. How, therefore, can a tradition in the midst of an epistemological crisis judge another tradition's internal final end as better without the aid of an external criterion? It cannot use its own criterion because that is exactly what is being trashed.

It is hard to understand MacIntyre's exclusive focus on internal rational coherence when the growth and exchange of traditions is based so clearly on harmonization of a culture's memes with its objective environment. Despite the fact that MacIntyre recognizes the possibility of new problems requiring new solutions, he apparently sees these problems as existing entirely on the rational plain, not in the empirical world of objects and events. Thus MacIntyre, like Rorty, rejects experience in favor of language. Problems arise and are overcome within particular vocabularies, discourses, or in MacIntyre's case, internally rational traditions. MacIntyre and Rorty reject Dewey's method because they reject the notion that experience can be anything other than an internal, or mental, construction—the former shared and the latter private. Both hold on to the same mind/body dualism that they profess to reject. Minus the mind/body dichotomy, experience must be seen, as Dewey sees it, as the mutual interaction of what dualists divide into mind and matter—concept and percept. While dualists must attribute experience to *either* mental concepts (idealists) *or* perceptions of the material world (empiricists), pragmatists such as Dewey see experience as the mutual interaction and adjustment of one to the other.

In summary, MacIntyre must accept Dewey's notion of a process of cultural evolution that transcends particular traditions because the components of the transcultural method are contained within MacIntyre's own theory of rational tradition—they are simply not brought together into a coherent theory. From my previous discussion of MacIntyre, we can derive the following: not all traditions have developed into a rational form of inquiry, but such development is the only means for a tradition to dialectically evolve. Thus, the concept of a rationally coherent and internally evolving moral tradition provides a method of cultural evolution that transcends any particular rational tradition.

MacIntyre argues that a tradition will, first, have to "institutionalize and regulate to some extent at least its methods of enquiry." MacIntyre adds that "insofar as a tradition of enquiry is such, it will tend to recognize what it shares as such with other traditions, and in the development of such traditions common characteristic, if not universal, patterns will appear." Second, MacIntyre hints at what those universal patterns are when he claims, for example, that all practices, regardless of their end or of their cultural context, require the moral virtues of honesty, courage, and justice. Third, MacIntyre explicitly states that criticism of existing beliefs and inventiveness for the creation of new, more adequate beliefs are necessary elements of the internal dialectic of a tradition qua tradition. And fourth, MacIntyre says that some traditions may prove, despite having developed into forms of rational moral inquiry, less adequate than others for solving the practical problems of a particular culture, implying the need for a criterion of adequacy that transcends any particular tradition.[58]

Why must MacIntyre accept that this transtraditional method is Dewey's pragmatic liberalism? The key is MacIntyre's recognition of the necessity of a universal method (which he calls tradition) and his recognition that this method requires the intellectual goods of criticism and inventiveness. Only a Deweyan liberal tradition—or, in other words, a tradition that is tolerant of a plurality of cultural idiosyncrasies and that encourages internal criticism and imaginative reconstruction of existing institutions, laws, and norms—is capable of providing all four of the requirements called for by MacIntyre's theory that are listed in the previous paragraph.

I remarked above that MacIntyre's notion of moral tradition is essentially the application of a Kuhnian theory of paradigms to cultural evolution. Reflecting on Kuhn's scientific paradigms, we can see that Dewey's universal method is still in force. The scientific community's dependence on the intellectual virtues of critical reflection, creative individuality, and communication (intersubjective verification) is not affected by the comings and goings of particular paradigms. Newton's physics may be superseded by Einstein's physics, which may be superseded by quantum physics, but the value of the intellectual virtues that are the basis of a method of inquiry remain constant. Deviation from these virtues, represented by the arbitrary authority that sometimes develops within a community to defend an existing paradigm from a potential newcomer, is deplored by Kuhn and is the real reason why science must sometimes advance by revolution rather than by evolution. MacIntyre may wish to argue that Dewey's conception of liberal culture is merely part of a particular (Darwinian) tradition, but Dewey can retort that pragmatic liberalism is the only tradition that can subject itself to criticism and imaginative reconstruction without risking extinction, because through such criticism and reconstruction its general applicability is confirmed. If it is just one of a variety of traditions, then it is that particular tradition whose components are the necessary and sufficient condition for the rational evolution of tradition qua tradition.

Conclusion. The function of culture is to provide meaning. Meaning is derived from experience. It cannot be generated by subjectivity alone; that is why Rorty refers to self-creation as fantasy. No single human being has the depth of experience to derive meaning from events and objects independent of communication with others. We know what meaning this object or that event has for us and for our community from our past collective experience with it. For this same reason, meaning cannot be derived from contemplation of abstract concepts. Genuine meaning cannot be abstracted from experience.[59]

The institutions, rules, and norms provided to us by our culture are practical biases or memes. This is so because all institutions, rules, and norms have practical consequences. Some consequences are more desirable to the ruling members of a culture than others. The culture is thus biased toward those more desirable consequences and the institutions, rules, and norms that lead to them. Only in a genuinely democratic culture can cultural bias reflect the needs of the community as a whole because only intersubjective verification serves to generalize the needs (demands, desires) of all, rather than those of a few. Pragmatic method, reflected in liberal culture, is the best way to assure that institutions, rules, and norms continue to evolve in such a way that they reflect the needs of the community.

Prior to the industrial revolution and the development of a corporate economy, laissez-faire economics *may* have had the consequence of a more free and just society. After the social environment was drastically changed by these developments, that same laissez-faire economy resulted in the loss of genuine freedom for millions of wage earners. The norms, rules, and institutions of laissez-faire required adjustment and/or replacement. Those who sought to preserve the existing system did so either because they profited from it or were among those who tend to absolutize cultural norms.

Because cultural institutions and norms are contingent on the social environment, they cannot be treated as universals. Because they do not exist prior to the time that they are called out by experience, they must be created, not discovered. Our creations, however, need be no less objective than our discoveries. They are based on the needs of the community.[60] Meanings are subjective only if they have no relation to objective needs. The only source of creativity are individuals. Individuality is thus the source of cultural innovation.

The cultivation of individuality is important because it gives a culture the advantage of a multitude of innovative perspectives when change is needed.[61] For the same reason, we find that a plurality of philosophical outlooks is valuable. The worst thing that can happen to a culture that is seeking to adjust its meanings to the contingencies of its environment is to become locked into a specific set of memes unless those memes are themselves a process of evolutionary growth. Dogmatism and practical problem solving are as incompatible in politics and society as they are in science. Market solutions may provide the answer in some questions of public policy, state-imposed equality may produce more desirable consequences in others, but for the doctrinaire follower of either of these notions of justice there can be only one answer to all questions, at all times, regardless of the conditions of the specific case.

Finding solutions to practical social problems (defined as hindrances to individual development) is the road by which cultures grow. If all of a culture's memes are producing consequences that optimize the development of each individual, then we can speak of that culture as being in a state of harmony with its environment. That such a state is unrealizable no more disqualifies it from being the final end of culture than the unattainability of perfect health, perfect virtue, or perfect wisdom makes the quests for a healthy body, a virtuous self, or a wise mind a waste of time and effort. It is the quest itself that is rewarding in each case. For it is not a matter of perfect wisdom or no wisdom, but rather degrees of wisdom that are attained by working toward the ideal.

Environmental change, usually technological, tends to produce gaps between some existing memes and the current needs of a people. One or a few of its memes no longer has the effect of producing desirable consequences. A kind of tension has now disturbed the harmony that once existed between the culture and its environment. Movement occurs. The culture seeks a solution to its problem. The many memes that have not become problematic provide a background for inquiry. They are the unquestioned assumptions necessary in order for all reasoning to take place. When a new meme has been found, one that has been intersubjectively verified to produce satisfactory consequences, the culture has, by the addition of the new meme, been changed. This change is considered growth because a tension has been resolved, a problem solved.

Another way in which a culture can grow is in relation to the method of growth itself. This type of growth may be seen as a form of maturation. Any change in cultural attitudes that makes critical reflection on existing meanings less likely (toward dogmatism or skepticism, for example) is a movement in the wrong direction. A change that makes the cultivation of individuality more likely (away from conformity or eccentricity, for example) is genuine growth. A change that moves away from the possibility of the interaction between individuals and culture that results in sociability (toward docility or rebelliousness, for example) is movement in the direction of immaturity. For although, as Dewey explains to us, the absolutization of cultural meanings prevents genuine moral inquiry, an general method of inquiry is a necessity.

Some claim that Dewey is inconsistent in simultaneously denying the existence of absolutes while advocating a general method of inquiry. But we might just as well accuse a carpenter of being inconsistent for cutting his boards to different lengths but using the same method of measuring each one or accuse a physician of being inconsistent for offering varying prognoses for different patients after using the same method of examination. The methods by which carpenters measure and physicians examine may be subject to change if better ways are found; however, it makes more sense to say that there is a single, objectively best way to measure or examine, regardless of whether we have yet discovered it, than it does to say that there is a single, objectively best length of board or that there is a single, objectively best prognosis for all patients. In a world characterized by time and contingency, processes, "ways," and methods can be generalized because they perform functions. Particular memes that do not serve as methods for adapting to change, however, cannot be generalized because they describe or explain the results of particular interactions between existences.

Based on the generic traits of nature, not to mention the historical accomplishments of the practical arts and sciences, Dewey concludes that the best method of inquiry requires the virtues of critical reflection, individuality, and intersubjective verification. When applied to the individual, these virtues produce Dewey's conception of the autonomous chooser. When applied to culture, these virtues require the norms, beliefs, and institutions associated with Dewey's conception of liberalism. The generic traits of nature include all of the traits associated with a contingent and changing conception of reality. Dewey's conceptions of the self and of liberalism are not, therefore, the products of historical contingency. Rather, his argument is that they are the necessary conceptions of the self and culture if we start with the premise that the world is characterized by contingency and change.

Conclusion

The Synthesis of Progress and Tradition

This inquiry began with my contention, in the introduction, that Dewey's pragmatic philosophy is capable of dissolving many of the problems that occupy contemporary liberals and communitarians. The claim was that many of the dichotomies that are the locus of debate between the two groups are pseudoproblems, the product of unnecessary dualisms. The most salient dichotomy was traced to the relative importance the two groups give to the concepts of "the good" and "the right."

Communitarians focus on and give priority to the "good." The good is defined variously as "the good life," "happiness," or "self-development" and is associated with perfectionist philosophies of the community. It is given priority over the right, which is usually understood as a political notion of justice. Communitarians give priority to the good because they understand the right, or justice, to be the *means* to the good—and thus undefinable until the concept of the good has been established. Another reason is that the right has been associated in modernity with the notion of presocial individual rights, and thus the right exists in direct opposition to community and the common good whenever it is accorded the priority that many liberals want to bestow upon it.

Liberals, on the other hand, give priority to the right, or justice, because of the importance they attach to the value of freedom. Liberals fear that collective quests for the good inevitably deprive individuals of the freedom to choose their own notion of the good life. When the community gives priority to the good, liberals warn, particular conceptions of the good life are imposed on individuals and groups by the community as a whole. By giving the principles of justice priority over the good, liberals believe they are protecting individual rights from meddling, and possibly authoritarian, communities.

176

What Dewey offers is a defense of the most valued liberal principles of right, and hence justice, *as a means to the communitarian perfectionist end.* He defends liberal principles not as goods in themselves but as the best means for individual quests for the good life. Dewey's educative community does in fact promote—although it does not impose—a particular conception of the good. The conception it promotes, however, is a liberal conception of individual autonomy. A Deweyan conception of autonomy is communitarian because it consists of virtues that are a product of personal effort within a context of shared beliefs. Because these liberal virtues—critical reflection, creative individuality, and sociability—are both the means to and partially constitutive of the good life, they can be used by Dewey to establish a communitarian form of liberal society.

As with communitarian theories generally, the end, or goal, of community is the good, or self-development, of individual members. The means, however, is a notion of autonomy that encourages individuals to create their own distinctive good. Dewey envisions a community where criticism and nonconformity are valued as positive benefits to the community as both a method of testing existing values, institutions, and rules and as a source of innovative alternatives.

From Dewey's classical pragmatism, we were thus able, in chapter 1, to derive a conception of individual autonomy that, while meeting all of the criteria for a *liberal* conception of autonomy, does not, as the dominant Kantian variants do, require transcendence from any particular language community. In fact, the Deweyan conception of autonomy requires that the individual be situated within a context of cultural beliefs. As we saw in chapter 2, this particular conception of autonomy is necessary if one wants to conceive of life, as communitarians do, as a quest for the good life within a social context. The Deweyan notion of individual autonomy, unlike the Kantian variants, is able to assure freedom of choice without having to fall back on an abstract and untenable conception of the self—the so-called disembodied and disembedded self that communitarians like Sandel are so fond of parodying.

In chapter 3, we saw how Dewey's conception of individuality is distinguished from various alternatives that overemphasize either the subjective or objective contributions to creativity. The autonomous self is one that can make and remake itself within the context of a shared tradition of meanings. Dewey's autonomous choosers can be simultaneously original and situated within a context of shared cultural values. Self-creation, as Dewey conceives of it, is not a flippant and superficial activity in which we continually reimagine ourselves from different perspectives, but rather one that is closely related to the classical philosophical goal of caring for the soul. Outside of a shared social context, the self is, using Charles Taylor's terminology, "morally disoriented." The noncontextual self has no means of judging its movement in one direction as better or worse than its movement in any other—there is no way to gauge growth in patience, for example, as being more or less worthy than growth in egoism. On the other hand, Dewey helps us to understand that a nonautonomous self within a context of shared meanings loses the means to self-creation and is thus created by others.

In part two, we focused on the community, and there we learned that these autonomous individuals are not the product of untutored human nature. The Deweyan notion of autonomy, consisting as it does of moral and intellectual virtues, is an achievement that can best be attained within a certain set of social and political institutions. In chapter 4, we saw that critical, imaginative, and participatory individuals both give rise to and are created by democratic and liberal institutions. We also saw that social intelligence has proven, historically, to be the best means for advancing knowledge in any practical endeavor. The pragmatic claim is this: the society or organization that does the best job of cultivating a population of critical, creative, and participatory members will have the competitive advantage in any kind of enterprise. For doubters, there is the pragmatic challenge: compare societies and organizations with unquestioning and unimaginative followers to those that encourage the virtues of Deweyan autonomy in their members—and see which work best at creating strong, energetic, and thriving communities.

In chapter 5, we were able to use the arguments from the previous four chapters to accomplish what we set out to do in the introduction: to explicate a Deweyan communitarian defense of liberal freedoms and toleration and compare it to Kantian and postmodern alternatives. The Deweyan defense, unlike that of Kantians and postmodernists, is able to justify liberal principles without opposing the individual to the community. Liberal freedoms and toleration are defended as being of *intrinsic* value both to the community as a whole and to the self-development of the community's individual members. Liberal freedoms need not be defended as freedoms *from* community but rather as freedoms that can only be exercised properly *in* the community.

Finally, in chapter 6, we saw how this communitarian notion of liberal democracy offers cultures a rational means of adapting to historical contingencies. Dewey's communitarian liberalism enables a culture to adapt and progress through changes while maintaining the continuity and stability of various and particular traditions. It is able to do this for the same reason it is able to reconcile the dichotomies in the liberal/ communitarian debate: because it balances and maintains a reciprocal relationship between forces of differentiation and integration—that is, the individual and the community. Differentiating forces such as criticism and individuality provide a culture with a means of continually reexamining and renewing its internal goods, while the integrating forces of participatory democracy and dialogical community—both necessary for intersubjective verification of criticisms and innovations—keep the community from disintegrating into a society of atomized individuals (of either the egoistic liberal or eccentric postmodern variety).

Dewey's communitarian defense of liberalism is, in short, an attempt to reconstruct a natural—in the Darwinian sense of the word—relationship between individuals and communities, where communities exist for no other reason than to meet the needs of their members and individuals, as a consequence, derive their identities—meanings, purposes—from the communities in which they are members.

Notes

Bibliography

Index

Notes

Introduction: Pragmatic Instrumentalism

1. Kymlicka compares his conception of liberalism to those of Mill, Green, Hobhouse, and Dewey, who "were concerned with community, but were not thereby communitarians. . . . They were as much concerned with the value of individual liberty as anyone before or since. Yet they recognized the importance of our cultural membership to the proper functioning of a well-ordered and just society." 209. Barber, in the preface to his *Strong Democracy*, writes that "I have been much helped by the tradition of American pragmatism. It is an oddity of American political thinking that it has turned to English and Continental modes of thought to ground a political experience notable for its radical break with the English and Continental ways of doing politics; at the same time it has neglected indigenous sources that have a natural affinity for the American way of doing politics—as anybody who reads Pierce or James or Dewey will recognize." xx.

Others, as Alan Ryan point out, are less aware of the antecedents of the tradition of thought they are exploring: "Of contemporary social theorists, the most 'Deweyan' is the German thinker Jurgen Habermas, for all that he has written enthusiastically about Pierce rather than Dewey. There are many connections between Habermas' ideas about emancipatory forms of social theory and Dewey's conception of philosophy as social criticism; there is a clear affinity between the way Dewey's *Democracy and Education* links human communication and democracy and the way Habermas develops an account of democracy in communicative terms in his enormous *Theory of Communicative Action*." Ryan also refers to the writings of Michael Sandel and Robert Bellah as "a rehearsal of Durkheim and Dewey" and claims that Charles Taylor "is for the most part a Deweyan without knowing it." *High Tide of Liberalism* 357, 359.

2. Macedo 280–304.
3. *Later Works* 1: 309.
4. *Later Works* 1: 55–57, 119.
5. *Middle Works* 12: 270, 260–61.
6. *Middle Works* 12: 114–15.
7. *Middle Works* 12: 92–94.
8. Dennett 21.
9. In discussing Thomas H. Huxley, Dewey remarked that

[t]he distinction between the struggle for existence and the struggle for happiness breaks down. It breaks down, I take it, none the less in animal life itself than it does in social life. If the struggle for existence on the part of the wolf meant simply the struggle on his part to keep from dying, I do not doubt that the sheep would gladly have compromised at any time upon the basis of furnishing him with the necessary food—including an occasional bowl of mutton broth. The fact is the wolf asserted himself as a wolf. No agent can draw this distinction between desire for mere life and desire for happy life for himself; and no more can the spectator intelligently draw it for another. "Evolution and Ethics," in Early Works 5: 45.

10. It must be stressed that the desire for harmony with the environment expressed in Dewey's theory is not a means of conserving the natural environment, it is a desire on the part of the individual organism to flourish in its environment whatever it is. A lack of harmony may require changing either the environment or the individual. Harmony is the goal, not the conservation of the environment as it is. Dewey explained that the natural tendency of even nonconscious life seems to point beyond mere survival.

Plants and non-human animals act *as if* they were concerned that their activity, their characteristic receptivity and response, should maintain itself. Even atoms and molecules show a selective bias in their indifferences, affinities and repulsions when exposed to other events. With respect to some things they are hungry to the point of greediness; in the presence of others they are sluggish and cold. It is not surprising that naive science imputed appetition to their own consummatory outcome to all natural processes, and that Spinoza identified inertia and momentum with the inherent tendency on the part of things to conserve themselves in being, and achieve such perfection as belongs to them. In a genuine *although not psychic sense,* natural beings exhibit preference and centeredness. *Later Works* 1: 162; my emphasis.

11. *Early Works* 5: 53.
12. *Later Works* 1: 194–200.
13. Aristotle, *Politics* 1252b9.
14. I see this as being essentially the same as Aristotle's description of the quest for the good life. It is not realization of the goal that results in a blessed life but the process of striving. For Dewey, his conception of growth is the only final end; all other ends are ends-in-view: turning points in growth rather than completions. Aristotle and Dewey diverge on the issue of essentialism. Dewey believed that Aristotle made the mistake of seeing the current development of things as their final and natural essence. Aristotle had no idea that species develop through time, nor that the city-state was a historical artifact.
15. The intellectual virtues of reflective criticism, creative individuality, and sociability (necessary for intersubjective verification) together comprise Dewey's conception of autonomy. They will be discussed in the first chapter. In regard

to the moral virtues, Dewey wrote that no activity that strives to attain a worthy end or goal is possible without being accompanied by an attitude that is wholehearted, persistent, and impartial. Wholeheartedness "requires consistency, continuity and community of purpose and effort." "We cannot be genuinely whole-hearted unless we are single-minded." Wholeheartedness can thus be equated with self-discipline because it means that our focus and desires are not divided. Persistence, on the other hand, "demands character to stick it out when conditions are adverse." Persistence can thus be equated with courage. Impartiality requires "an equal and even measure of value"; it means to measure justly. Such intellectual and moral virtues comprise Dewey's general method of inquiry. See *Later Works* 7: 255–58, 290, 295.

16. Despite the cosmic significance that we habitually attach to the phrase "the purpose of life," realistically it should be accorded a much more mundane significance. In our everyday lives, when we go about our routine daily activities, is our activity purposeless and thus meaningless? Unless we attach some purpose to our getting out of bed, washing and dressing, then heading off to work or school, it is doubtful that we would even have the will to perform these activities. Rather than seeing these routine activities as having some cosmic significance such as "serving God" or "sacrificing ourselves for humanity," we may also see them as having the purpose of a daily quest, in concert with others, of seeking a harmony between our physical and psychical needs as human beings and the natural and social environment that we have created and are continually re-creating for ourselves. Finding "the purpose of life" seems less dramatic when we think of it this way, but it is the very unattainableness of discovering the purpose of life in its more cosmic dimensions that makes this more practical formulation all the more necessary if we are to escape the existentialist conclusion that life is absurd.

17. Burke 99–112.

1. The Unity of Freedom and Virtue: A Deweyan Conception of Autonomy

1. *Later Works* 11: 41. Thomas Alexander describes "the human eros" found within Dewey's philosophy as a "drive to live with a funded sense of meaning and value." By "funded," Alexander refers to the need to exist within a context of meaning and value that is provided or supplied to us by culture. This funded sense of meaning is not in lieu of autonomy but its starting point—individuals cannot start from scratch. "Human Eros" 203–22.

2. *Middle Works* 12: 181.

3. *Middle Works* 12: 119–20.

4. *The Blackwell Encyclopaedia of Political Thought,* ed. David Miller (Cambridge: Blackwell Publishers, 1991), 31.

5. *Later Works* 7: 166.

6. *The Oxford Companion to Philosophy,* ed. Ted Honderich (Oxford: Oxford University Press, 1995), 69.

7. Kant, "Metaphysical Foundations" 140–209.

8. Kant, "Metaphysical Foundations" 197–98.

9. Kant, "Metaphysical Foundations" 156, 158.

10. Locke, *Two Treatises* 271.

11. Rawls, *A Theory of Justice* 253–57.

12. Habermas 123–24.

13. By "soft," I mean communitarians who are more concerned with offering a corrective prescription for liberalism rather than an alternative. They want to warn liberal society of the dangers of overemphasizing individualism and competition, but they do not want to trash political liberalism wholesale. "Hard" communitarians believe that liberal society is a failed social experiment based on an inadequate Enlightenment worldview.

14. See, for example, T. Levine's "Individuation and Unification."

15. Ryan, *High Tide of Liberalism* 359

16. MacIntyre, *After Virtue* 260.

17. MacIntyre, *After Virtue* 126–27, 160–61.

18. MacIntyre, *After Virtue* 147.

19. MacIntyre, *After Virtue* 191 (author's emphasis).

20. Although MacIntyre says that liberalism has itself been transformed into a tradition with its own conception of the good, that is, toleration for rival conceptions of the good (*Whose Justice?* 335–36), apparently he does see this as sufficient to eliminate the moral chaos. Dewey would agree that liberalism represents a cultural tradition with a shared good. He argues, however, that the good of liberalism, as the name implies, is the liberation of individuals to realize their capacities. Autonomy and moral wisdom are both the means to this good and, in their practice, the good itself.

21. MacIntyre, *After Virtue* 191, 149, 219.

22. MacIntyre, *Whose Justice?* 362.

23. MacIntyre includes philosophical activity in his notion of a practice. "In the ancient and medieval worlds the creation and sustaining of human communities—of households, cities, nations—is generally taken to be a practice in the sense that I have defined it." *After Virtue* 187–88.

24. MacIntyre, *After Virtue* 190. "A practice involves *standards* of excellence and obedience to rules as well as the achievement of goods" (my emphasis).

25. MacIntyre, *After Virtue* 222.

26. MacIntyre, *Whose Justice?* 362.

27. MacIntyre, *After Virtue* 198.

28. Aristotle, *Nicomachean Ethics* 1115b25–1116a7.

29. *Later Works* 1: 296–97, 298, 299, 300, 303–4, 298, 304, 306.

30. *Later Works* 7: 263–64, 273–74.

31. I do not believe that Dewey's notion of reflective desire is susceptible to the criticism of infinite regress that has been made frequently in regard to Harry Frankfurt's notion of ordered desires (first, second, third, and so on). For Dewey, a desire is either immediate or reflective. It would serve no purpose to speak of reflecting on one's reflective desires except in the sense of reconstructing them—not, however, in the sense of adding higher-order desires.

32. As quoted in Feinberg 42.

33. Nietzsche, *Genealogy* 36.

34. *Later Works* 7: 219.

35. Feinberg 33–34.

36. Dworkin, *The Theory and Practice of Autonomy* 25. In Neurath's metaphor, each individual part of a ship is replaced, one at a time while the ship is in mid-ocean, so that eventually every single part is new, but the ship as a whole is the same. It has been transformed rather than replaced.

37. Dworkin, *The Theory and Practice of Autonomy* 160.

38. *Middle Works* 9: 312.

39. Riesman ch. 18. Alan Ryan credits Dewey with anticipating "a view later made famous by David Riesman's best-selling book of 1950 *The Lonely Crowd.*" *High Tide of Liberalism* 320.

40. *Later Works* 5: 85. *Individualism* refers to the type of isolated egoism that is instrumentalized in rational choice theory. *Individuality,* on the other hand, refers to uniqueness, creativity, innovativeness.

41. Feinberg 41.

42. Rorty, *Contingency, Irony, and Solidarity* xiv.

43. *Later Works* 5: 109.

44. *Later Works* 10: 286.

45. Dworkin, *The Theory and Practice of Autonomy* 158.

46. *Later Works* 1: 168.

47. *Later Works* 1: 164. Rorty speaks of Dewey as a precursor to postmodern thought because he clings to the half of Dewey's thought that is concerned with criticism and ignores the half concerned with reconstruction.

48. *Later Works* 1: 170–71.

49. Ryan, *High Tide of Liberalism* 361.

50. Taylor, *Ethics of Authenticity* ch. 4.

51. *Later Works* 1: 135.

52. *Middle Works* 9: 7.

53. In chapter 6 of Taylor's *Ethics of Authenticity,* "The Slide to Subjectivism," he explains that the quest for self-fulfillment without external moral demands or commitments to others is the epitome of narcissism and that a narcissistic culture, because of the rejection of all horizons of significance, is also in danger of sliding into nihilism.

54. *Middle Works* 9: 314.

55. *Later Works* 7: 227.

56. *Later Works* 13: 82.

57. *Later Works* 2: 328.

58. *Later Works* 7: 257.

59. Taylor writes that the "manner" of self-fulfillment is "self-referential," while the matter is "something beyond the self." The something beyond the self that Taylor is referring to is God, nature, a cause, a cultural horizon, or the like. *Ethics of Authenticity,* 82.

60. MacIntyre, *After Virtue* 191 (author's emphasis). MacIntyre's conception of virtue is essentially Aristotelian. See also page 219.

61. MacIntyre, *After Virtue* 154. By "through teaching," MacIntyre and Aristotle mean through being systematically instructed. MacIntyre is referring specifically to *phronesis,* or practical judgment.

62. Dworkin is considered by the philosophical community to be one of the most important writers on the concept of autonomy. His book *The Theory and Practice of Autonomy* is necessary reading for anyone interested in the contemporary discussion of the concept of autonomy. The criteria I am using here is from his "Concept of Autonomy" 56.

2. The Context of Freedom: A Deweyan Conception of the Self

1. I am referring to the conceptions of the self found in MacIntyre's *After Virtue* and in Taylor's *Sources of the Self* and *Ethics of Authenticity*.

2. For an explanation of the relationship between meaning, feeling, and action see Taylor's "Interpretation and the Sciences of Man," *Philosophical Papers* 15–57.

3. *Later Works* 13: 286.

4. Nietzsche, *Thus Spake Zarathustra* 60.

5. *Middle Works* 14: 65, 16.

6. *Later Works* 1: 71.

7. *Middle Works* 12: 139; see also pp. 81–84.

8. Alexander, "Human Eros" 206.

9. *Later Works* 1: 196–97; see also ch. 2 of *Democracy and Education,* in *Middle Works* 9.

10. *Middle Works* 12: 181–86.

11. *Later Works* 6: 4.

12. *Later Works* 4: 11–12.

13. *Later Works* 1: 198.

14. *Later Works* 1: 199–200.

15. *Later Works* 1: 231, 170, 231, 147.

16. *Later Works* 3: 13. How does Dewey know that mind consists of this relatively stable body of norms and values and that consciousness consists of immediate awareness? The answer is that he doesn't. *Mind* and *consciousness* are words that Dewey uses to label those two respective functions. He could have made up his own words, but he used words already in common use to better communicate his particular interpretation. Dewey does not ask us to compare his interpretation of the cognitive process to the truth, for no interpretation is even necessary; he asks us instead to compare his interpretation to alternative interpretations in order to determine which one fits better with actual experience, which one enables us to understand and predict better. There may not be a single best interpretation—it will depend on the interests or ends of the observer. A jockey and a working cowboy will probably give different, but not incompatible, descriptions of the same horse.

17. *Later Works* 1: 12.

18. MacIntyre, *After Virtue* 220.

19. MacIntyre, *After Virtue* 222.

20. Taylor, *Sources of the Self* 27, 35.

21. *Later Works* 5: 75.

22. *Later Works* 7: 185.

23. *Later Works* 1: 322.

24. *Later Works* 10: 286.

25. *Later Works* 14: 114.

26. Dewey does not use the term *authenticity*. He speaks of "communication." I am borrowing Taylor's use of the word because it fits Dewey's meaning and its use makes comparison to other thinkers easier.

27. See Taylor's *Ethics of Authenticity,* ch. 4, "Inescapable Horizons."

28. Heidegger, *Being and Time* 213, 224, 345–46, 435.

29. *Later Works* 10: 88–89.

30. MacIntyre, *After Virtue* 206.

31. *Later Works* 14: 102.

32. *Later Works* 5: 73.

33. *Later Works* 7: 306; 1: 167.

34. From Joad's discussion of Bergson in the chapter, "The Problem of Change," in his *Guide to Philosophy.*

35. MacIntyre, *After Virtue* 219.

36. Taylor, *Sources of the Self* 51–52.

37. *Middle Works* 12: 81.

38. *Later Works* 7: 307–8.

39. MacIntyre, *After Virtue* 222.

40. By voluntarism, I mean the theory that beliefs are voluntary acts of will as opposed to the involuntary effects of causes. If all beliefs are involuntary effects, it follows that it is impossible to critically assess and alter our current set of beliefs.

41. MacIntyre, *After Virtue* 221.

42. Taylor, *Sources of the Self* 86–88.

43. MacIntyre, *After Virtue* 187, 194, 191, 192 (author's emphasis). MacIntyre explains that "notoriously the cultivation of truthfulness, justice and courage will often, the world being what it contingently is, bar us from being rich or famous or powerful. . . . We should therefore expect that, if in a particular society the pursuit of external goods were to become dominant, the concept of the virtues might suffer first attrition and then perhaps something near total effacement." 196.

44. *Later Works* 7: 256.

45. *Later Works* 7: 290.

46. MacIntyre, *After Virtue* 187.

47. *Later Works* 7: 256–58.

48. MacIntyre, *After Virtue* 195.

49. By conceptualizing autonomy as a means to the good life rather than as an end in itself, Dewey escapes the problems encountered by theorists such as S. I. Benn. Benn's conception of autonomy is similar to Dewey's in that it requires "a continuing process of criticism and re-evaluation" within a "conceptual scheme" provided by a tradition. The autonomous person is one "committed to a *critical and creative* [my emphasis] conscious search for coherence." "He will appraise one aspect of his tradition by critical canons derived from another." But unlike Dewey's conception of autonomy, which provides a method of moral decision making, Benn's says nothing about "the content of the autonomous man's principles and ideals." Cesare Borgia could turn out "to have been no less autonomous than Socrates." Benn 124, 126, 128–29.

Joseph Raz tries to avoid this conclusion by making autonomy a perfectionist ideal. Still, it seems contradictory for him to say that autonomy is itself a final end (381) while also claiming: "Autonomous life is valuable only if it is spent in the pursuit of acceptable and valuable projects and relationships" (417). A Deweyan notion of autonomy, on the other hand, *consists of* the intellectual and moral virtues.

50. Taylor, *Sources of the Self* 63, 35.

51. Rorty, *Consequences of Pragmatism* xviii.

52. Taylor, *Sources of the Self* 27.

53. *Later Works* 7: 227.

54. Rorty, *Contingency, Irony, and Solidarity* 26–43. By "private," Rorty does not mean merely nonpolitical but noncultural as well. If it were simply a matter of not wanting the state to get involved in the creation of identity, then Rorty's position would not differ from that of Mennonite communities that want their children to be excused from public education so that they can be socialized within their own closed societies. But Rorty sees all social influence as nonauthentic—as someone else's creation rather than one's own. As Dewey and Taylor argue, however, the pure subjectivity that postmodernists such as Rorty aspire to results in an identity that is insignificant, trivial, and eccentric.

55. Rorty, *Contingency, Irony, and Solidarity* 27, 29.

56. Rorty, *Contingency, Irony, and Solidarity* 29.

57. Rorty, *Contingency, Irony, and Solidarity* 36.

58. It is true that for Rorty most people do not attain the ideal of self-creation but live within an inherited language game; but can this be considered a saving grace? The strong poet is, after all, the ideal of Rorty's liberal utopia. Those whose identities are embedded in a cultural context and, thus, for Dewey are those for whom the notion of a quest for the good remains a real possibility, are for Rorty those who have *failed* to escape from other people's descriptions of them and from other people's standards of judgment. According to Rorty's interpretation, the ideal is to overcome this embeddedness so that one might be the product of "idiosyncratic fantasy."

59. *Later Works* 14: 114.

60. Rorty, *Contingency, Irony, and Solidarity* 41.

61. *Later Works* 7: 303–9.

62. Boisvert, "Heteronomous Freedom" 143.

63. *Later Works* 7: 302–3.

3. The Freedom of Creativity: A Deweyan Conception of Individuality

1. Thus, Dewey's insistence on including among the generic traits of nature contingency, change, and qualitative individuality alongside regularity, lawlike predictability, and commonality.

2. The nineteenth-century institution of economic individualism has manifold economic, social, and political consequences in twentieth-century corporate society. What changes must take place to compensate for the loss of extended families, local communities, and churches, the economic independence and creative opportunities of the individual artisan and entrepreneur, the po-

litical inequality caused by the growth of giant multinational corporations, and the stultifying alienation that is caused by a life of monotonous wage labor? Dewey believed that the same creative innovation that produced the technological changes could, if allowed to, provide answers to these economic, social, and political problems.

3. See part 3, section 5 of *Human Nature and Conduct* in the *Middle Works* 14: 146–53 under the heading of "The Uniqueness of Good." Dewey's cyclical view of progress—the continual cycle of tension, growth, consummation—is based on the notion that the future will always present us with novel situations/problems with which we have to deal. Is this a cultural bias? No, it is universal experience.

4. *Middle Works* 12: 260–61.

5. *Later Works* 7: 165–66.

6. *Later Works* 1: 164.

7. *Later Works* 1: 188.

8. *Later Works* 10: 276.

9. *Later Works* 1: 229.

10. *Later Works* 1: 167.

11. Kallen 8, 10, 4.

12. *Later Works* 10: 53.

13. *Later Works* 10: 277.

14. If the creation is practical (the steam engine, private property), intersubjective verification is necessary in regard to its usefulness for achieving practical results. If the creation is aesthetic (painting, literature), intersubjective verification is necessary in regard to its meaningfulness. Verification of the usefulness of a concept such as private property is likely to be slower and more ambiguous than that of a technological innovation such as the steam engine. Verification of the meaningfulness of an aesthetic creation is often much slower than the more immediate verification of the usefulness of practical tools or concepts. For example, Vincent van Gogh and Herman Melville both died in relative obscurity despite the subsequent recognition of the value of their aesthetic works.

The alternative to intersubjective verification is to state that an aesthetic or practical creation is meaningful or useful despite the fact that neither the creator's own (nor any other) community that has experienced the work recognizes or verifies its meaningfulness or usefulness. While this can be true, as in the case of van Gogh and Melville before their works were eventually appreciated, who is to say which particular works fall into this category until after their meaningfulness or usefulness has been recognized?

15. *Later Works* 10: 281.

16. This is not to say that classical art involves no creativity, but rather that the *conception* classical philosophy has of art as imitation of objective truth is wrong. If the classical conception of art is correct, then neither classical nor any other type of art *can* be characterized as creative, because according to the classical view, only God, or the gods, can create.

17. *Later Works* 10: 298; *Later Works* 10: 280.

18. *Later Works* 10: 287.

19. *Later Works* 1: 165.

20. *Later Works* 10: 271.

21. *Later Works* 10: 284.

22. *Later Works* 10: 285.

23. Plato, *Sophist* 234–36.

24. According to Plato, if an artist employs perspective he or she is deceiving the audience by not representing things as they really are. Perspectivism in painting or sculpture is analogous to contextualism in norms and goods. "Plato is in search of a beauty which is not relative to context or person." *Dictionary of the History of Ideas,* vol. 1 (New York: Charles Scribner's Sons, 1973), 581.

25. Plato, *Republic* 596–97; 278–80.

26. To find creativity in Plato, one must turn to his discussion of beauty in the *Symposium.* Speaking of the demigod Eros, Socrates says, "in the first place he is a poet. . . , and he is also the source of poesy in others, which he could not be if he were not himself a poet. And at the touch of him everyone becomes a poet, even though he had no music in him before." *"Symposium" and "Phaedrus"* 21.

27. Plato, *Laws* 719b–c.

28. Kant, "Critique of Judgment" 284. "[T]he judgment of taste is not an intellectual judgment and so not logical, but is aesthetic—which means that it is one whose determining grounds *cannot be other than subjective.*"

29. Bernstein, *Beyond Objectivism and Relativism* 120.

30. *Later Works* 10: 310.

31. Boisvert is correct in concluding that Rorty's insistence that knowledge of the real is impossible necessarily implies a dualistic framework. "Without the dualistic assumption of a knowing subject that is both distinct and separate from a known object there would be no context within which such questions as 'Is knowledge possible?' 'How are knowledge claims to be justified?' or "What are the most accurate representations?' would make sense." "Dewey," on the other hand, "is not interested . . . in ascertaining whether knowledge is possible. Intelligence in the service of modifying the environment/organism interaction is an ongoing and obvious fact. What he seeks to discover is the manner in which human beings can increase, improve, and manipulate what is known in order to attain more security, harmony, and satisfaction. Dewey wants to examine 'how we think.'" *Dewey's Metaphysics* 199–200.

32. Rorty, *Contingency, Irony, and Solidarity* 40.

33. Rorty, *Contingency, Irony, and Solidarity* 25–27.

34. Boisvert, "Heteronomous Freedom" 144.

35. In *Contingency, Irony, and Solidarity,* Rorty claims that realization of the fact that socialization "goes all the way down" has helped to "free us, gradually, from theology and metaphysics." xiii. But Dewey recognized that, although natural needs and impulses can be channeled in a variety of different directions by different cultures, pure, unsocialized needs and impulses are common to all humans. Besides the obvious physical needs, there are numerous psychological ones—companionship, aesthetic expression, to learn by emulating others, cooperation, to lead, to follow. There are also such common natural impulses

as pity, sympathy, pugnacity, and fear. "Does Human Nature Change?," in *Later Works* 13: 286–93.

36. Aristotle, *Physics* 199a15–18. Barker explains the role played by human agency in Aristotle's conception of art: "But movement may . . . take place by art as well as by Nature, by external agencies as well as by an immanent force. Things not possessing in themselves a source of movement are changed by human agency: the marble becomes a statue by the hand of the sculptor. But human agency acts not only within this province: it also acts within the province of things which have in themselves a source of movement. It may act to thwart Nature: it may act to realize Nature." 222.

37. Aristotle speaks of poets representing men as "better than we know," (1461b) and as creating ideal models (1448a) in G. M. A. Grube's translation of Aristotle's *Poetics;* Aristotle, *Nicomachean Ethics* 1140a.

38. Aristotle, *Poetics* 1449a.

39. Dewey understands the process by which things and practices develop as having a natural form, but not the things and practices in themselves. Thus, for Dewey, the Greek practice of tragic drama developed contingently according to natural methods of criticism, creativity, and communication until its growth was arrested by being sanctified at a particular stage of its development. For Aristotle, because creativity (individuality) is reserved for the gods, criticism and communication are useful only for discovering the preexisting natural form of tragedy.

40. *Later Works* 14: 108–9.

41. *Later Works* 14: 109.

42. Barker 223–26.

43. *Middle Works* 12: 112–13.

44. *Middle Works* 14: 138.

45. Hinchman 763–64.

46. Bowman 16.

47. Bowman 19.

48. Hinchman 766.

49. *Middle Works* 14: 204.

50. Goethe, *Autobiography* 423.

51. Hinchman 766.

52. Emerson 22.

53. Dewey is referring to Henri Bergson's *élan vital. Middle Works* 14: 53.

54. Emerson 17. Unlike romanticists such as Emerson, Dewey was not locked into a conception of nature that is beyond good and evil because the initial premise of his philosophical system is that the end of nature is development or growth—which for humanity means self-fulfillment. Good is what we label things and practices whose consequences bring individuals and cultures closer to this end—evil is what we label things and practices whose consequences tend to hinder it.

55. *Later Works* 1: 187.

56. Westbrook, *American Democracy* 337. If art is the condition of the means-end relationship as opposed to the cause-effect relationship of natural

Darwinism, what must we make of the Aristotelian notion of preexisting natural ends? Are antecedent natural ends logical without a supreme artist? Do not natural ends, therefore, presuppose a divine realm and a divine maker?

57. Rorty, *Contingency, Irony, and Solidarity* 48.

58. Rorty, *Contingency, Irony, and Solidarity* 7.

59. Rorty, *Contingency, Irony, and Solidarity* 20, 80.

60. Rorty, *Contingency, Irony, and Solidarity* 55.

61. Rorty, *Contingency, Irony, and Solidarity* 37.

62. "Do not despair of life. You have no doubt force enough to overcome your obstacles. Think of the fox prowling through wood and field in a winter night for something to satisfy his hunger. Notwithstanding cold and hounds and traps, his race survives. I do not believe any of them ever committed suicide." *Thoreau on Man and Nature* (New York: Peter Pauper Press, 1960), 34.

63. Dewey's notion of historical and cultural progress as outlined here is essentially Hegelian *(The Phenomenology of Mind),* except that while Hegel understands the process as a linear one that ends when equal freedom is attained, Dewey understands it as a cyclical readaptation of the means (superstructure) required to assure equal freedom in a continually changing environment (substructure). Hegel argues that changes in substructure are the result of work and that work must be performed by a slave (thus in the service of an idea rather than instinct). Work thus ends when equal freedom is attained. Hegel's explanation does not provide for substructural change after the attainment of equal freedom and the end of history. For Hegel, history ends because the slave is now satisfied. Being satisfied, he no longer strives to transcend himself. Dewey, in much the same manner as Nietzsche, equates satisfaction with stagnation and mediocrity. The only end (or goal) of growth is more growth; eternal satisfaction can only mean the once-and-for-all overcoming of all problems, which Dewey can only equate with death. In life, problems are not something to be overcome once and for all, they are the essence of life itself—the continual cycle of problem, growth, and harmony (or tension, movement, and rest)—a never-ending process that provides the groundmap for a general method.

64. *Later Works* 14: 103.

65. MacIntyre, *After Virtue* 206.

66. *Later Works* 10: 286.

67. *Later Works* 14: 110–12.

68. MacIntyre, *After Virtue* 215–16.

69. "[T]he Many are also better judges [than the few] of music and the writings of the poets: some appreciate one part, some another, and all together appreciate all." Aristotle, *Politics* 1281b.

70. *Later Works* 1: 171.

71. I suppose it is theoretically possible for a person's identity to be explained in a wholly deterministic manner with no sign of individuality—that is, conforming absolutely to social influences—and yet for that person to have freely chosen to do what everyone else is doing in every aspect of their life. It is also theoretically possible for a person who is bound and gagged, with a gun pointed at his or her head, to have freely chosen to be put into that situation. However, in both cases, intuition derived from experience serves us better than ab-

stract theory. Intuition tells us that both of these persons are outside of the realm of freedom.

72. *Middle Works* 9: 311.

4. The Unity of Freedom and Authority: A Deweyan Conception of Social Intelligence

1. *Later Works* 2: 366.

2. Gouinlock, *Excellence in Public Discourse* 57.

3. *Later Works* 1: 172. It is important to understand that Dewey says that "*some portion* of an apparently stable world" (my emphasis) is put into peril whenever we start to think autonomously. "Some portion" occupies the ground between "no portion" and "every portion." If every portion of our apparently stable world was in peril, the social instability would be too great. If no portion was in peril, then no social reform would ever take place. Meliorative reform requires that some portion, but not the whole, of our established beliefs be in peril of being reconstructed.

4. See Weber 113; Schumpeter 269; and Lippmann, *Public Opinion* and *Phantom Public*.

5. Those who take an optimistic view of human nature are often accused of relieving individuals of personal responsibility for their behavior by tracing dispositions and attitudes to social circumstances. Finding the conditions that promote greater antisocial behavior, however, does not imply that the antisocial individual was determined to be that way, thus relieving him of responsibility. In fact, the opposite is true. It is only if we believe that individuals lack the capacity to be educated or to transform themselves that we are led to the necessary conclusion that they are not responsible for their behavior.

6. *Middle Works* 9: 197. In fact, Socrates may be the ideal personification of the Deweyan conception of the autonomous thinker with its virtues of critical reflection, creative individuality, and sociability. He was arrested and executed for teaching the youth of Athens to reflect critically on their community's existing beliefs in their search for the truth, and he often repeated that the only thing he knew for sure was his own ignorance—he could not thus be accused of being either a dogmatist or a skeptic. His arrogance in Plato's *Apology* coupled with his refusal to escape the consequences of his behavior in the *Crito* show him to be neither docile nor rebellious, but sociable. The virtue of self-reliant individuality, I believe, is manifested in Socrates' obedience to his *daimon*. Goethe, as I discussed in the previous chapter, also referred to his unique inner voice as a demon. Friedlander, referring to Plato's discussion of Socrates' demon, explains: "In Plato, the demonic in Socrates determines primarily his educational mission. It is not merely a remarkable peculiarity of a single individual, but an integral part of the nature of a great teacher. As an extralogical influence, it protects education progressing through the realm of the *Logos* from becoming a purely rational pursuit, and secures a connection with that element of mystery which is lacking in the Sophist's instruction. Thus Plato must have regarded it as part of the normal, not as something abnormal." 36.

7. *Middle Works* 9: ch. 12, "Thinking in Education."

8. *Later Works* 5: 102.

9. The labels "lost community" and "long revolution" are from Featherstone 7.

10. Shklar 33.

11. Frankel 10.

12. Shklar 24–25.

13. *Later Works* 2. 210.

14. Shklar 33.

15. Dewey, quoted in Gouinlock, "Dewey and Contemporary Moral Philosophy" 83.

16. *Later Works* 13: 186.

17. *Later Works* 13: 98.

18. In the family, the call for greater participation results in the eclipse of the assumption that paternal authority is absolute. In the more participatory family, both spouses contribute to decision making. And child rearing, while authoritative, is designed to cultivate autonomous future adults as opposed to those who have been habituated to obey authority unquestioningly.

19. *Middle Works* 12: 187.

20. Unless, of course, like realists, we are worried about the consequences of a more autonomous citizenry.

21. Realists fear that citizens will demand more participation without the necessary moral and intellectual virtues to perform the tasks more participation will require of them. If they are correct, those institutions (business, educational, religious, interest- or value-based associations, and so on) that do not value reflective and imaginative members will outperform those that do. Hence, the market will decide. In politics the same rule applies. When dealing with education issues, for example, some communities will tend to have more participation from the citizenry in regard to criticizing existing institutions and methods, suggesting imaginative solutions, and arriving at a community consensus, perhaps after the trial-and-error process of experimenting with different methods and techniques. Other communities will tend to allow public officials to authoritatively prescribe educational policies. Once again, experience will show which method of determining public policy is better able to produce solutions that work.

22. As Benjamin Constant, another minimalist liberal democrat, claims. 327.

23. *Later Works* 2: 266.

24. *Later Works* 2: 243–45.

25. *Middle Works* 12: 196.

26. *Later Works* 2: 245.

27. Walzer expresses a similar view in "Civil Society Argument" 103–5.

> The network of associations incorporates, but it cannot dispense with the agencies of state power. . . . There can be no victory at all that does not involve some control over, or use of, the state apparatus. . . . It compels association members to think about the common good, beyond their own conceptions of the good life . . . across the entire range of association, individual men and women need

to be protected against the power of officials, employers, experts, party bosses, factory supervisors, directors, priests, parents, patrons; and small and weak groups need to be protected against large and powerful ones. For civil society, left to itself, generates radically unequal power relationships, which only state power can challenge. . . . The state can never be what it appears to be in liberal theory, a mere framework for civil society. It is also the instrument of the struggle, used to give particular shape to the common life. Hence citizenship has a certain practical pre-eminence among all our actual and possible memberships.

28. *Later Works* 2: 328.

29. *Middle Works* 9: 89–105.

30. *Later Works* 2: 256.

31. *Later Works* 5: 66–76.

32. Dahl lists three criteria for procedural democracy: political equality, effective participation, and enlightened understanding. Enlightened understanding is the end served by communication in Dewey's theory of democracy. Dahl argues that a "democratic government ought to be evaluated according to the opportunities it furnishes for the acquisition of knowledge of ends and means, of oneself and other selves, by the demos." He also calls it "the most challenging of the criteria of procedural democracy," but without it, political equality and effective participation are of limited value. 10, 18.

33. Lippmann, *Public Opinion* 10.

34. Schumpeter 256–68; Herman and Chomsky.

35. *Later Works* 5: 62; 2: 348: "The smoothest road to control political conduct is by control of opinion."

36. *Middle Works* 14: 49–50.

37. *Later Works* 13: 168.

38. *Later Works* 2: 351.

39. I believe that Dewey would have approved of the idea of public television. That conservative interests want to cut public funding for it is hardly surprising. It is one of the few sources of information available to the general public that does not operate on the profit motive and thus is not dependent on private interests.

40. Wain 399.

41. *Later Works* 2: 349–50.

42. It should be pointed out, however, that the most widely read serial publication in the world prints a mixture of fiction (art) and research findings. The *Reader's Digest* (a conservative-leaning profit-making venture) is aimed at a lowbrow audience and yet at least a quarter of its entries each month is a nonfiction account of research.

43. *Later Works* 10: 331.

44. "Shelley did not exaggerate when he said that moral science only 'arranges the elements that poetry has created,' if we extend 'poetry' to include all products of imaginative experience. The sum total of the effect of all reflective treatises on morals is insignificant in comparison with the influence of ar-

chitecture, novel, drama, on life, becoming important when 'intellectual' products formulate the tendencies of these arts and provide them with an intellectual base." *Later Works* 10: 350.

45. *Later Works* 5: 103–4, 107.

46. Mills 300–2. Mills goes on to say that the many are passive "receivers" of opinion from a few "givers of opinion."

47. Sleeper, "Dewey and the Metaphysics of American Democracy" 124.

48. *Later Works* 13: 153–54.

49. Diamond. Dewey also rejected the distinction between facts and values in science.

50. *Middle Works* 9: 155.

51. *Middle Works* 12: 197.

52. As Macedo points out: "Liberalism requires . . . not merely an overlapping consensus but a consensus that practically *overrides* all competing values. . . . The success and stability of liberal politics depends, therefore, on people's private beliefs and commitments becoming importantly liberalized— becoming, that is, congruent with and supportive of liberal politics." 285.

53. Gouinlock, *Excellence in Public Discourse* 77.

54. Dewey, *Moral Writings* 269–70.

55. Dewey, *Moral Writings* 270.

56. *Later Works* 13: 161–63.

57. Gouinlock observes that "when principles cannot be disputed we cannot hope to find a high scale of mental activity." *Excellence in Public Discourse* 17. Thus ideological commitment tends to lower the level of public discourse.

58. *Later Works* 13: 131. Taylor voiced the same sentiment after the collapse of the Soviet Union. "What should have died along with communism is the belief . . . [in] a single principle, whether that of planning under the general will or that of free-market allocations." *Ethics of Authenticity* 110–11.

59. *Later Works* 2: 329–30.

60. *Middle Works* 9: 310.

61. *Later Works* 2: 329–30.

62. *Middle Works* 9: 128.

63. *Later Works* 7: 251–52.

64. *Later Works* 2: 330. "In order to have a large number of values in common, all the members of the group must have an equable opportunity to receive and to take from others. There must be a large variety of shared undertakings and experiences." *Middle Works* 9: 90.

65. *Later Works* 7: 299.

66. *Later Works* 7: 299.

67. *Middle Works* 12: 199.

68. Charles Anderson's *Pragmatic Liberalism* provides the best example of what a pragmatic liberalism would be like.

69. *Middle Works* 14: 199.

70. "As with Aristotle's golden mean, liberalism should be governed by a logic of just proportion." C. Anderson, *Pragmatic Liberalism* 153. Anderson list those values as freedom, equality, justice, and social efficiency.

71. C. Anderson, *Pragmatic Liberalism* 169–74.

72. The ideal does not seem to be peculiar to Dewey. Dahl, for example, lists the criteria of procedural democracy as political equality, effective participation, enlightened understanding, inclusiveness, and full final control by the demos. 4–12. Barber's notion of "strong democracy" also follows along the same lines. In fact, in the preface to the first printing of *Strong Democracy,* Barber writes: "My task in this book has been to try to find an approach to democracy suitable to human relations rather than to truth. I have been much helped by the tradition of American pragmatism."

73. Not that it may not gradually lead to major or radical changes, but it does not require the introduction of immediate radical and destabilizing change.

74. Dewey, *Moral Writings* 261–62.

75. Dewey, *Moral Writings* 263–64.

76. The unattainable ideal that provided the publican with a direction for growth was the example given by the life of Jesus. The unattainable ideal that Dewey believes should provide us with a direction of growth is the community of autonomous participators. The Pharisee compared himself to the publican in much the same way Americans tend to compare their nation to less open and less democratic nations. Such comparisons result in complacency rather than in the quest for excellence.

5. The Unity of Freedom and the Good: A Deweyan Justification of Liberalism

1. *Middle Works* 12: 186.

2. *Middle Works* 12: 91.

3. For example, Rawls's "overlapping consensus" in *A Theory of Justice* and Rorty's ironic liberalism in *Contingency, Irony, and Solidarity.*

4. MacIntyre, *After Virtue* 11–12.

5. Tocqueville, *Democracy in America* 110–13.

6. *Middle Works* 9: 305. Dewey adds that "this state of affairs suggests a definition of the role of the individual, or the self, in knowledge; namely, the redirection, or reconstruction of accepted beliefs."

7. *Middle Works* 9: 315.

8. See "America—By Formula," ch. 2 of *Individualism: Old and New,* in *Later Works* 5.

9. *Middle Works* 12: 198.

10. *Middle Works* 12: 196.

11. MacIntyre, *After Virtue* 253; *Later Works* 7: 179.

12. See Lee 367.

13. Feinberg, quoted in Lee 368.

14. *Later Works* 13: 67–68.

15. Rawls, *Political Liberalism,* lecture 5, "Priority of Right and Ideas of the Good"; see also *A Theory of Justice* 25, 30–31, 111, 184–85, 446–47.

16. Macedo 280–304.

17. Rawls, *Political Liberalism* 173–207.

18. Rawls, *Political Liberalism* 181.

19. Rawls, *Political Liberalism* 173.

20. Rawls, "Reply to Alexander and Musgrave" 641.

21. Rawls, *A Theory of Justice* 25–27, 31. In a note on page 31, Rawls traces the concept of the priority of right to Kant.

22. *Later Works* 7: 224–25. Because the liberal conception of the good life includes the virtues of critical reflection and individuality, difference and idiosyncrasy will be protected as means to the good. The end of perfectionist liberalism is equal liberation.

23. Kymlikca 21, 40.

24. Rawls, *Political Liberalism* 201–4.

25. *Middle Works* 12: 191.

26. MacIntyre, *After Virtue* 52–55.

27. *Later Works* 7: 186–99.

28. Rawls, *Political Liberalism* 81, 19.

29. Rawls, *Political Liberalism* 189.

30. It must be remembered that Rawls does not claim that the moral powers are exercised merely by believing in a particular comprehensive doctrine; he says that a necessary prerequisite to the exercise of the two moral powers is "the intellectual powers of judgment, thought, and inference." *Political Liberalism* 19. The prerequisite implies that some conceptions of the good constitute more intelligent choices than others.

31. See Dewey's "Liberty and Social Control," in *Later Works* 11: 360–63.

32. *Later Works* 11: 41.

33. Rawls, *Political Liberalism* 77.

34. I say "the achievement of some measure of autonomy" because autonomy, as Dewey conceives it, is not a state that someone can achieve in perfection and rest in. Rather, it is a way of living one's life. Different people can operate at different levels of autonomy, and a single person can be more or less autonomous at different times in his or her life.

35. Berlin; and Taylor, "What's Wrong with Negative Liberty."

36. Rorty, *Contingency, Irony, and Solidarity* 57.

37. Rorty, *Contingency, Irony, and Solidarity* xiii.

38. Rorty, *Contingency, Irony, and Solidarity* 26.

39. Rorty, *Contingency, Irony, and Solidarity* 47, 53.

40. Rorty, *Contingency, Irony, and Solidarity* 58; see also his article "Solidarity or Objectivity" 21–35.

41. Rorty, *Contingency, Irony, and Solidarity* 46.

42. Rorty, *Contingency, Irony, and Solidarity* 146.

43. Rorty, *Contingency, Irony, and Solidarity* 190–92.

44. See Shklar.

45. Rorty, *Contingency, Irony, and Solidarity* 48.

46. Rorty, *Contingency, Irony, and Solidarity* 192.

47. Rorty, *Contingency, Irony, and Solidarity* xiv, 65.

48. Rorty, *Contingency, Irony, and Solidarity* 65.

49. Rorty, *Contingency, Irony, and Solidarity* xiii.

50. "Does Human Nature Change?" in *Later Works* 13: 286–93.

51. Rorty, *Contingency, Irony, and Solidarity* xiii–xiv.

52. Rorty, *Contingency, Irony, and Solidarity* xiv.

53. Rorty, *Contingency, Irony, and Solidarity* xiii–xiv.
54. Rorty, *Contingency, Irony, and Solidarity* 36–37.
55. Rorty, *Contingency, Irony, and Solidarity* 37.
56. Rorty, *Contingency, Irony, and Solidarity* 37.
57. *Later Works* 13: 292.
58. Taylor, *Ethics of Authenticity* 35–39.
59. Rorty, *Contingency, Irony, and Solidarity* 94.
60. Rorty, *Contingency, Irony, and Solidarity* 60–61.
61. Rorty, *Contingency, Irony, and Solidarity* 13. Rorty also refers to shared vocabularies as "poetic achievements." 77. Once again, a shared vocabulary is the opposite of an idiosyncratic fantasy. The notion that one person's idiosyncratic fantasy should "just happen" to meet the need for a new public vocabulary is absurd.
62. Rorty writes that the "social glue holding together the ideal liberal society . . . consists in little more than a consensus that the point of social organization is to let everybody have a chance at self-creation to the best of his or her abilities, and that that goal requires, besides peace and wealth, the standard of 'bourgeois freedoms.'" *Contingency, Irony, and Solidarity* 84–85.
63. Rawls, "Justice as Fairness."
64. See Neal and Paris 419–49.

6. Cultural Evolution

1. A culture may also be said to be in a state of harmony with its circumstances when its members are satisfied, that is, there is no social dissonance. This would be harmony in the descriptive sense.
2. A meme is "a unit of cultural information comparable in its effects on society to those of the chemically coded instructions contained in the gene of the human organism." The word is derived from the Greek *mimesis* to refer to a cultural institution, rule, or norm that is passed from one generation to another "by example and imitation." Csikszentmihalyi 120.
3. *Middle Works* 9: 5–7.
4. "Moral Theory and Practice," in *Early Works* 3: 102–3.
5. By aesthetic standard, I do not mean that matters of good and bad, right and wrong are merely aesthetic matters, I mean that people tend to internalize the standard emotionally rather than cognitively. That is why we speak of the "intuitions" of people socialized into a particular culture or encourage people to listen to their conscience rather than the voice of reason. While many people will find it difficult to rationally defend their culturally ingrained standards of right and wrong, that does not mean that they cannot be defended, only that, in general, we tend to feel the difference between right and wrong before we consider reasons.
6. "Context and Thought," in *Later Works,* 6: 4, 11–12.
7. *Later Works* 1: 231.
8. MacIntyre, *Whose Justice?* 371; *After Virtue* 220, 222.
9. While not all of MacIntyre's "traditions" or Rorty's "vocabularies" are cultures, all cultures fall under the definition MacIntyre gives of tradition and Rorty gives of vocabulary.

10. *Middle Works* 14: 9.

11. *Later Works* 10: 276.

12. *Later Works* 7: 176–77.

13. *Middle Works* 9: 24.

14. MacIntyre, *After Virtue* 146; *Whose Justice?* 358.

15. MacIntyre, *After Virtue* 39.

16. MacIntyre, *Whose Justice?* 117.

17. MacIntyre, *Whose Justice?* 355.

18. Bronowski 19–20.

19. Rorty, *Contingency, Irony, and Solidarity* 37, 55.

20. Rorty, *Contingency, Irony, and Solidarity* 55.

21. Rorty, *Contingency, Irony, and Solidarity* 20.

22. Rorty, *Contingency, Irony, and Solidarity* 19.

23. MacIntyre, *Whose Justice?* 355–58. By making tradition a functional concept, he necessarily subjects it to a standard of evaluation, as MacIntyre himself points out in regard to the functional conception of the self. *After Virtue* 58.

24. MacIntyre, *Whose Justice?* 362.

25. MacIntyre, *Whose Justice?* 358.

26. Rorty, *Contingency, Irony, and Solidarity* 9.

27. Rorty, *Contingency, Irony, and Solidarity* 16–20.

28. Rorty, *Contingency, Irony, and Solidarity* 55.

29. Rorty, *Contingency, Irony, and Solidarity* 192.

30. Rorty, *Contingency, Irony, and Solidarity* xv.

31. Rorty, *Contingency, Irony, and Solidarity* 192.

32. By saying that liberals *are* individuals who believe that cruelty is the worst thing we can do, Rorty absolutizes this supposedly contingent characteristic of liberalism which, if it is a blindly evolving vocabulary, may be determined by new characteristics in the next century. If there is no criteria for evaluating alternative metaphors, then a new metaphor that devalues private perfection and is indifferent to cruelty may be liberalism's next defining direction of growth. If this is not possible because it violates the essence of liberalism, then there is a criterion for judging between alternative metaphors.

33. Rorty, *Contingency, Irony, and Solidarity* 93.

34. Rorty, *Consequences of Pragmatism* 84.

35. Rorty, *Contingency, Irony, and Solidarity* 25–26.

36. *Middle Works* 14: 199.

37. In chapter 2 of *Contingency, Irony, and Solidarity*, Rorty approvingly explains how Freud democratizes Nietzsche's conception of the strong poet, in which "to fail as a human being—is to accept somebody else's description of oneself." 28.

38. *Later Works* 10: 305–10.

39. *Later Works* 10: 286.

40. See Dewey's "Time and Individuality," in *Later Works* 14: 98–114.

41. Rosenthal, "Individual, Community, and Reconstruction of Values" 61. Dewey describes the interaction as being between structure and process. "The rate of change of some things is so slow, or is so rhythmic, that these changes

have all the advantages of stability in dealing with more transitory and irregular happenings. . . . To designate the slower and regular rhythmic events 'structure,' and more rapid and irregular ones 'process,' is sound practical sense. It expresses the function of one in respect to the other. . . . [T]he issue of living depends upon the art with which these things are adjusted to each other." *Later Works* 1: 64–67.

42. *Middle Works* 14: 117.

43. *Later Works* 1: 165.

44. Rorty, *Contingency, Irony, and Solidarity* xiv, 60–61, 65, 84.

45. Rorty, *Contingency, Irony, and Solidarity* 37, 55.

46. Rorty, *Contingency, Irony, and Solidarity* xvi, 94.

47. Rorty, *Contingency, Irony, and Solidarity* 48.

48. Rorty, *Contingency, Irony, and Solidarity* 41.

49. Rorty, *Contingency, Irony, and Solidarity* 53, 61.

50. Rorty, *Contingency, Irony, and Solidarity* 60. Rorty goes on to say that because the strong poet and the revolutionary appeal to a society's own self-image, they, in essence, "cancel out the difference between the revolutionary and the reformer. But one can define the *ideally* liberal society as one in which this difference *is* canceled out." All successful metaphors, then, must in some sense be continuous with existing vocabularies. They cannot, therefore, be idiosyncratic fantasies.

51. Rorty, *Contingency, Irony, and Solidarity* 48.

52. Rorty, *Contingency, Irony, and Solidarity* 60–61.

53. In that Rorty is talking about a liberal utopia and in that he speaks of strong poets and revolutionaries helping to guide society in the direction provided by his utopia, it matters very much if his method of self-perfection produces only trivial fantasies rather than meaningful insights.

54. Taylor, *Ethics of Authenticity* 39.

55. Rorty, *Contingency, Irony, and Solidarity* 36–37.

56. Rorty, *Contingency, Irony, and Solidarity* xiv.

57. MacIntyre, *After Virtue* 159–61.

58. MacIntyre, *Whose Justice?* 358–62.

59. We must not confuse meanings with principles. While principles have meanings, not all meanings are principles. Meanings are necessary for communication: we must agree on the meanings of at least some words and principles before we can have a rational discussion regarding other moral principles. Common meanings are derived from interactive experience and are thus cultural. Principles, such as equality, can be abstracted from experience and generalized, although what specific actions, or rules, the general principle of equality calls for in a specific situation or context is determined by practical method.

60. While some might argue that laissez-faire economics met an objective need by its creation of wealth, there are a few problems with this argument. First, it is not verified by experience. A regulated economy is the only proven means to a genuinely competitive marketplace, and competitive markets have proven to be more conducive to the creation of wealth than economies that are monopolized and controlled by a few centers of power—private or public. Second, the end of culture is not the production of wealth. No moral or political

theory that I know of explicitly posits the creation of wealth as an end in itself. Laissez-faire theory itself values wealth as a means to individual happiness and independence. Any system in which individuals are merely the means to an end of wealth creation is a perversity. The relegation of individuals, many of them children, to the position of expendable means to the end of creating wealth that is to be controlled by a relatively small number of private individuals has been the result whenever laissez-faire theory has been put into practice in an industrial society.

61. Evolutionists tell us that it is not the strongest organism that survives but the organism that is most complex. Complexity is defined as the simultaneous possession of differentiation and integration. Differentiation is necessary for adaptation to change; a simple undifferentiated, but integrated, organism is less likely to be able to produce the innovations that allow an organism to adapt to change. A differentiated organism that is not integrated, however, is unlikely to survive because it is necessarily chaotic—the differentiated elements do not work together and thus tend toward *dis*integration. A differentiated organism in which the various elements are integrated by a single purpose has the highest likelihood of survival. If we transfer this evolutionary logic to the evolution of cultures, we see that a culture of shared values and norms that lacks differentiation in the form of the diversity produced by individuality and pluralism possesses fewer sources of innovation should change become necessary. On the other hand, a differentiated culture (of idiosyncratic individuals or multiple incommensurable cultures) that is not integrated by a common purpose and language is in danger of disintegration. Thus, a healthy culture must seek to promote individuality, but in the Deweyan rather than in the Rortyan or postmodern sense. See Csikszentmihalyi 150–59.

Bibliography

Works by John Dewey

Art as Experience. New York: Minton, Balch and Co., 1934.
A Common Faith. New Haven: Yale University Press, 1960.
Democracy and Education. New York: Free Press, 1966.
The Early, Middle, and Later Works, 1882–1953. Edited by Jo Ann Boyston. 37 vols. Carbondale: Southern Illinois University Press.
Experience and Education. New York: Collier Books, 1963.
Experience and Nature. New York: Dover Publishing Publications, 1958.
Freedom and Culture. New York: G. P. Putnam's Sons, 1963.
German Philosophy and Politics. New York: Henry Holt and Co., 1915.
Human Nature and Conduct. New York: Henry Holt and Co., 1922.
Individualism, Old and New. New York: G. P. Putnam's Sons, 1962.
The Influence of Darwin on Philosophy. New York: Peter Smith, 1951.
John Dewey: The Political Writings. Edited by Debra Morris and Ian Shapiro. Indianapolis: Hackett Publishing Co., 1993.
Liberalism and Social Action. New York: G. P. Putnam's Sons, 1963.
Logic: The Theory of Inquiry. New York: Henry Holt and Co., 1938.
The Moral Writings of John Dewey. Edited by James Gouinlock. Amherst: Prometheus Books, 1994.
On Experience, Nature, and Freedom. Edited by Richard Bernstein. New York: Bobbs-Merrill Co., 1960.
Philosophy and Civilization. New York: Peter Smith, 1968.
The Philosophy of John Dewey. 2 vols. Edited by John J. McDermott. Chicago: University of Chicago Press, 1973.
Problems of Men. New York: Philosophical Library, 1946.
The Public and Its Problems. Chicago: Swallow Press, 1946.
The Quest for Certainty. New York: Minton, Balch and Co., 1929.
Reconstruction in Philosophy. Boston: Beacon Press, 1957.
"The School and Society" and "The Child and the Curriculum." Chicago: University of Chicago Press, 1990.
Theory of the Moral Life. New York: Holt, Rinehart and Winston, 1960.
Theory of Valuation. Chicago: University of Chicago Press, 1939.

Secondary Sources

Alexander, Thomas. "The Human Eros." In *Philosophy and the Reconstruction of Culture*, edited by John Stuhr, 203–23. Albany: State University of New York Press, 1993.

———. *John Dewey's Theory of Art, Experience and Nature: The Horizons of Feeling*. Albany: State University of New York Press, 1987.

Anderson, Charles W. *Pragmatic Liberalism*. Chicago: University of Chicago Press, 1990.

———. "Pragmatism and Liberalism, Rationalism and Irrationalism: A Response to Richard Rorty." *Polity* 23.3 (1991): 357–71.

Anderson, Quentin. "John Dewey's American Democrat." *Daedalus* 108 (1979): 145–59.

Aristotle. *Nicomachean Ethics*. Translated by Terence Irwin. Indianapolis: Hackett Publishing, 1985.

———. *On Poetry and Style*. Translated by G. M. A. Grube. New York: Bobbs-Merrill Co., 1958.

———. *The Politics of Aristotle*. Translated by Ernest Barker. Oxford: Oxford University Press, 1958.

Barber, Benjamin. *Strong Democracy*. Berkeley: University of California Press, 1984.

Barker, Ernest. *The Political Thought of Plato and Aristotle*. New York: Dover Publications, 1959.

Bellah, Robert N., et al. *Habits of the Heart: Individualism and Commitment on American Life*. New York: Harper and Row, 1985.

Benn, S. I. "Freedom, Autonomy, and the Concept of a Person." *Proceedings of the Aristotelian Society* 76 (1975–76): 109–30.

Benson, Peter. "Rawls, Hegel, and Personhood." *Political Theory* 22.3 (1994): 491–500.

Berlin, Isaiah. *Four Essays on Liberty*. Oxford: Oxford University Press, 1969.

Bernstein, Richard J. *Beyond Objectivism and Relativism: Science, Hermeneutics, and Praxis*. Philadelphia: University of Pennsylvania Press, 1983.

———. *John Dewey*. New York: Washington Square Press, 1966.

———. "One Step Forward, Two Steps Backward: Richard Rorty on Liberal Democracy and Philosophy." *Political Theory* 15.4 (1987): 538–63.

———. *Philosophical Profiles: Essays in a Pragmatic Mode*. Cambridge, England: Polity Press, 1986.

———. "Rorty's Liberal Utopia." *Social Research* 57.1 (1990): 31–72.

Blau, Joseph L. "John Dewey's Theory of History." *Journal of Philosophy* 7.3 (1960): 89–100.

Blewett, John. "Democracy as Religion: Unity in Human Relations." In *John Dewey: His Thought and Influence*, edited by John Blewett, 36–55. New York: Fordham University Press, 1960.

Boisvert, Raymond D. *Dewey's Metaphysics*. New York: Fordham University Press, 1988.

———. "Heteronomous Freedom." In *Philosophy and the Reconstruction of Culture*, edited by John Stuhr, 131–51. Albany: State University of New York Press, 1993.

Bontekoe, Ron. "Rorty's Pragmatism and the Pursuit of Truth." *International Philosophical Quarterly* 30.2 (1990): 221–44.

Bordeau, Edward J. "John Dewey's Ideas about the Great Depression." *Journal of the History of Ideas* 23 (1971): 67–84.

Bourne, Randolph. "Twilight of Idols." In *War and the Intellectuals: Collected Essays, 1915–1918,* edited by Carl Resek, 53–64. New York: Harper, 1969.

Bowman, Derek. *Life into Autobiography: A Study of Goethe's "Dichtung und Wahrheit."* Bern: Herbert Lang and Co., 1971.

Bronowski, Jacob. *The Ascent of Man.* Boston: Little, Brown, and Co., 1973.

Burke, Edmund. *Reflections on the Revolution in France.* Edited by Conor Cruise O'Brien. Middlesex, England: Penguin Books, 1968.

Burtt, Edwin A. "The Core of Dewey's Way of Thinking." *Journal of Philosophy* 57.13 (1960): 401–19.

Buscemi, William I. "The Ironic Politics of Richard Rorty." *Review of Politics* 55.1 (1994): 141–57.

Campbell, James. "Democracy as Cooperative Inquiry." In *Philosophy and the Reconstruction of Culture,* edited by John Stuhr, 17–36. Albany: State University of New York Press, 1993.

Cascardi, Anthony J. "The Genealogy of Pragmatism." *Philosophy and Literature* 14.2 (1990): 295–303.

Childs, John L. "John Dewey and Education." In *John Dewey: Philosopher of Science and Freedom,* edited by Sidney Hooks, 154–64. New York: Barnes and Noble, 1950.

Colapietro, Vincent M. "The Vanishing Subject of Contemporary Discourse: A Pragmatic Response." *Journal of Philosophy* 22 (1990): 644–55.

Collins, James. "The Genesis of John Dewey's Naturalism." In *John Dewey: His Thought and Influence,* edited by John Blewett, 9–26. New York: Fordham University Press, 1960.

Connolly, William E. "Mirror of America." *Raritan* 3.1 (1983): 124–35.

Constant, Benjamin. *The Political Writings of Benjamin Constant.* Edited by Biancamaria Fontana. London: Cambridge University Press, 1988.

Conway, Daniel W. "Taking Irony Seriously: Rorty's Postmetaphysical Liberalism." *American Literary History* 3 (1991): 198–208.

Cork, Jim. "John Dewey and Karl Marx." In *John Dewey: Philosopher of Science and Freedom,* edited by Sidney Hooks, 333–48. New York: Barnes and Noble, 1950.

Cotkin, George. "Middle-Ground Pragmatists: The Popularization of Philosophy in American Culture." *Journal of the History of Ideas* 55.2 (1994): 283–302.

Coughlan, Neil. *Young John Dewey.* Chicago: University of Chicago Press, 1975.

Csikszentmihalyi, Mihaly. *The Evolving Self.* New York: Harper Collins, 1993.

Cywar, Alan. "John Dewey: Toward Domestic Reconstruction, 1915–1920." *Journal of the History of Ideas* 30.2 (1969): 385–400.

Dahl, Robert. "On Removing Certain Impediments to Democracy in the United States." *Political Science Quarterly* 92.1 (spring 1977): 1–19.

Damico, Alfonso J. "Analysis and Advocacy: Pragmatism and the Study of Politics." *Polity* 7.2 (1974): 193–208.

———. *Individuality and Community: The Social and Political Thought of John Dewey.* Gainesville: University Presses of Florida, 1978.

Dennett, Daniel. *Darwin's Dangerous Idea: Evolution and the Meanings of Life.* New York: Simon and Schuster, 1995.

Diamond, Martin. "The Dependence of Fact upon 'Value.'" In *Loyola Series on Political Analysis: Interpretation,* 226–35. Chicago: F. E. Peacock, 1971.

Dicker, Georges. "Knowing and Coming-To-Know in John Dewey's Theory of Knowledge." *Monist* 57 (1973): 191–219.

Diggins, John Patrick. "From Pragmatism to Natural Law." *Political Theory* 19.4 (1991): 519–38.

———. *The Promise of Pragmatism: Modernism and the Crisis of Knowledge and Authority.* Chicago: University of Chicago Press, 1994.

Dupre, Louis. "Postmodernity or Late Modernity? Ambiguities in Richard Rorty's Thought." *Review of Metaphysics* 47 (December 1993): 277–95.

Dworkin, Gerald. "Autonomy and Behavior Control." In *Hastings Center Report* 6, 23–28. New York: Hastings Center, 1976.

———. "The Concept of Autonomy." In *The Inner Citadel: Essays on Individual Autonomy,* edited by John Christman, 54–62. New York: Oxford University Press, 1989.

———. *The Theory and Practice of Autonomy.* Cambridge: Cambridge University Press, 1988.

Emerson, Ralph Waldo. "Self-Reliance." In *Essays of Ralph Waldo Emerson,* 15–31. New York: Book League of America, 1941.

Eodice, Alexander R. "Dewey and Wittgenstein on the Idea of Certainty." *Philosophy Today* (spring 1990): 30–38.

Featherstone, Joseph. "John Dewey and David Riesman: From the Lost Individual to the Lonely Crowd." In *On the Making of Americans,* edited by Herbert Gans et al., 3–39. Philadelphia: University of Pennsylvania Press, 1979.

Feinberg, Joel. "Autonomy." In *The Inner Citadel: Essays on Individual Autonomy,* edited by John Christman, 27–53. New York: Oxford University Press, 1989.

Flathman, Richard. *The Philosophy and Politics of Freedom.* Chicago: University of Chicago Press, 1987.

Fott, David. *John Dewey: America's Philosopher of Democracy.* Lanham, Md.: Rowman and Littlefield, 1998.

———. "John Dewey and the Philosophical Foundations of Democracy." *Social Science Journal* 28.1 (1991): 29–44.

Frank, Lawrence K. "Culture and Personality." In *John Dewey: Philosopher of Science and Freedom,* edited by Sidney Hooks, 89–102. New York: Barnes and Noble, 1950.

Frankel, Charles. "John Dewey's Social Philosophy." In *New Studies in the Philosophy of John Dewey,* edited by Steven M. Cahn, 5–38. Hanover, N.H.: University Press of New England, 1977.

Frankfurt, Harry G. "Freedom of the Will and the Concept of a Person." In *The Inner Citadel: Essays on Individual Autonomy,* edited by John Christman, 63–76. New York: Oxford University Press, 1989.

Friedlander, Paul. *Plato: An Introduction.* New York: Harper and Row, 1958.

Frisina, Warren G. "Knowledge as Active, Aesthetic, and Hypothetical." *Philosophy Today* (fall 1989): 245–63.

Geiger, George. *John Dewey in Perspective.* New York: Oxford University Press, 1958.

Gellner, Ernest. *Spectacles and Predicaments: Essays in Social Theory.* New York: Cambridge University Press, 1979.

Goethe, Johann Wolfgang von. *The Autobiography of Johann Wolfgang von Goethe.* 2 vols. New York: Horizon, 1969.

Goodman, Jesse. "Education for Critical Democracy." *Journal of Education* 171.2 (1989): 88–116.

Goudge, T. A. "Pragmatism's Contribution to an Evolutionary View of Mind." *Monist* 57 (1973): 133–50.

Gouinlock, James. "Dewey and Contemporary Moral Philosophy." In *Philosophy and the Reconstruction of Culture*, edited by John Stuhr, 79–96. Albany: State University of New York Press, 1993.

———. "Dewey's Theory of Moral Deliberation." *Ethics* 88.3 (1978): 218–28.

———. *Excellence in Public Discourse: John Stuart Mill, John Dewey, and Social Intelligence.* New York: Teacher's College Press, Columbia University, 1986.

———. "What is the Legacy of Instrumentalism? Rorty's Interpretation of Dewey." *Journal of the History of Philosophy* 28.2 (1990): 251–69.

Green, Thomas Hill. *The Works of T. H. Green.* Edited by R. L. Nettleship. London: Longmans, Green, and Co., 1894.

Grube, G. M. A. *On Poetry and Style.* New York: Library of Liberal Arts, 1958.

Gunn, Giles. "Rorty's Novum Organum." *Raritan* 10.1 (1994): 80–103.

Haack, Susan. "Recent Obituaries of Epistemology." *American Philosophical Quarterly* 27.3 (1990): 199–212.

Habermas, Jurgen. "Reconciliation through the Public Use of Reason: Remarks on John Rawls' Political Liberalism." *Journal of Philosophy* 42.3 (1995): 109–32.

Hance, Allen. "Pragmatism as Naturalized Hegelianism: Overcoming Transcendental Philosophy?" *Review of Metaphysics* 46 (December 1992): 343–68.

Heidegger, Martin. *Being and Time.* Translated by John Macquarrie and Edward Robinson. New York: Harper and Row, 1962.

Herman, Edward S., and Noam Chomsky. *Manufacturing Consent: The Political Economy and the Mass Media.* New York: Pantheon Books, 1988.

Hickman, Larry A. "Liberal Irony and Social Reform." In *Philosophy and the Reconstruction of Culture,* edited by John Stuhr, 224–40. Albany: State University of New York Press, 1993.

Himmelfarb, Gertrude. "The Abyss Revisited." *American Scholar* 16 (1992): 337–49.

Hinchman, Lewis. "The Idea of Individuality: Origins, Meaning, and Political Significance." *Journal of Politics* 52.3 (1990): 759–81.

Hofstadter, Albert. "Concerning a Certain Deweyan Conception of Metaphysics." In *John Dewey: Philosopher of Science and Freedom,* edited by Sidney Hooks, 252–71. New York: Barnes and Noble, 1950.

Hollinger, David A. "The Problem of Pragmatism in American History." *Journal of American History* 67.1 (1980): 88–107.

Holmes, Robert L. "John Dewey's Moral Philosophy in Contemporary Perspective." *Review of Metaphysics* 22 (1966): 42–70.

Hook, Sidney. "The Desirable and Emotive in Dewey's Ethics." In *John Dewey:*

Philosopher of Science and Freedom, edited by Sidney Hooks, 196–217. New York: Barnes and Noble, 1950.

———. "John Dewey and the Crisis of American Liberalism." *Antioch Review* 29 (summer 1969): 218–32.

———. *John Dewey: An Intellectual Perspective.* New York: John Day Co., 1939.

Jasper, James M. "The Politics of Abstractions: Instrumental and Moralist Rhetorics in Public Debate." *Social Research* 59.2 (1992). 315–44.

Joad, C. E. M. *Guide to Philosophy.* New York: Dover Publications, 1957.

Kadish, Mortimer. "John Dewey and the Theory of the Aesthetic Practice." In *New Studies in the Philosophy of John Dewey,* edited by Steven M. Cahn, 78–95. Hanover, N.H.: University Press of New England, 1977.

Kallen, Horace M. "John Dewey and the Spirit of Pragmatism." In *John Dewey: Philosopher of Science and Freedom,* edited by Sidney Hooks, 4–41. New York: Barnes and Noble, 1950.

Kant, Immanuel. "Critique of Judgment." In *The Philosophy of Kant,* edited by Carl J. Friedrich, 265–364. New York: Modern Library, 1977.

———. "Metaphysical Foundations of Morals." In *The Philosophy of Kant,* edited by Carl J. Friedrich, 140–209. New York: Modern Library, 1977.

Kaufmann, Felix. "John Dewey's Theory of Inquiry." In *John Dewey: Philosopher of Science and Freedom,* edited by Sidney Hooks, 218–31. New York: Barnes and Noble, 1950.

Kaufman-Osborn, Timothy V. "John Dewey and the Liberal Science of Community." *Journal of Politics* 46.1 (1984): 1142–65.

———. "Pragmatism, Policy Science, and the State." *American Journal of Political Science* 29.4 (1985): 827–49.

Kennedy, Gail. "The Hidden Link in Dewey's Theory of Evaluation." *Journal of Philosophy* 52.4 (1955): 85–94.

Kestenbaum, Victor. *The Phenomenological Sense of John Dewey.* Atlantic Highlands, N.J.: Humanities Press, 1977.

Konvitz, Milton R. "Dewey's Revision of Jefferson." In *John Dewey: Philosopher of Science and Freedom,* edited by Sidney Hooks, 165–95. New York: Barnes and Noble, 1950.

Kymlicka, Will. *Liberalism, Community, and Culture.* Oxford: Oxford University Press, 1989.

Lachs, John. "Aristotle and Dewey on the Rat Race." In *Philosophy and the Reconstruction of Culture,* edited by John Stuhr, 97–113. Albany: State University of New York Press, 1993.

Lavine, Thelma Z. "American Philosophy, Socialism, and the Contradictions of Modernity." In *Philosophy and the Reconstruction of Culture,* edited by John Stuhr, 4–16. Albany: State University of New York Press, 1993.

———. "Individuation and Unification in Dewey and Sartre." In *Doctrine and Experience,* edited by Victor G. Potter, 149–64. New York: Fordham University Press, 1988.

Lee, Seung-hwan. "Liberal Rights or/and Confucian Virtues?" *Philosophy of East and West* 46.3 (1996): 367–79.

Lentricchia, Frank. "Rorty's Cultural Conversation." *Raritan* 3.1 (1983): 136–41.

Levine, Daniel. "Randolph Bourne, John Dewey, and the Legacy of Liberalism." *Antioch Review* 29 (1969): 234–44.

Lippmann, Walter. *The Phantom Public.* New York: Macmillan, 1925.

———. *Public Opinion.* New York: Free Press, 1965.

Locke, John. *Two Treatises of Government.* Edited by Peter Laslett. Cambridge: Cambridge University Press, 1990.

Macedo, Stephen. "The Politics of Justification." *Political Theory* 18.4 (1990): 280–304.

MacIntyre, Alasdair. *After Virtue: A Study in Moral Theory.* 2d ed. Notre Dame: University of Notre Dame Press, 1984.

———. *Whose Justice? Which Rationality?* Notre Dame: University of Notre Dame Press, 1988.

Manasse, Ernest. "Moral Principles and Alternatives in Max Weber and John Dewey." *Journal of Philosophy* 41.2 (1944): 29–48, 57–68.

Manicus, Peter. "Naturalizing Epistemology: Reconstructing Philosophy." In *Philosophy and the Reconstruction of Culture,* edited by John Stuhr, 152–66. Albany: State University of New York Press, 1993.

Margolis, Joseph. "The Relevance of Dewey's Epistemology." In *New Studies in the Philosophy of John Dewey,* edited by Steven M. Cahn, 120–51. Hanover, N.H.: University Press of New England, 1977.

McGill, V. J. "Pragmatism Reconsidered: An Aspect of John Dewey's Philosophy." *Science and Society* 3 (summer 1939): 289–322.

Mills, C. Wright. *Power Elite.* New York: Oxford University Press, 1956.

Murphy, Arthur E. "John Dewey and American Liberalism." *Journal of Philosophy* 57.13 (1961): 420–36.

Nathanson, Jerome. *John Dewey: The Reconstruction of Democratic Life.* New York: Frederick Ungar Publishing Co., 1951.

Neal, Patrick. "Vulgar Liberalism." *Political Theory* 21.4 (1993): 623–43.

Neal, Patrick, and David Paris. "Liberalism and the Communitarian Critique: A Guide for the Perplexed." *Canadian Journal of Political Science* 23.3 (1990): 419–39.

Nichols, James H. "Pragmatism and the U.S. Constitution." In *Confronting the Constitution,* edited by Allen Bloom, 369–88. Washington, D.C.: AEI Press, 1990.

Nietzsche, Friedrich. *"On the Genealogy of Morals" and "Ecce Homo."* Translated by Walter Kaufmann and R. J. Hollingdale. New York: Vintage Books, 1989.

———. *Thus Spake Zarathustra.* New York: Modern Library, 1972.

Nitecki, Matthew H., and Doris V. Nitecki. *Evolutionary Ethics.* New York: State University of New York Press, 1993.

Nozick, Robert. *Anarchy, State, and Utopia.* New York: Basic Books, 1974.

Olafson, Frederick A. "The School and Society: Reflections on John Dewey's Philosophy of Education." In *New Studies in the Philosophy of John Dewey,* edited by Steven M. Cahn, 178–94. Hanover, N.H.: University Press of New England, 1977.

Oppenheim, Felix. "Relativism, Absolutism, and Democracy." *American Political Science Review* 44 (1950): 951–60.

Peerenboom, R. P. "Reasons, Rationales, and Relativisms: What's at Stake in the Conversation over Scientific Rationality?" *Philosophy Today* 34.1 (1990): 3–19.

Phillips, D. Z. "Reclaiming the Conversations of Mankind." *Philosophy* 69.267 (1994): 35–53.

Plato. *The Laws of Plato.* Translated by Thomas L. Pangle. Chicago: University of Chicago Press, 1988.

———. *Plato's Theory of Knowledge: "The Theaetetus" and "The Sophist" of Plato.* Translated by Francis Cornford. New York: Library of Liberal Arts, 1957.

———. *The Republic of Plato.* Translated by Allan Bloom. New York: Basic Books, 1968.

———. *"Symposium" and "Phaedrus."* Translated by Benjamin Jowett. New York: Dover Publications, 1993.

Posnock, Ross. "The Politics of Nonidentity: A Genealogy." *Boundary 2* 19.1 (1992): 34–68.

Price, David E. "Community and Control: Critical Democratic Theory in the Progressive Period." *American Political Science Review* 68 (1974): 1663–78.

Rachels, James. "John Dewey and the Truth about Ethics." In *New Studies in the Philosophy of John Dewey,* edited by Steven M. Cahn, 152–77. Hanover, N.H.: University Press of New England, 1977.

Rawls, John. "Justice as Fairness: Political Not Metaphysical." *Philosophy and Public Affairs* 14.3 (1985): 223–51.

———. *Political Liberalism.* New York: Columbia University Press, 1993.

———. *A Theory of Justice.* Cambridge: Harvard University Press, 1971.

Raz, Joseph. *The Morality of Freedom.* Oxford: Clarendon Press, 1986.

Riesman, David. *The Lonely Crowd.* New Haven: Yale University Press, 1950.

Rockefeller, Steven C. *John Dewey: Religious Faith and Democratic Humanism.* New York: Columbia University Press, 1991.

———. John Dewey, Spiritual Democracy, and the Human Future." *Cross Currents* (fall 1989): 300–21.

Rorty, Richard. *Consequences of Pragmatism.* Minneapolis: University of Minnesota Press, 1982.

———. *Contingency, Irony, and Solidarity.* Cambridge: Cambridge University Press, 1989.

———. *Philosophy and the Mirror of Nature.* Princeton: Princeton University Press, 1979.

———. "Putnam and the Relativist Menace." *Journal of Philosophy* 90.9 (1993): 443–61.

———. "Realism and Reference." *Monist* 59 (1976): 321–40.

———. "Solidarity or Objectivity." In *Objectivity, Relativism, and Truth,* 21–34. Cambridge: Cambridge University Press, 1991.

———. "Thugs and Theorists: A Reply to Bernstein." *Political Theory* 15.4 (1987): 564–80.

Rosenblum, Nancy L. *Liberalism and the Moral Life.* Cambridge: Harvard University Press, 1991.

Rosenthal, Sandra B. "The Individual, the Community, and the Reconstruction of Values." In *Philosophy and the Reconstruction of Culture,* edited by John Stuhr, 59–78. Albany: State University of New York Press, 1993.

———. *Pragmatism and Phenomenology.* Amsterdam: B. R. Gruner Publishing Co., 1980.

Roth, Robert J. *John Dewey and Self-Realization.* Englewood Cliffs, N.J.: Prentice Hall, 1962.

Ryan, Alan. *John Dewey and the High Tide of American Liberalism.* New York: W. W. Norton and Co., 1995.

———. "The Legacy of John Dewey." *Dissent* (spring 1992): 273–78.

Sabine, George H. "The Pragmatic Approach to Politics." *American Political Science Review* 24.4 (1930): 865–85.

Sandel, Michael. *Liberalism and the Limits of Justice.* Cambridge: Cambridge University Press, 1982.

———. "The Procedural Republic and the Unencumbered Self." *Political Theory* 12.1 (1984): 81–96.

Schick, Frederic. "Liberty, Equality, and Diversity: Some Reflections on Rorty." *Social Research* 59.2 (1992): 297–314.

Schick, Theodore W. "How Is Philosophy Possible?" *International Philosophical Quarterly* 31.2 (1991): 203–12.

Schumpeter, Joseph A. *Capitalism, Socialism, and Democracy.* London: Allen and Unwin, 1976.

Schwarzenbach, Sibyl. "Rawls, Hegel, and Communitarianism." *Political Theory* 19.4 (1991): 539–71.

Sellars, Wilfred. "Language, Rules, and Behavior." In *John Dewey: Philosopher of Science and Freedom,* edited by Sidney Hooks, 289–313. New York: Barnes and Noble, 1950.

Shklar, Judith. "The Liberalism of Fear." In *Liberalism and the Moral Life,* edited by Nancy Rosenblum, 21–38. Cambridge: Harvard University Press, 1991.

Shusterman, Richard. "Pragmatism and Liberalism between Dewey and Rorty." *Political Theory* 22.3 (1994): 391–413.

Sleeper, R. W. "Dewey's Metaphysical Perspective: A Note on White, Geiger, and the Problem of Obligation." *Journal of Philosophy* 57.3 (1960): 100–15.

———. "John Dewey and the Metaphysics of American Democracy." In *Doctrine and Experience: Essays in American Philosophy,* edited by Vincent G. Potter, 122–48. New York: Fordham University Press, 1988.

———. *The Necessity of Pragmatism.* New Haven: Yale University Press, 1986.

Somjee, A. H. *The Political Theory of John Dewey.* New York: Teachers College Press, Columbia University, 1968.

Spits, David. "Politics and the Critical Imagination." *Review of Politics* 32 (1970): 419–35.

Spitzer, Alan B. "John Dewey, the 'Trial' of Leon Trotsky, and the Search for Historical Truth." *History and Theory* 29 (1990): 16–37.

Strauss, Leo. "Progress or Return?" In *The Rebirth of Classical Political Rationalism,* edited by Thomas L. Pangle, 227–70. Chicago: University of Chicago Press, 1989.

Stuhr, John J. "Democracy as a Way of Life." In *Philosophy and the Reconstruction of Culture,* edited by John Stuhr, 37–58. Albany: State University of New York Press, 1993.

Taylor, Charles. *The Ethics of Authenticity.* Cambridge: Harvard University Press, 1991.

———. *Hegel and Modern Society.* Cambridge: Cambridge University Press, 1979.

———. *Philosophical Papers.* Vol. 2, *Philosophy and the Human Sciences.* Cambridge: Cambridge University Press, 1985.

———. *Sources of the Self: The Making of the Modern Identity.* Cambridge: Harvard University Press, 1989.

———. "What's Wrong with Negative Liberty." In *The Idea of Freedom,* edited by Alan Ryan, 211–29. Oxford: Oxford University Press, 1979.

Thayer, H. S. *Meaning and Action.* 2d. ed. Indianapolis: Hackett Publishing Co., 1981.

———. "Objects of Knowledge." In *Philosophy and the Reconstruction of Culture,* edited by John Stuhr, 189–202. Albany: State University of New York Press, 1993.

Tilman, Rick. "New Light on John Dewey, Clarence Ayres, and the Development of Evolutionary Economics." *Journal of Economic Issues* 24.4 (1990): 963–79.

Tocqueville, Alexis de. *Democracy in America.* Indianapolis: Hackett Publishing, 2000.

Trotsky, Leon. "Their Morals and Ours." *New International* 4.6 (1938): 163–73.

Wain, Kenneth. "Strong Poets and Utopia: Rorty's Liberalism, Dewey, and Democracy." *Political Studies* 41 (1993): 394–407.

Wallach, John R. "Liberals, Communitarians, and the Tasks of Political Theory." *Political Theory* 15.4 (1987): 581–611.

Walzer, Michael. "The Civil Society Argument." In *Dimensions of Radical Democracy,* edited by Chantal Mouffe, 89–107. London: Verso Press, 1992.

———. "Philosophy and Democracy." *Political Theory* 9.3 (1981): 379–99.

Weber, Max. "Politics as a Vocation." In *From Max Weber: Essays in Sociology,* edited by H. H. Gerth and C. Wright Mills, 77–128. New York: Oxford University Press, 1946.

West, Cornel. *The American Evasion of Philosophy: A Genealogy of Pragmatism.* Madison: University of Wisconsin Press, 1989.

Westbrook, Robert B. *John Dewey and American Democracy.* Ithaca: Cornell University Press, 1991.

———. "Schools for Industrial Democrats: The Social Origins of John Dewey's Philosophy of Education." *American Journal of Education* 100 (August 1992): 401–19.

Wienpahl, Paul. "Dewey's Theory of Language and Meaning." In *John Dewey: Philosopher of Science and Freedom,* edited by Sidney Hooks, 272–88. New York: Barnes and Noble, 1950.

Wilshire, Bruce. "Body-Mind and Subconsciousness: Tragedy in Dewey's Life and Work." In *Philosophy and the Reconstruction of Culture*, edited by John Stuhr, 262–80. Albany: State University of New York Press, 1993.

Wolin, Sheldon S. "Democracy in the Discourse of Postmodernism." *Social Research* 57.1 (1990): 5–30.

———. "Paradigms and Political Theories." In *Politics and Experience*, edited by Preston King and Bhikhu Parekh, 125–52. London: Cambridge University Press, 1968.

Zedler, Beatrice H. "Dewey's Theory of Knowledge." In *John Dewey: His Thought and Influence*, edited by John Blewett, 60–77. New York: Fordham University Press, 1960.

Index

absolutes, 8–9, 65–67; in method, 2–4
aesthetic standard, 151, 166, 201n. 5
Alexander, Thomas, 43, 185n. 1
Anderson, Charles, 118, 198n. 70
art, 46, 48, 109–10, 197–98n. 44; Dewey's theory of, 67–70
authenticity, 31–34, 46–47, 57–59, 143–47, 168
autonomy, 2–3, 11–12, 17–41, 46–48, 86–87, 136–38, 177–78; Kantian, 19–23

Barber, Benjamin, 183n. 1, 199n. 72
Benn, S. I., 189n. 49
Bergson, Henri Louis, 50
Berlin, Isaiah, 139
Bernstein, Richard, 72
Boisvert, Raymond, 60, 73, 192n. 31
Burke, Edmund, 11

chance, 64–67, 139
change, 3–4, 8–9, 17–18, 27, 40–41, 42, 49–50, 61–67, 76–77, 83–84, 139, 152–53, 156, 163–64, 173–75, 190n. 2, 202–3n. 41
civil society, 94, 103–6, 126–27, 136, 196n. 27
communication, 10–11, 26–27, 79, 94–96, 104–14, 127–28, 145, 197n. 32. See also sociability
communitarianism, 186n. 13; Mac-Intyre's, 23–27
community, 117–18, 122
complexity, 28, 61–62, 173–74, 204n. 61
conflict, 94, 110–14

consciousness, 44–45
contextualism, 41–45. See also cultural context
contingency. See chance
creative individuality, 31–34, 125–27. See also creativity; individuality
creativity, 46–48, 61–89, 143–47, 164–69. See also creative individuality
critical reflection, 28–31, 125
Csikszentmihalyi, Mihaly, 201n. 2, 204n. 61
cultural context, 11–12, 28–31, 40–60, 83–84, 173–74, 203n. 59
cultural growth, 152–56, 162–72; measuring of, 156–75
culture, 150–52
cyclical growth, 6–7, 17, 149, 154, 191n. 3

Dahl, Robert, 197n. 32, 199n. 72
Darwin, Charles, 5–8, 61, 80, 82, 98, 155, 159, 162, 165
Davidson, Donald, 156
democracy, 127–28, 196n. 21, 197n. 32, 199n. 72; and social intelligence, 93–120
Dennett, Daniel, 5
docility, 35
dualism, 1–2, 5, 20–21, 68, 70–83, 132, 142–43, 171, 192n. 31
Dworkin, Gerald, 31–33, 38, 187n. 36, 188n. 62

eccentricity, 31–32, 126
education, 99–102
equality, 116

Daniel M. Savage is an assistant professor of political science at the University of Science and Arts of Oklahoma, where he teaches political theory and American politics.